The American Novel After Ideology, 1961–2000

The American Novel After Ideology, 1961–2000

Laurie A. Rodrigues

BLOOMSBURY ACADEMIC
NEW YORK • LONDON • OXFORD • NEW DELHI • SYDNEY

BLOOMSBURY ACADEMIC
Bloomsbury Publishing Inc
1385 Broadway, New York, NY 10018, USA
50 Bedford Square, London, WC1B 3DP, UK

BLOOMSBURY, BLOOMSBURY ACADEMIC and the Diana logo are
trademarks of Bloomsbury Publishing Plc

First published in the United States of America 2021
This paperback edition published 2022

Copyright © Laurie A. Rodrigues, 2021

Cover design by Namkwan Cho
Cover image: Getty Images

All rights reserved. No part of this publication may be reproduced or transmitted in any form or by any means, electronic or mechanical, including photocopying, recording, or any information storage or retrieval system, without prior permission in writing from the publishers.

Bloomsbury Publishing Inc does not have any control over, or responsibility for, any third-party websites referred to or in this book. All internet addresses given in this book were correct at the time of going to press. The author and publisher regret any inconvenience caused if addresses have changed or sites have ceased to exist, but can accept no responsibility for any such changes.

Library of Congress Cataloging-in-Publication Data
Names: Rodrigues, Laurie A., author.
Title: The American novel after ideology, 1961-2000 / Laurie A. Rodrigues.
Description: New York, NY : Bloomsbury Academic, 2020. | Includes bibliographical references and index. |
Summary: "Argues that while political and sociological discourses in late 20th-century America made multilateral assertions of the "end of ideology," novels of the Cold War and post-Cold War years conflicted with satisfied postures that claimed the completeness, or unity, of American society"– Provided by publisher.
Identifiers: LCCN 2020031358 (print) | LCCN 2020031359 (ebook) | ISBN 9781501361869 (hardback) | ISBN 9781501371417 (paperback) | ISBN 9781501361876 (epub) | ISBN 9781501361883 (pdf)
Subjects: LCSH: American fiction–20th century–History and criticism. | Ideology in literature. | Society in literature.
Classification: LCC PS379 .R57 2020 (print) | LCC PS379 (ebook) | DDC 813/.5409–dc23
LC record available at https://lccn.loc.gov/2020031358
LC ebook record available at https://lccn.loc.gov/2020031359

ISBN:	HB:	978-1-5013-6186-9
	PB:	978-1-5013-7141-7
	ePDF:	978-1-5013-6188-3
	eBook:	978-1-5013-6187-6

Typeset by Integra Software Services Pvt. Ltd.

To find out more about our authors and books visit www.bloomsbury.com and sign up for our newsletters.

For Wayne, Langston and my Great Mentors.

Contents

	Introduction: Ideology and American Literary Studies, 1950s–2000	1
1	Cliché and Modern Womanhood: J. D. Salinger's *Franny and Zooey*	29
	"Franny": Cliché as Characterization	33
	"Zooey's" (False) Alternative	41
2	Ideology and Nostalgist Aesthetics: Carlene Hatcher Polite's *The Flagellants*	55
	Polite's Organic Community	64
	Cyclical Aesthetics and Ideological Operations	68
	The Problem of Inscription	77
3	"Sorcery" and Historical Narrative: Leslie Marmon Silko's *Almanac of the Dead*	83
	A Glyphic Grundrisse: The "Five Hundred Year Map"	93
	One World, Many Tribes	122
4	Color-Blindness and the Trouble of Depiction in Philip Roth's *The Human Stain*	129
	Zuckerman's Late 1990s and Racial Discourse's Omissions	137
	Coleman Silk and Women (According to Zuckerman)	152
	Conclusion: Toward Renewing Readers' Experiences of American Novels	167
	Notes	177
	Bibliography	208
	Index	215

Introduction:
Ideology and American Literary Studies, 1950s–2000

Literary interpretation can be as difficult to teach as it can be to perform. To begin with, not all literary texts seem to cry out for interpretation: regardless of genre, some literatures (and in particular, the contemporary) may appear straightforward, transparent. By the same token, however, the temptation to procure answers concerning a text's *meaning* (with which interpretation inevitably teases) can drive readers' impulses to "short-circuit," as Fredric Jameson puts it, a text's obscurity with abstract thought; and this, of course, allots rather limited clarity to the text in question.[1] For all its trickiness, literary interpretation implicitly directs readers' attention to *history*: that is, the place of the text within a particular scope, the text as an artifact in-itself, its writer's personal history, and so on.[2] However, particularly in America following the Second World War, this issue of *history* (along with its alluring fellow, *interpretation*) becomes tricky business, as well: During and after the Cold War, the rise of mass cultures, the Civil Rights Movement, actions for indigenous sovereignty, and acknowledgments of intersectionality altered the image and concept of American history, both domestically and abroad. The variety of distinct experiences revealed in these diverse portions of recent American history reveal the difficulty inherent to imagining that history as *either* cohesive or harmonious. And yet, simultaneous with the social and political (not to speak of cultural) variety associated with the post-Second World War age in America, there reverberated an uncanny, para-cultural consensus. That consensus aggressively (if counterintuitively) asserted an *accord* intrinsic to the Cold War and post–Cold War years in America. Thus, the proverbial *plot* of American literary interpretation thickens—particularly in light of the various ways this historical moment has itself been interpreted.

The urge to interpret *or* to determine that a text does not need interpretation are both revealing and important historical impulses. When critics or scholars historically encounter a particular text as facile, or middlebrow, and thus determine it is not (worthy of, or) in need of interpretation (as critics considered of J. D. Salinger's *Franny and Zooey*), today's scholars of American literatures and cultures should pause; a similar awkward moment will arise when some of those same critics (and several others) dismiss certain other novels as opaque or *difficult* (as was the case with Carlene Hatcher Polite's *The Flagellants* (c. 1967).[3] This deprives the texts in question of concerted engagement with the critical and historical contexts of their emergence. Today's readers of American literatures might be reminded of a prescient point, made by Rita Felski, about American studies: In *Beyond Critique*, Felski notes that it is difficult to "dodge the bullet of the accusation that [critics and scholars] are shoring up the very ideology of American exceptionalism they [claim to] call into question."[4] Dismissals or refusals to potentially enrich certain texts (or methodologies) via interpretation reveal readers' generalized *suspicions* toward the American novels they encounter (or, at the very least, *certain* American novels they encounter); in turn, this misplaced suspicion reveals exchanges between literature and the humanistic, critical disciplines that are (problematically, if not compellingly) inseparable from their ideological milieux. Embedded within critical and scholarly dismissals are important sign-posts illuminating details that concern the moment of a text's publication, its writer's critical (if sometimes inarticulate) impulses, and matrices of norms surrounding art and literary value that have systematically (and historically) excluded certain styles, modes of discourse, and characterizations from the canonical, or traditional (and therefore, pedagogically disseminated), *contemporary American* literary milieu.

In contemporary, scholarly pursuits of interpretation via *close reading*, for instance, works of literature, are often historicized or encountered and read as formal, historical objects in and of themselves. And many compelling debates, particularly on Cold War and post–Cold War American novels, have been borne of readers' historicizations of texts; from this approach, valuable debates around canonization, literary value, and narrative experimentation have been generated. However, formalist approaches of this ilk share a tendency to flatten the cultural and social variety inherent to particular turning points, peculiarities, and crises that may be found within broader, historical moments. Conventional historicization elides deep analyses of novels' aesthetic complexities, as well as the socio-cultural fluxes and movements toward which aesthetics have been argued to gesture (consider the work of Esther Leslie, for instance). In this way, formalist and/or historicist approaches to American Cold War and post–Cold War novels may (paradoxically) foreclose broadened historical insights that are generated *within* these cultural productions. In addition to Felski, Susan Sontag and Frederic Jameson have also explored this point.[5] That is to say, if one follows certain rules (or modes, such as historicism) of interpretation, one's readings lend oneself to specific (presumably favorable) analytical outcomes; and while following such rules may succeed in extracting elements from texts that showcase a writer's artistry or profundity (e.g., exceptionalism), as Sontag teaches, they ultimately operate to render the text (perhaps disingenuously) *familiar*—and thus, delimited.[6] In this way (recalling Felski's issues with *critique*), indiscriminate decoding of disparate works of art with a single interpretive matrix may generate a troubling resonance, or equivalency, where such may not actually exist (by the same token, this also relates to why certain texts may have been excluded from specific discussions within American literary studies).

By contrast, in this study, I apply to the problem of interpretation a commentary on the conditions of that problem, itself. Reaching beyond conventional historicization, I historicize the specific postwar moments in which novels were published and initially received, adding new dimension to literary considerations of the postwar years' shifting social and cultural values. By offering readings that are rigorously interdisciplinary (i.e., exploratory, but *not* suspicious), this approach expands readers' experiences of the texts I engage, as well as understandings of the texts' embeddedness in specific, important historical narratives. And while the novels I string together in *American Novel after Ideology* are, indeed, intentionally disparate (popular, experimental, conceptual, and academic), my readings and the interpretive matrices from which I draw are *also* disparate; from this formal cacophony,

I bring out uncanny resonances among diverse novels published during America's Cold War and post–Cold War periods, from 1961 to 2000.

An important, common element connecting the precarious moments in which these dissimilar novels were published is their emergence amid various, dominant discourses of national cohesion and progress, found both in American literary studies and in sociological debates: Within historical, philosophical, and sociological fields, the years following the close of the Second World War have been described by many as "the end of ideology"; and subsequently, the post–Cold War age has been dubbed, first by Francis Fukuyama, the "end of history." These descriptions comprise historical signposts that make provocative, if paradoxical, claims concerning the definitive "ends"—or, as I define them, transformations and qualitative changes—of ideology. Claims of ideology's "end" in the postwar years were first popularized by sociologist Daniel Bell. According to Bell, socially supported totalizing systems of comprehensive reality, or ideologies (e.g., Marxism, socialism, communism), ended with the allied triumph in the Second World War. Bell made this argument in various forms, in discussions on various topics, in articles published across the 1950s and in his 1960 collection *The End of Ideology: On the Exhaustion of Political Ideas in the Fifties*. Bell's claim, along with Francis Fukuyama's assertion of "the end of history," offers compelling historical narratives with resonances in society and, I argue, American culture, that is, as representations of historical progress and political consensus, or (ironically) ideological representations in and of themselves. After all, claims such as Bell's (and Fukuyama's, explored in Chapter 3) comprise performative denials of ideology's inability to ever fully draw to a close; while, paradoxically, they also reiterate the idea that ending (or, transforming) is simply what all ideologies eventually do, classically defined ideologies typically forecast their own end(s).

While the works of Bell and Fukuyama (along with the topic of ideology, more generally) are rarely engaged in twentieth-century American literary scholarship, their definitive assertions concerning the American postwar condition (i.e., a shared situation, or an objective position, to which various creative responses irrupted) directly contradict the cultural variety that *also* hallmarks the Cold War and post–Cold War years. Cultural and critical innovations including mass media and its respondent, McLuhanism; the Black Arts Movement (BAM); stylistic innovations in Native American literatures, reclamations of ancient and modern myth, literary histories; and the early-21st century's engagements with intersectionality, encompass but a few of the ways novels published in American after 1960 have artfully challenged satisfied postures, like those of Bell and Fukuyama, that insist on the unity or completeness of American society and culture.

Bell's assertions reflected the country's relative economic success in the first decades following the war; or, his assertions reflected a strident, associated *claim* concerning the supposed achievement of general affluence across America. Bell's exceptionalist argument, maintained alongside other neoconservative figures of the 1960s onward, claimed that given the precipitant excess within American life following the Second World War the country's "people of plenty" were not concerned with either class-related or economic issues—but rather, if anything, with issues of "status."[7] Perhaps surprisingly, Bell's and others' presumptions of positive economic change precipitating negative cultural and social consequences *were also* echoed in contemporaneous literary debates. These claimed the proverbial death of the American *novel*—apparently, alongside Bell's "end" of ideology. In *Partisan Review*, for instance, literary critic Lionel Trilling claimed of the novel in America: "It has been of all literary forms the most devoted to the celebration and investigation of the human will; and the will of our society is dying of its own excess."[8] Trilling's comment reminds readers that, awash in (presumed) general prosperity, Americans' concerns for principled self-preservation, and their capacities for (not to mention the necessity of) prioritizing among desires, have atrophied to damning cultural effect. Of course, neither the claim of ideology's demise nor that of America's abundance encapsulates fully developed views of the totality of postwar American economic or political structures. Importantly, economic "excess" was not general among all people living in America (whether fictional or actual) following the Second World War. Furthermore, sociologists since the 1960s have noted the notion of "status politics," resulting from economic change, as problematic insofar as it overlooks the instrumental significance of status in issues such as the desegregation of schools and the religious question of the 1960 presidential election.

Nevertheless, the excess perceived by Bell, Trilling, and others did not only come in economic forms—rather, in light of the American novel's purported decline in readership, the "excess" indicated by Trilling and echoed by his contemporaries was likely related to the expansion of technology and new, more accessible forms of entertainment beyond reading. I further develop this claim in Chapter 1. The novel's audience was disappearing and without these readers, such arguments generally ran, the form's moral and aesthetic values were likewise dissolving into discursive chaos. The alleged mid-twentieth-century *death of the American novel* encompasses a collection of generally anti-populist claims, asserting the cultural degradation of American literature as a result of: on the one hand, a boom in popular and ephemeral publications (e.g., women's magazines, mass-market paperback fiction, self-help literature) and on the other, the sudden, technologically driven omnipresence of mass culture in American life—which of course includes mass-produced, popular, and ephemeral publications.

Commenting on the encroaching superficiality of mass culture, writer, and critic, Mary McCarthy pointed out a problem, similar to Trilling's, with contemporaneous American novels: characters reflecting modern images of womanhood were few and far-between, she asserted, seemingly having not been updated since the pre-war heydays of John Dos Passos and William Faulkner.[9] McCarthy's denunciation obliquely references the popularity in the 1950s and 1960s of sociological and managerial studies, including John Burnham's *Managerial Revolution* (1941) and William Whyte's *The Organization Man* (1956); such studies charted sweeping changes in American social structures that were a result of the wartime and postwar growth of corporate economic centrality in the United States. However, McCarthy contended, despite these great (if alleged) changes to private and public American lives, contemporary literary characters drawn from American life barely resembled these changes. In spite of (or perhaps because of) the 1950s' and 60s' soaring production rates for mass-market paperbacks, to many cultural and literary commentators of the day, the American novel's slow but apparently inevitable death was a troubling sign of more sweeping, cultural, and even social issues afoot. Some critical strains implicated the American *mass* as potential crucible for the germs of fascism, calling to mind the European *crowds* and *mobs* of the wartime years. However, along with Trilling, McCarthy's complaints miss the uncanny preoccupations with social, political, and historical spheres emerging in fiction writers' transformed iterations of the novel during the early 1960s and onward.

McCarthy's comments in particular presume that the alternative historical theories offered by Burnham, the descriptions of capital-driven conformity described in Whyte's work (without an alternative in sight), and so on in fact comprise accurate models of contemporary American lives that would *also* be compelling to read in fictionalized form. Moreover, and perhaps more troubling, McCarthy's comment also presumes that, within models like those of Burnham and Whyte, an artistic critique or satirical rendering could or would not be generated; Burnham's, Whyte's, and others' images of social progress or change, McCarthy seems to suggest, ought simply to be *faithfully* (or, realistically) reproduced in contemporary American literatures. Along with Trilling, McCarthy's complaints thus read as an aesthetic (if not desubliminized) stand against economic and social changes that were actually taking place in America—changes, in fact, which *directly challenged* cohesive, unified images of American life, work, and society. While critics' and scholar's mid-century complaints against the American novel seem to plead for a new voice, their pleas carry the hidden premise that this voice should coincide with a limited critical lexicon—that is, a voice already-defined (so, not new at all), to follow Trilling and McCarthy's logic.

While political, managerial, and sociological discourses made multilateral assertions of consensus concerning the "end of ideology" during the years following the Second World War, expressions in novels of the Cold War and post–Cold War years jangled with the discontinuities inherent to these attitudes. Dominant modes and methods of interpretation widely applied at the time, however, were unable to access these expressions. Many postwar cultural critics and influencers—within and beyond the field of literature— supported systematic (if paradoxical) denials like Bell's and Trilling's (though more implicit) of deep-level changes in American culture *and* power relations "after ideology." As a result, I claim, many timely narrative innovations were unevenly comprehended, and much less often appreciated. Against claims like Trilling's, writers of novels published after 1960 did, indeed, offer readers ample innovations in voice, character, and form. Beginning with J. D. Salinger's critically despised *Franny and Zooey* (1961), a composite novel published within a year of Bell's *End of Ideology*, I dig into the tension between literary taste and innovation in the age "after ideology" by examining the form's various engagements with this paradoxical assertion.

In Chapter 1, I open a renewed discussion around Salinger's text, examining how *Franny and Zooey* presents an unexpected, feminist commentary on the individual effects of mass cultural images and representations of women. Salinger's composite novel, I claim, refracts dominant sociological theories of the 1950s (such as Bell's), whose deliberations on society "after ideology" omit women's experiences. In "Franny," Salinger depicts Franny Glass as protagonist-in-crisis via carefully curated clichés drawn from various media such as fashion, epistolary, and popular film. This collection of clichés guides readers' interpretations of the text's central cliché: Franny's crisis, which comes to a head in the text's first section and is protracted as a breakdown through the remainder of the composite text. Through Bell's ideas on generational divides (e.g., between Franny and her brothers) among postwar youth; in combination with analyses by Alva Myrdal, Viola Klein, and Betty Friedan on women's lack of personal, social, and professional options; and Marshall McLuhan's reflections on mass culture's social effects vis-à-vis the "cultural cliché": I read the remainder of *Franny and Zooey* as reflecting the blind spots inherent to post-ideological discourses that construct feminine identity and maturity along a spectrum of clichés.[10] Through its host of resonances with representations of women "after ideology," *Franny and Zooey* illustrates the ways outdated social norms and troubling mass cultural frameworks formulate women's options concerning professional and personal success. *Franny and Zooey* highlights the (unwittingly) comic distortions and blind spots inherent to depictions of modern leading ladies, like Franny Glass.

However incisive or surprisingly sensitive *Franny and Zooey* may seem to twenty-first-century readers in Chapter 1, Salinger's contemporaries regarded the book as extensive, clumsy, and arguably cult-like in its subject matter. In fact, a 2001 article by Janet Malcolm ("Justice for J. D. Salinger") specifically focuses on the critical onslaught received by Salinger's later fiction, like *Franny and Zooey*.[11] In this piece, Malcolm notes: "I don't know of any other case where literary characters have aroused such animosity, and where a writer of fiction has been so severely censured for [apparently] failing to understand the offensiveness of his creations." In fact, Malcolm points out, the ire of several critics may well have "set forth the terms on which Salinger would be relegated to the margins of literature."[12] Alfred Kazin, Joan Didion, and Mary McCarthy along with Leslie Fielder, John Updike, and other titans of literary criticism and discourse negatively responded to *Franny and Zooey*, registering marked annoyance with the Glass family characters in particular.[13]

Interestingly, while few directly critiqued the character of Franny or her "little nervous breakdown" to many of Salinger's contemporaries, the Glass family stories generally comprised an extensive creative indulgence, lowering the degree of artistic accomplishment that this work could achieve. Some of *Franny and Zooey*'s reviewers even read Salinger's text as one of many middlebrow novels that were ultimately "too paltry to create a literary tradition" that could compete with either the greatness of the previous generation's literature *or* the growing presence of mass cultures, like television.[14] Indeed, in *Love and Death in the American Novel* (1960), Leslie Fielder refers to Salinger's fiction, particularly his then-recent work toward *Franny and Zooey*, as "middlebrow."[15] As a result, *Franny and Zooey* fell out of favor for years, but the text did not go without voluminous academic engagements. Yet, for the wealth of critical viewpoints and interpretive treatments of *Franny and Zooey* that have emerged since its publication in 1961, few scholars of Salinger have honed in on his depiction of Franny Glass, whose ladies room breakdown motors the text's action and (what it possesses of) plot.

Chapter 1's exploration of Franny Glass and her clichéd, critically overlooked nervous breakdown thus begins to reveal uncanny, discursive continuities (or really, omissions) among several influential fields of the postwar years, including sociology, literary criticism, and advertising. Thus, Salinger's contemporaries' rejection of *Franny and Zooey* by way of its supposed, aesthetic resonances with middlebrow (or, popular, mass-marketed) literatures reveals a troubling blindness to the cultural importance of clichés to processes of identity-formation for women at this same time—as well as what this cultural importance might indicate. By extension, this blindness systematically avoids confronting women's experiences in the postwar age (or, "after ideology") as potentially diverse from those of American men of any generation. Combined with women's limited ontological options after ideology, these elisions essentially amount to a systemic erasure of the existence and operations of power relations (particularly via gender relations) at this time.

This move may call to mind the New Critical principle of self-contained literary critique, or solely examining the formal elements of a text; according to this principle, any social, political, or historical factors that bear on a text's creative inception, the context of its publication, or find reference in its content, are beyond the jurisdiction of literary scholarship. And interestingly, by the time complainants against the American novel's demise began publishing their concerns in the *New Republic*, *Partisan Review*, and elsewhere, the New Criticism had already been methodologically normalized: that is, widely taught in top American universities. Given the New Criticism's methodological standardization well before the mid-1960s, as well as its (and other contemporaneous discourses') systematic blindness to power relations, it is therefore perhaps unsurprising to twenty-first-century readers that, through the 1960s, the field's most well-known literary critics could generate but scant constructive responses to, or critical engagements with, certain, apparently opaque, long-form works of literary fiction—including the impetuously toned *Franny and Zooey* and Carlene Hatcher Polite's experimental first novel *The Flagellants*. Like Daniel Bell's claims of ideology's definitive "end," mid-century complaints concerning the American novel's death and the New Criticism's omission of contextual and intertextual considerations from literary scholarship should, to twenty-first-century readers, appear limiting.

Indeed, the New Critics' methodology is ill-equipped for critically engaging (beyond description) representations of unsettling power relations. Furthermore, like Bell's definition of ideology and its end, claims concerning the novel's end presume that the American novel itself is a finished, definitive aesthetic that can be neither improved upon nor changed; similarly, as Bell's theories would have it, "ideology" also comprises finished and productive, socially supported systems that (due to their presumed "exhaustion" via repeated failures) simply ended with the close of the Second World War. The trouble, then, with Bell's mid-century claims as well as those within literature, is that they proceed from limited perspectives of, on the one hand, American society and, on the other, literature. This would not be an issue were it not clear that these limited perspectives cannot (or will not) engage with the cultural codes and principles that survived "the end of ideology" and were adapted in mass culture, the social sciences, and nationalist discourses, that is, codes and ideological formulations that retain power relations, despite efforts to ignore them. This shortfall, I claim, is precisely what post-1960 American novels aesthetically demonstrate. According to Salinger, Carlene Hatcher Polite, Leslie Marmon Silko, Philip Roth, and the numerous discussions and texts with which their creations intersect, the period at the end of ideology is a time of partial, interested viewpoints that are no less ideological than, for instance, the New Criticism, Marxism, or Daniel Bell's critiques thereof.

In Chapter 2, I extend *Franny and Zooey*'s discussion of American women's limited prospects by taking up a nuanced novel by BAM-era writer Carlene Hatcher Polite. Like *Franny and Zooey*, *The Flagellants*' forced conjunctions of partially dissolved ideological formulations distort its narrative and (perhaps ironically) curtail its capacity for plot development and resolution—or, *progress* and *consensus*. Concurrent with McLuhan and Friedan's critiques of cliché's predominance in American conceptions of women "after ideology," women of color writers explored ways black women were hemmed in by their position at the interstices of race, class, and gender discourses (all of which are ideological). This would be studied for decades following the 1960s, through projects of literary recovery and black feminisms' academic consolidation during the 1980s, which I also discuss in Chapter 2. However, *The Flagellants* pushes upon the critical values, stylistic elements, and purported functions of American and African American literatures, while the novel also anticipates (and prophetically critiques) potentially problematic aesthetics that would be developed by black women writers later, particularly in the 1970s.

Before womanism and other women of color feminisms of the 1970s and 1980s, Polite's *The Flagellants* questioned the urban, masculinist culture espoused by the BAM, particularly the notion of a naturalized revolutionary subject that excluded black women. Her novel notes the ways black nationalist discourses absorbed American mass culture's often racist discourses on black families and gender relations, as in Daniel Patrick Moynihan's contemporaneous, *The Negro Family: A Case for National Action* (1965), to cite one example.[16] Polite's

Flagellants also satirizes expectations pertaining to realist characterizations in black literature. For instance, the novel may present naturalist settings—a dingy apartment, a street corner, the local bar—but it draws on non-realist traditions of parody, surrealism, and the distortions of American culture itself, which rely on interpretations of African American culture. Moreover, Polite populates her novel with stubbornly static, projective characters, making obvious their inculcation and inscription by ideological processes, and thereby intentionally compromising readers' abilities to encounter them as figures imbued with affirmative agency. Polite's main characters, Ideal and Jimson, are black New York City transplants who, in the context of their crumbling romance, torment each other in the present with traumatic allegories and concepts from their respective pasts. Their dysfunctional relationship is mediated by Polite's biased narrator, driving readers to sadly wonder if there will be any escape for either party, from their poverty, themselves, *or* each other.

It therefore may not surprise readers that Polite's first novel, which received critical acclaim in France (where it was first published in 1966), was all but ignored (according to surviving reviews) in both area-specific and general American literary journals; and it was largely denigrated by mainstream (i.e., then, the most widely read) reviewers. This is all likely, at least in part, due to the problematic fact *The Flagellants'* American release was in 1967, at the height of the BAM.[17] Only a handful of reviews were written in the States, but the similitude among their points of praise and critique for *The Flagellants* is uncanny: American reviewers seemed to appreciate the depth with which Polite expresses her protagonists' respective agonies. In a review for *The American Scholar*, Roger Ebert compared Polite to Richard Wright, claiming, with the publication of *The Flagellants*, that "there is now a novel that throughout its length remains at [a] pitch of endurance and despair" comparable to Wright's *Black Boy* (1945).[18] Nora Sayre, on the other hand, extended her praise of the novel's moving affectivity beyond racialized agony. The sincerity and immediacy of Jimson and Ideal's painful relationship, Sayre wrote in *The Nation*, are effective because they are constituted by "agonies that are uniquely Negro" and "torments which can afflict lovers of any color."[19] Mainstream readers praised Polite's ability to render human emotion into the tumultuous story of a poor American couple's failing marriage.

Yet, while emotional impact was praised as the novel's greatest asset, the same reviewers *also* articulated a greater, more general dissatisfaction with *The Flagellants*, as well as with Polite's abilities as a writer. Polite's prose style, along with her mode of characterization, was repeatedly critiqued as the novel's greatest flaws. Elsewhere in the review cited above, Sayre refers to Polite as "careless of characterization." Frederic Raphael, author of the novel's most negative review, expounds upon this complaint; in his piece, he distastefully comments on Polite's inattention to character development—as well as to all "standardized methods of Creative Writing." As the narrative tone vacillates, according to Raphael, between "whimsy" and "two-fisted rant," Polite betrays her stylistic uncertainty. Thus, the novel demonstrates the author's difficulties with expression and intention—that is, Raphael asserts, Polite did not seem to know her "ideal audience." Ebert comments similarly, linking Polite's "strange" writing style to the difficulties he faced in reading her two protagonists: "Jimson and Ideal speak by turns in elevated language, in jargon, in gutter idiom, in poetic incantation, and in obscenity."[20] Ebert notes that the narrative's frequent tonal shifts place too much emphasis upon the characters' "masochism." Polite's unsettlingly self-aware characters "watch their own lives deteriorate"—and this, for Ebert, too closely resembles "the flagellants of classic pornography." The result, as Raphael points out, is a "smoke screen of words," behind which the protagonists' "fire" is neutralized by Polite's convoluted and inconsistent prose style.

Although scholarship engaging BAM literature and art has been undertaken by more recent scholars such as Aldon Nielsen, James Edward Smethurst, and Cynthia Young, and works by BAM-era women writers have enjoyed attention by current researchers like Madhu Dubey, Polite's socially oriented, non-realist novel has nevertheless fallen to the margins of discussions emerging around the representations and interpretations of 1960s black nationalisms and their interactions/intersections with American cultures.[21] Polite's first novel has virtually disappeared from American literary history, unable to leave its mark on readers' understandings of the context of its publication. While critics in Polite's own time may have found discomfort in reading *The Flagellants'* often dysfunctional, one-dimensional characters, in Chapter 2, I clarify that the text's difficulty for readers likely did not lie in what it depicts, but in the challenge that it presents to interpreting its ideological position via Polite's characters. Against conventions and reader expectations, in *The Flagellants*, characters become devices that allow the novel to represent ideology's transfer of distorting, oppressive values as (not only destructive forces against black solidarity, but also) complex dynamics of consent and misogynoir; by normalizing the characters' dysfunction through consistent, disorienting narrative strategies (e.g., extended flashbacks, fantasy, fugue states), Polite's *The Flagellants* questions several of the mid-Cold War years' ironically ideological responses to the purported end of ideology.[22]

Salinger's and Polite's novels may appear to have little other than the decade of their publication in common. However, despite their clear representational distinctions along lines of race and privilege, the experiences of both Salinger's and Polite's main characters are uncannily similar: that is, their worlds are constituted by structures, laws, and forces that are beyond their control. Moreover, via their respective struggles to attain agency over their lives, Franny, Ideal (and Jimson, though differently) are contentious characterizations: that is, each aesthetically suitable to, but discursively problematic within, the contexts of their respective worlds. Their separately "high strung and willful nature[s]" (as Polite's narrator puts it) seem to critique the value of obedience (e.g., "bowing" for Ideal and "good sportsmanship" for Franny), which implicitly underwrites their existences as women.[23] These dispositions fly in the face of the 1960s' "spirit of capitalism"—that is, social actors' productive and uncritical cooperation with various laws, structures, and forces that are beyond their own control.[24]

This important mis-match in *Franny and Zooey* and *The Flagellants* reveals the characters' troubling self-awareness (coupled with intermittent denial) that she is but a surrogate for narratives that already exist: in the case of Franny, gendered clichés; and for Ideal, the same clichéd expectations, in addition to intersectional racial stereotypes and other complications. For Franny, the sole alternative to conventional, biologically determined destinies (or Zooey's "low-grade spiritual counsel") is the distracting allure of perpetual prayer via her deceased brother's copy of *The Way of the Pilgrim*. As for Ideal, alternatives to her "substandard life" lie in her vivid reminiscences and workday flirtations. In both cases, the alternatives offered by these worlds either are defined by others (e.g., brother Zooey, partner Jimson) or merely serve as distractions from the realities of the characters' circumstances (e.g., raccoon coats, the Jesus Prayer, Ideal's fantasies). This is precisely why neither Polite's Ideal nor Salinger's Franny experiences growth or much self-assertion in their respective narratives. Importantly, these narratives end in stalemates suited to their irreconcilable conflicts; at the ends of their stories, Franny and Ideal are left to contemplate and nevertheless bear their unbearable circumstances, leaving readers only to hope for a better future—in their fictional worlds, as well as in actuality.

Interestingly, during the decade of *Franny and Zooey*'s and *The Flagellants*' publication, literary critics and intellectuals such as Kazin, Trilling, McCarthy, many New Critics, and others decrying the death of long-form American literature did not necessarily count themselves among Daniel Bell's conceptual or political supporters (nor, surely, vice versa). However, these perceived opponents' claims concerning the ends of ideology and the American novel nevertheless converge and participate in establishing a broader, intellectual status quo during the initial decades following the Second World War. This trans-partisan wave constituted a critical push-back, in various idioms, against postwar forms of populism, however loosely defined: for neoconservatives, largely social movements, and protests; for many on the left, mass culture. This shift in American critical attitudes, in many ways, reflects intellectuals' shift in critical focus: from the powers behind economics (or, capitalism) during wartime, to the cultural values associated with capitalism's productivity (and, in some cases, those products themselves), after the war. It may therefore not surprise readers that Daniel Bell, John Burnham, and several other preeminent intellectuals of this status quo were former scholars of Marxist theory, as well as its political supporters prior to the conclusion of the Second World War; however, given the insights of the war's end, rather than "endorsing a system of total terror," as Sidney Hook put it in *Partisan Review*, intellectuals of this trans-partisan status quo operated in the interest of "*critically* supporting our own imperfect democratic culture with all its promises and dangers."[25]

However, this brand of critique, more often than not, would operate to indignantly expose presumably ideological impulses residing at the heart of, for instance, moral values and ideals (which often attend social movements, protests, and may also inform mass cultures). It may not be surprising, then, that the subtle, non-realist strategies introduced by Salinger and Polite were either lost on, or the source of ire to, many such readers of the time; their ironic reflections of mass culture, their exposure of the New Criticism's interpretive limitations, and the BAM's imperfect models comprise critical responses to the cultural stasis and homogeneity insisted upon, at least, by the literary status quo. And much to the annoyance of many, texts such as Salinger's and Polite's began to demonstrate for American readers not only that the American novel was alive and well, but (dangerously) that ideology was, as well—although transformed from its customary configurations.

Thus, in their respective worlds, Franny's and Ideal's personal values and principles are dismissed, by narrators as well as by other characters; moreover, their critical impulses are perceived as potentially rogue, undead ideological revenants—that is, threats to the stability of their worlds' structures, laws, and relations of force. Through their fictional worlds' respective intolerances for characters' clashing critical impulses, the novels reveal unspoken relations of power between and within characters' relationships. Simultaneously, through their pretenses of realism, the novels absorb and refract the ways models of history, sociology, and social movements may enrich (but also constrict) characters' desires, values, and experiences. The intentionally scientific, critical models abounding in American social sciences, managerial theory, and in literary studies thus become fodder for these novels; they aesthetically question the point (or, the ends) of this form of critique (particularly in the absence of power relations), if all relations are supposedly otherwise reducible to conflicts of interest and/or relations of force.[26]

By the end of the 1960s, *The Flagellants* suggests, new models were needed—at least in the literary world—toward expressing and contextualizing heretofore overlooked lives and experiences in American society. While Salinger's and Polite's texts do not argue against end of ideology claims, they do question lines of logic that would assert ideology's end and (though more subtly) the potential future consequences of claims of this sort. In this way, Salinger's and Polite's texts grope for some beyond, away from the distorting prescriptions of mass culture that form Franny's characterization and away from the brutal, nostalgist "motherwit" and contradictory stereotypes, which inform Ideal.[27]

In this way, both texts look (so to speak) outward—toward actuality and the future—for assurances and resolutions for their narratives. The texts coax (in characters and readers alike) questions concerning the potential quality and meaning of lives lived beyond the boundaries and circuits of conventional existences, such as Franny's or Ideal's. As neither young woman is able to recognize (and then pursue) a more desirable state of affairs, their critical impulses become incapable of engendering meaningful change in their lives (thus, like the literary status quo, their complaints on society, family, or their personal lives may read as rather aesthetic).

The troubled perspectives showcased in Salinger's and Polite's texts reach for futures in which antithetical views have been overcome, that is, in which ideology's "end" is reimagined as its transformation, from a productive operation, to a malleable problematic by which citizens may make or remake meaning in their lives, in accordance with personal interest. And eerily, by the late 1980s and the end of the Cold War, this is precisely what Francis Fukuyama would claim had occurred in America: given the discursive multi-vocality of the 1970s and 1980s vis-à-vis Black Power, women of color feminisms, the induction of poststructuralist and postcolonial thought into the American academy (etc.), Fukuyama claimed, ideology as such had dissolved into an atomized array of unproductive, clashing discourses. In his 1989 article for *The National Interest*, Fukuyama asserted that such theories, which construct historical progress as series of ideologically motivated struggles for supremacy, were exhausted by the Cold War victory of capitalist democracy; although not without critics by the time he published *The End of History and the Last Man* in 1992, Fukuyama nevertheless compelled many with his assertion, as it aligned with optimistic interpretations of the Cold War's end as an assured triumph for the United States, Western democracy, and capitalism alike. Indeed, by the late 1980s, Ronald Reagan's revolution in American politics and policy was already the stuff of living lore, lodged in the popular imagination of many as paving America's way out of the energy crisis, its international affairs issues, the growth of international terrorism, and the malaise which some would claim hallmarked the Carter administration. At the dawn of the 1990s, the patriotic conservatism branded by Reagan echoed in triumphalist historical narratives like Fukuyama's; and this established for many *the way* to America's future prosperity (and how fortunate, as not long before, that future appeared quite uncertain).

Through the 1970s and 1980s, the American literary academy was also undergoing significant changes in the form and structure of its collegiate departments and programs, as well as in the style and directions of its pedagogies and scholarship.[28] Founded largely on the intellectual work of women of color artists and writers in the early decades of the Cold War, and the gradual introduction of critical theories (e.g., Jacques Derrida, Michel Foucault, Gilles Deleuze et al.) into American literary lexica in the 1970s and 1980s, scholars of American literatures and cultures compellingly contrasted with Fukuyama's totalizing triumphalism, as writing on cultural productions via power relations (i.e., their motives, sources, pathologies) became more prominent in the academy. This convergence of renewed critical and artistic perspectives also helped to engender the establishment of postcolonial studies, cultural studies, and ethnic studies in the American academy. At the same time, however, on the ground in America (both within and beyond the academy's walls) class tensions mounted, recession loomed, and an American "underclass" continued to grow beyond urban centers; highlighting the historical irony of economic reason, conservative approaches abounded in international relations and domestic economic policies.[29]

The discursive heterogeneity beginning to take off in the American academy by the early 1990s was considered, by Fukuyama, as *part and parcel to* the atomized, politically unproductive ideological discourses that are aligned in *The End of History and The Last Man* with telltale signs of history's end. Thus, Fukuyama's claims concerning the effects of the Cold War on American society, economy, and politics presented a stridently optimistic, assured perspective on the present (c. early 1990s). Akin in structure and function to Bell's arguments decades before, Fukuyama's assertions of history's end befit a particular outlook of America for the time in which it was published; I further unpack this consideration alongside Leslie Marmon Silko's second novel in Chapter 3. In his formulation, Fukuyama does not engage *ideology*, as such (reminiscent of *capital* in managerial theories of the 1970s and 1980s); but rather, this concept is distilled down to diverse and benign, if hypocritical, veils for power relations (which are never explained by Fukuyama insofar as power's impulse toward concealment).³⁰ However, Fukuyama's definition of the post–Cold War condition as the "end of history," much like Daniel Bell's claims concerning the "end" of ideology, elides the return of 1960s' civil rights battles—sexuality, race, gender equality—to the national stage during the 1990s.³¹ In this way, Fukuyama's influential (if incendiary) claims do not fulfill the preferential states alluded to in either *Franny and Zooey* or *The Flagellants*. While Fukuyama considers contexts in which all Americans' individual identities, personal and professional options, transcend descriptively critical orientations (such as those found in theories from the 1950s and 1960s), like Daniel Bell, his work does not consider any difference that gender may make to his theorizations, nor is his image of the American context capable of contending with the concept of culture, or multiple cultures, coexisting therein.

Rather, in Fukuyama's historical narrative of post–Cold War America, there is no alternative to the capitalist democratic state—and interestingly, there are presumably *no oppositions* to it, either. In this formulation, capitalist democracy comes to stand in for culture as "universal homogeneity," to use Fukuyama's terminology; here, differences among cultures are problematically imagined as part of their *essence*, or essential to culture, as such. This construction may call to mind President Clinton's Executive Order #13050 in 1997, also known as his "Initiative on Race," *One America in the 21st Century*. This executive order generated a commissions document defining the crux of America's race problem as "intrinsic racial/cultural differences" among American citizens; Clinton's Initiative thus proposed "dialogue" as the best means for American citizens to adopt toward the resolution of these "differences."³² The effect of this (essentialist) literalized, reductive concept of culture is a theory of history (much like Marx's or Hegel's, as I explore in Chapter 3) that reflects developmental, linear progressions of ages or eras which encapsulate humanity's progress within inevitable waves toward some ultimate end—such as Fukuyama's "universal homogeneity," or democratic and capitalist forms of government.

By contrast, I argue in Chapter 3, Leslie Marmon Silko's second novel, *Almanac of the Dead* (1991), conceptualizes history as a variety of discourses, or forms of communication.³³ Like Fukuyama, *Almanac of the Dead* shifts its focus off of ideology, but also reminds readers of the predominating influence of *narrative* (i.e., of theorization and formulation) on broad, often hegemonic understandings of history. Some of these discourses, readers find, are framed in the novel as real, or expository, while others figure as mythical, sacred, and so on; interestingly, in this formulation, the primary equivalency among these discourses is *not* a single, "homogenizing" or "ultimate" discourse, as in Fukuyama (and Marx, Hegel), for instance. Instead, in *Almanac of the Dead*, historical narratives proceed from the potentially unfamiliar, cyclical coordinates of "sorcery." Actuality's continual shuttling between the ideal and the real (i.e., the *illusory* ability of ideals to exist, for better or worse, in the material realm) is referred to as "sorcery" in Silko's *Almanac*. Sorcery's distorting influence on characters and their senses of actuality thus generates a negative portrait of Fukuyama's "coherent and directional History of mankind"[34]—that is, a depiction of humanity's path through history as paved by *accident*, immanent to the compounding effects of projective humanity's self-interested pursuits under sorcery's influence.[35] In fact, *Almanac*'s number of echoing plotlines and stories correspond through the generality of sorcery's influence, as a seemingly omnipresent social and political force, over all of the characters in the novel.

Almanac of the Dead is a complex, extensive text composed of uncannily reverberating, interweaving stories and mythologies. Rather than placing specific politics of race and gender at the forefront of the novel (as in *The Flagellants*) or cliché-laden expressions assembling characterization (as in *Franny and Zooey*), Silko paints an even more nuanced landscape for transmuted ideology's work in the post–Cold War age. Although deploying a much larger cast than either Polite or Salinger, *Almanac of the Dead* also engages surprisingly flat characters; and as in Polite's novel, Silko's characters do not serve plot(s), but rather operate as sign-posts by which readers may perceive ideological processes unfold through the stories that characters embody and share, the beliefs that they internalize, and the subsequent actions and choices these characters make (often with little consideration of consequences). Through the novel's spiraling narrative structure, readers come to see that the social, racial, and economic differences among Silko's characters (indeed, differences to which many stubbornly adhere) formulate a compelling ground for their material generality. Silko's novel suggests that ideology's operations are challenged by *economic* circumstances that materially contribute to individuals' desires to either mobilize against or protect a status quo; interestingly, this directly challenges Fukuyama's contention that ideology's productivity is hindered by its dissolution (or, transformation) into incongruous discourses.

Thus, the causes and interests for which characters work in the novel (in lieu of conventional jobs or careers) are non-necessary, or free; it is done, in other words, because characters believe these pursuits (including vocations such as drug dealing, weapons smuggling, etc.) will fulfill their personal interests and material desires.[36] In contrast with Franny, Ideal, or Jimson, *Almanac*'s massive cast has access to a seemingly exhaustive array of tools toward self-actualization and revolt; in sharp contrast with my readings of Salinger's and Polite's texts from the 1960s, countless *ways out* of unhappy, degrading, or inconvenient circumstances exist in *Almanac* for all of Silko's characters—one need only be willing to pay the price. In this way, I encounter *Almanac of the Dead* as a rebuttal to claims like Fukuyama's (following Bell) that define history's end with the early 1990s. *Almanac*'s expression emerges from its depiction of a post-1960s America (and wider world) in which the 1960s' revolutionary ideas, existential rebellions, and Marxist critiques (particularly regarding sexuality, gender, and racial equality) have been marketized and, as a result, fatally neutralized; engendered by the very system they profess to overthrow, the various *styles* (or ways out) from which characters choose can never be politically productive, nor can their commodified pseudo-critiques encapsulate the totality of anything they approach.

In contrast to Fukuyama's optimism, then, non-mundane work in *Almanac* constitutes characters' impotent struggles for recognition (or, status). Through the text's gradual unfolding, Silko reveals "sorcery" as the processes and effects of the circulation of standardized knowledge (as in cartography, for instance) and shared stories (or religion, myths) that ultimately comprise potent and long-standing social forces. Beginning with the "Five Hundred Year Map," Silko bares the representational powers that distort characters' senses of space, territory, and identity; and through the unfolding of *Almanac*, Silko reveals that the engulfing force of "sorcery" is (not the work of witches or the supernatural, but) perpetuated by the novel's projective characters themselves, unwitting makers of history held in sway by the distorting influences of the stories they hold dear—but over which they seemingly have little control. Thus, *Almanac*'s conceptual sorcery leaves readers with an overwhelming sense that history will be repeated until its core impulses—the stories people share—are accounted for and operationally examined.

Despite emerging amid the culture wars and the quinquennial of Christopher Columbus' colonial exploits, Silko's *Almanac of the Dead* did win some critical praise from certain circles in the American literary academy; however, most early critics, particularly in the mainstream, seemed to take greatest issue with the novel's lack of realism and its scarcity of character development. According to early reviews, *Almanac* did not make a splash among general readers of popular fiction, as Silko had hoped while writing it during the 1980s. John Skow, for instance, writing for *Time* in 1991, described *Almanac*'s characters as "half-explained" and referred to their stories as amounting to little more than a "dull headache." As for the values held by *Almanac*'s characters, Skow claimed to find only absence because, he asserted, the novel's characters are all either "drunk, doped, or crazy" and thus incomprehensible; this makes their plotlines not only difficult to follow, he claimed, but difficult to read with gravity, as the characters often read as devoid of both morality and direction.[37] Many critics' difficulties with *Almanac of the Dead* may have arisen as a result of the text's publication coinciding with the culture wars, a precarious moment in American intellectual history "during which English departments embraced minority literatures as part of multicultural studies initiatives within the U.S. academy"; however, as *Almanac* sharply departed from "what had become by then expected representations of Native American cultures," it was "doubly distanced" from accepted canonical criteria.[38] For instance, other critics of Silko's second novel, including Alan Ryan writing for *USA Today*, charged *Almanac* with failing in the area of character development by refusing to offer "that special insight into the lives and minds of Native Americans that we have come to expect."[39] Ryan problematically claims that reading *Almanac* left him knowing even less about America's marginalized populations than before having encountered the novel.

Early critics' presumptions of realism via characterization in *Almanac* were certainly misguided; and recent scholars have made much critical use of early reviews which took disapproving aim at the origins, political outlooks, and lifestyles of *Almanac*'s characters. Particularly over the last fifteen years, scholars have reminded twenty-first-century readers of *Almanac*'s early reception, using objections like those from Skow, Ryan, and others as provocative springboards into discussions of the novel's wider, cultural significance.[40] For example, Rebecca Tillett's collection of new scholarship on *Almanac* finds its critical fulcrum in *Almanac*'s negative receptions by large and mainstream publications such as *Time* and *USA Today*. In her introduction to *Howling for Justice* (2014), Tillett notes: "Silko's depiction of a social uprising that draws together the indigenous People's Army of the Americas and the American Army of the Homeless [...] triggered, and continues to trigger, some very loud socio-political alarm bells."[41] Tillett draws readers' attention to *Almanac*'s subtext of preordained revolution and end-times for "all things European," noting that, while this may have outraged many readers, still more have found inspiration for treatments of *Almanac* in this feature of the novel.

Although the critical tide has turned concerning scholars' attitudes toward and expectations of *Almanac of the Dead*, a critical gap nevertheless remains (or perhaps it is a discursive difficulty) with regard to interpreting this novel, beyond paradigms linked to indigenous or other American multiethnic literary epistemes—that is, beyond dialectal and comparative modes. Operating toward an upheaval of the comparisons and divisions for which this historical moment is so well known, and utilizing the context of its publication as an aesthetic medium, I claim that it is no wonder that *Almanac of the Dead* was so angrily received by the mainstream in 1991 (and continues to cause difficulty today). In Chapter 3, I approach a conceptual reading of *Almanac* beyond critical designations of, or generic discourses on, indigenous American multiethnic, or American, literatures.

In Chapter 4, I read Philip Roth's *The Human Stain* (2000) as Nathan Zuckerman's quizzical (if telling) response to *Almanac*'s rebuttal á Fukuyama.[42] That is, while *Almanac* presents a compellingly multi-vocal response to essentialist and linear conceptions of history like Fukuyama's, troublingly, Silko's second novel does *not* ask whether the socially constructed issue of race may be conceptualized *beyond* signifiers (e.g., symbolism) and material formulas of recognition. In *The Human Stain*, Philip Roth's foremost ghost writer, Nathan Zuckerman, reaches beyond materialist and symbolic definitions of racial difference, drawing readers' attention to his characters' generalized involvement in (and inculcation by) racial ideology (i.e., racist structures and discourses) *since* the Cold War. In this way, Roth's novel engages the imaginative (and often problematic) dimensions of history- and community-making by depicting his own implication in ideology's most troubling transformation at the end of the twentieth century: into a political instrument and structuring agent for official discourses on race and racism (e.g., as in commissions documents, dating from the 1940s through 1990s).

Where *Almanac* draws readers' attention to the broad, conceptual importance of the stories that people tell (particularly concerning representations of history), *The Human Stain* focuses on *one* man's story—specifically, Coleman Silk's story of racial passing—and its problematic entanglement with the transformed ideological remnants of Jim Crow laws and commissions politics.[43] According to Zuckerman, Coleman abandoned his African American family as a young man in the early 1950s, choosing instead to pass as white. Readers of *The Human Stain* are thus offered Coleman's passing narrative, and late professional ruin for uttering a racial slur, via Zuckerman's authorial perspective. In his rendering, race is central to the social, economic, and educational structures that shape Coleman Silk's late-1990s narrative present; and, Zuckerman suggests, this centrality transcends this specific, late-century context.

The Human Stain thus alights on the problem of storytelling, insofar as a story's narrator holds the central role in shaping both form and content of any story he or she shares. In the case of Coleman Silk, race is central to Zuckerman's rendition of his subject's life, which the writer (not Coleman) shapes; in addition, it is Zuckerman who decides *how* passing functions and takes form in the text, specifically as strategy and structuring agent. As a result, Zuckerman's narrative of racial passing (which, itself, attempts to pass) presents possibilities for his subject's social mobility that are strictly ideological. As a writer who does not share Coleman's social or racial designations, Zuckerman's understanding (and therefore his narrative) of Coleman's race travel and social integration is limited to abstract identity politics. However, through this depiction, the self-conscious Zuckerman carefully implies his distaste for racial essentialism by limiting discussion of material or economic dimensions of racialized life (likely helping him to duck some of the criticism Silko incurred), focusing instead on Coleman's ideological individuality. And while this depiction is insightfully attentive to non-material, social dimensions of race and incisively credits Coleman's success in passing to his ability to *discursively* and *psychically* inhabit conscious privilege, Zuckerman's imaginative reconstruction is nevertheless most compelling for all that it seems to intentionally *miss*. That is, not only does the writer misguidedly fold Coleman's ideological individuality into his *interiority* (i.e., often rendering his subject surprisingly unfeeling), but Zuckerman also seems self-consciously uncritical, concerning the operations of racial ideology in America since the Cold War of his (as well as Coleman's) youth.

Zuckerman's narratological perspective on self-invention, combined with his (often inattentively conjectural) focus on Coleman's motivations, results in his story ignoring the material and economic circumstances (or consequences) of Coleman's life as *either* an African or white American man. Thus, while the writer *seems* to self-consciously de-link his narrative from essentialism by omitting discussion of material and economic conditions, Zuckerman simultaneously manages to subsume the material goals pursued by, for instance, the Civil Rights Movement, in which Coleman's family (and particularly his elder brother, Walter) was involved. Coleman's estranged sister, Ernestine Silk (the writer's late informant on Coleman's heritage), mentions that the Silks have historically dealt with economic and housing-related difficulties in their New Jersey hometown (not far from where Zuckerman was raised); but beyond Ernestine's conversational mention, Zuckerman does nothing with this information in his depictions of Coleman's youth. Precipitating from this omission, Zuckerman's story can only scratch the surface of the deep insult to the Silk family that is constituted by Coleman's *c.* 1950s race travel. Particularly in light of the Civil Rights Movement, the concept of race travel to acquire social and/or material privileges reads as deeply disrespectful, implying bad faith in (not only politicians' willingness to meet citizens' demands, but) black communities' and activists' abilities to effectively convince officials to sustainably fulfill their petitions. Yet, the discriminatory practices and conditions afforded by particular institutions (e.g., higher education, athletics) are *also* not explored by Zuckerman, at least not beyond Coleman's (misdirected) rage at feeling he must resign from his long career at Athena College "for being white."[44] Through Zuckerman's concurrent emphasis on the atmospheric and ideological parameters of Coleman's race travel in the 1950s, and his professional ruin during the late 1990s, the writer nevertheless involves his narrative of Coleman's passing in a drama of *fixing* racial meaning and making *known* the identities of his characters. I note this in Chapter 4, not to claim that Zuckerman is an ineffective or racially discriminatory writer, but rather that Roth (like Salinger) intentionally embeds narratological limitations in *The Human Stain* as a commentary on late-twentieth-century American culture.

In contrast with the other texts in this study (rather ironically), Roth's *The Human Stain* received a relatively positive reception upon release; since its publication in 2000, the novel has been widely read and referred to by many as a tale of racial passing. Some of the novel's most positive readings have touted its revolutionary and inventive appeal in its adaptation of this important, and often overlooked, African American literary genre. Jonathan Freedman, for example, credits *The Human Stain* with moving beyond the often-sentimental formulas of the conventional passing narrative, for instance, by including Ernestine only briefly in, and near the end of, the novel.[45] Similarly, Mark Maslan suggests that the novel productively departs from its predecessors in early-twentieth-century fiction by "rejecting the idea of a racial identity persisting beneath the performance of inauthentic social roles," and instead, imagining through Coleman "the idea of a national identity" that is founded on "historical discontinuity."[46] Maslan asserts that Coleman's decision to pass conceals a wish neither to re-join his African American family nor to acknowledge his past in any way; therefore, he demonstrates to readers that there are no viable means for deploying history toward defining oneself or others. Dean Franco reads Roth's story of passing in *The Human Stain* as a means for dislodging the notion of race, and especially blackness, from any "larger, stable, and knowable social condition or way of being" that is based in history or convention, whether familial, communal, or literary.[47] Franco argues that Coleman's choice to dissociate from his parentage does not reflect the genre's conventional, tragic "muting or repressing of something rich and knowable."⁴⁸ Rather, the blackness passing into Jewishness that readers encounter in Coleman represents an image of "fluid and malleable" ethnicity within the social sphere's "zero-sum game" of racial relations.⁴⁹ Derek Parker Royal, whom Franco cites, also maintains that Roth's fiction (even beyond his work in *The Human Stain*) directly confronts "the ways in which issues of identity formation help to establish the subject within certain ethnic-specific assumptions."⁵⁰

Readers addressing the roles of passing and race within the novel all credit Roth with confronting, through Coleman, the fact that a choice between one historically pre-determined position and another is really no choice at all. Yet, while readers alternately credit and critique *The Human Stain* for Roth's bold confrontation of race's limits and his slanted depiction of multiculturalism, very few have held Roth's self-disclosing, unreliable narrator, Nathan Zuckerman, in any way accountable for this. Zuckerman's embedded position on the novel's landscape has provoked nary a single reader to investigate the stakes of *his* narratological work. To take this consideration for granted is to overlook Zuckerman's personal investment, and his own inculcation, in the story he relays. Thus, Zuckerman's self-appointed task of sketching Coleman's life quickly becomes a projective and creative pursuit—not unlike Buddy Glass's in *Franny and Zooey*. Embedded in history alongside his subject, Zuckerman recreates Coleman's life through the filters of *his* experiences, difficulties, and perceptions. This is the central difficulty of Zuckerman's expression in *The Human Stain* (i.e., not *really* moving past the passing genre's formulas, so to speak).

In the novel's narrative present (approximately 1998–2000), official American discourses on racism were largely relegated to discriminatory phenomena of the historical past; at this same time, racial/cultural "differences" (*not* racism) were framed as the crux of the "American race problem."⁵¹ In this context, *dialogue* was suggested as an effective means by which Americans could reach the Clinton administration's goal of "One America"—or, "national unity with a multicultural gloss."⁵² *The Human Stain* thus straddles late-century political correctness (the novel's present) and the racially fraught mid-century of Coleman's youth; Chapter 4 asks if this contrast is false, a narrative misdirection by Zuckerman as he struggles to define his *own* values and social standing as a solitary, aging American writer. Dissembling through narrative a privileged intimacy with Coleman that he never actually establishes, via his subject's life story, Zuckerman processes questions about the ends of ideology, history, and the twentieth century. *The Human Stain* is thus conspicuously aware of its construction via Zuckerman's imagination and, as a result, ultimately asks readers to consider how *meaning* might be conceptualized in the creative life, if existence is not bound to social models or stabilized by attachments to institutional structures. Particularly in light of its embeddedness in the ends of both ideology and history, the text offers readers no easy solution to this query.

In light of the fact that ideology (its existence, its end, etc.) is so rarely directly engaged in studies of contemporary American literatures, its various qualitative transmutations during the latter half of the twentieth century may inspire readers to reconsider ideology's place in (not only shaping scholars' interpretations of literature, but) generating literary expression. I obliquely return to this consideration in the Conclusion, where I reflect on ideology's operational elision from literary studies, an elision that suggests (in concert with Daniel Bell and Francis Fukuyama) both historical narrative and literary expression are separate from ideology, rather than emerging from within it.

1

Cliché and Modern Womanhood: J. D. Salinger's *Franny and Zooey*

In *Franny and Zooey* (1961), main character Franny Glass realizes herself to be trapped. An unwilling pledge to external forces that define and seek to refine her, Franny finds herself caught between social choices that offer her no choice at all. On the one hand, she seems to half-heartedly participate in specific feminine stereotypes and clichés (particularly through her fashion choices); but on the other, Franny reacts to the contexts created by these clichés, as well as the auxiliary expectations placed upon her by them.[1] As a result (following a ladies room breakdown, fainting spell, and a retreat home to Manhattan), the remainder of *Franny and Zooey* dismisses Franny and her cliché predicament in a fashion uncannily resonant with Daniel Bell's *The End of Ideology* (1960), particularly Chapter 13 ("Mood of Three Generations").

    Bell's text offers scant consideration of women in American society, only exploring their social, civic, and cultural experiences insofar as their roles in the family's social organization and "dynastic" marriages.[2] Bell's lack of commentary on women's social circumstances, or the Second World War's impacts on their lives (beyond sexual "emancipation") is reprised in "Zooey," the concluding narrative that comprises the bulk of *Franny and Zooey*. Published within a year of Salinger's composite novel, *The End of Ideology* observes the bureaucratization of institutions and the dissolution of social ties that followed the end of the Second World War; this, Bell claimed, resulted in widespread social feelings of dependency and disillusionment in America. According to Bell, a college-aged "after-born" generation was formed, who misconstrue personal experiences according to psychological impact and importance.[3] These young adults, Bell claimed, subsequently misidentify the causes of their psychological discomfort due to the inaccessibility, to their generation, of "a genuine experience that transform[s] one's life" (which had, presumably, once been provided by ideologies). An American citizen of Franny's generation could thus only reach "infinite regress" via ineffective or partial expressions of revolt (such as the ladies room breakdown, or her recitations of the Jesus Prayer).[4] At this compelling historical moment, I claim that Salinger uses "Franny" to reflect and critique clichés that assemble postwar womanhood; and "Zooey," to probe the operations of these cultural clichés. To do this, Salinger transforms "Franny's" nameless, mass culture-reminiscent narrative voice to "Zooey's" dismissive, socio-politically mature narrator, Franny's eldest living brother and writer, Buddy Glass.

In the context of this chapter, my use of "cliché" refers to the work of literary and cultural critic, Marshall McLuhan. According to McLuhan, the "cultural cliché" appears and proliferates through various media, contributing to the construction of cultural environments: cliché may appear as an homage implied by character wardrobe, in the composition of a letter, or may manifest as setting.[5] Thus, clichés are pervasive and, through the environments they construct, can eventually forge breakthroughs in cultural understanding. McLuhan's work with cliché began with his first book, *The Mechanical Bride* (1951), an analysis of the sexist distortions of postwar images promoting better living; and his later work explores the cliché's various roles, uses, and effects on American society and culture. McLuhan's work on the cultural cliché echoes an implicit ethos of Salinger's notorious Glasses, asserting that America's culture demands "greater exertions of intelligence and a much higher level of personal and social integrity than have existed previously."[6] McLuhan's work on the social effects of mass culture gained prominence around the time of *Franny and Zooey*'s release, and McLuhan's relevance to the text resides with its popularity among general readers in 1961 (a *New York Times* bestseller). McLuhan's work explores paradigm shifts in interpretive values that are stylistically reflected in Salinger's prose; and both McLuhan and Salinger use their work to express (and sometimes ironize) the centrality of the cliché to American culture, society, and the relation between the two. Importantly, McLuhan did not seek to offer a theory of communications, but to probe the effects of mass communications on American culture and subjectivity.[7]

Read through the discourses in which Salinger's composite novel is couched, Franny Glass's crisis emerges as a derivative trope, reminiscent of middlebrow culture; and this likely contributed to critics' dismissal of Franny as worthy of scholarly engagement. Upon its initial release, Alfred Kazin, Joan Didion, Mary McCarthy, Leslie Fielder, John Updike, and other major figures in American literary criticism negatively responded to J. D. Salinger's second, long-form fictional work.[8] *Franny and Zooey* emerged in a historical context framed by intellectual and popular debates focused on the topic of women's problems. Although none of Salinger's literary contemporaries engaged the implications, causes, or results of Franny's crisis in their articles on *Franny and Zooey*, from the mid-1950s to early 1960s the general subject of women's problems (i.e., some women's experiences of despair and anxiety in adult life) was a popular boon among America's (largely female) general readership, and discussions of the implications, causes, and results of women's problems were topics that found broad engagement in popular media. For instance, in "women's films" (a genre dating from the 1930s through the 1960s) women's problems were presented, explained, and resolved within the neat parameters of mainstream social values.[9] A "leading lady" was transferred from a conflicted or troubled state, to "a state of normal, ordinary womanhood"—usually in the name of love for a man.[10]

However, as Jeanine Basinger explains, a major difficulty of women's film was its framing of women's problems as inevitabilities of the female gender, often couched in an idiom that implied a woman's "irresponsibility" (sometimes explained as emblematic of delayed "sexual responsiveness," or immaturity), defined by her presumed negligence of her "true" concerns as a woman.[11] In this way, suffering beyond the concerns of one's prescribed feminine roles (Freudian experts explained) indicated a gendered abnormality.[12] On television, in magazines and American paperbacks, working women were depicted discarding successful careers or leaving college if married or, in some cases, if presented with a proposal of marriage.[13] Via popular media, women were often urged to conform to their presumed feminine instincts in order to attain self-fulfillment. And this may contribute additional cause for Salinger's contemporaries' repulsion by the text; Salinger plays the role of narrator in *Franny and Zooey*'s shorter, "Franny" section, applying a third-person voice that occasionally adopts Franny's perspective. Readers gain an understanding of her general sense of things, but are denied access to *either* Franny's interiority or the story's world through her eyes. By adopting this anonymous narrative voice, Salinger is able to occasionally "impersonate" Franny while still directing the scene through his performance of her perspective.[14]

In "Franny," Salinger's narrative stylization creates a unique context through which Franny Glass and her dilemma are made central, but not resolved; indeed, the titular character of the text's opening narrative falls sharply out of focus in its concluding story, "Zooey." Salinger turns over narrative authority to Franny's elder brother, Buddy, in "Zooey" and his overall discourse on his sister reads as a dismissal of her social and personal concerns. Indeed, Buddy's tone and framing of Franny are comparable to (and seem to anticipate) a 1962 review of *Franny and Zooey* that appeared in *The Partisan Review*; here, Leslie Fielder drolly compares Salinger's readers to Franny, mocking them for expecting Salinger's work to answer their most pressing social questions: "Does my date for the Harvard weekend really understand what poetry is?" and "Is it possible that my English instructor hates literature after all?"[15] Buddy's perspective in "Zooey" reflects a philosophy of pragmatic compromise, sharply contrasting with Franny's (presumed) crusading idealism, which he reads in her breakdown at Sickler's, and precipitating crisis at home in Manhattan. Buddy's narrative reflects an interpretation of "Franny" that perceives no cause(s) for his sister's outburst and/or fainting; further, Buddy's interpretation is inflected by prevailing sociological and historical discourses of the time.

According to my reading, as Franny is nearly done with college, her breakdown reflects an inability to face the limited options (as a first-generation woman college student in the humanities, *c*. 1955) that she faces: that is, marrying Lane or refusing marriage to become a professional actress (neither she claims to desire). Buddy's narration and Bell's claims frame breakdowns like Franny's as invalid and incapable of authenticity comparable to "the Christian trials of conversion."[16] Yet, like Bell, Buddy's narration does not reveal attentiveness to the gender-specific, historical, and social forces bearing upon Franny—and my aim is not to critique his narrative for this. Rather, this narrative blind spot opens up new avenues by which readers may explore the context in which the text emerged, as well as the deeper textures of the values and ideals portrayed therein.[17] For instance, Buddy's failure to provide a resolution to Franny's crisis illuminates an additional cultural cliché: intellectuals' failure to critically engage the importance of clichés to American culture and identity formation.

"Franny": Cliché as Characterization

Salinger applies Franny's "sheared raccoon coat" as a primary cultural cliché in defining his protagonist at the outset of *Franny and Zooey*. This cliché begins to formulate not only Franny herself, but readers' initial interpretations of her environment and ensuing crisis:

> [Franny] was wearing a sheared racoon coat, and Lane, walking toward her quickly but with a slow face, reasoned to himself, with suppressed excitement, that he was the only one on the platform who really knew Franny's coat. He remembered that once, in a borrowed car, after kissing Franny for a half hour or so, he had kissed her coat lapel, as though it were a perfectly desirable, organic extension of the person herself.[18]

Acclimating readers to Franny and her environment, Salinger adorns his protagonist with an expansive cliché for 1955: the raccoon coat. Franny's date, Lane Coutell spots her on a train platform where she arrives to spend the weekend of a Yale football game in an unnamed college town. Lanes' reaction to Franny's coat sparks Salinger's expression of cultural work that the garment performs for his protagonist; the coat's place in fashion is key to Salinger's work in "Franny," contributing to the narrative ground in which Franny's crisis unfolds.

In 1955 (when *Franny and Zooey* is set), Franny's coat (likely vintage, if not vintage reproduction) would have been considered very chic.[19] Franny's "sheared raccoon coat" recalls Sue Salzman, a New York socialite whose sudden desire to find "a true raccoon" turned her personal preoccupation with pre-Depression style into a short-lived craze.[20] A famous symbol of 1920s jazz age extravagance and rebellion, in the 1920s, raccoon coats became "lush symbols of a new democratic ideal of consumer luxury" during the decade.[21] Favored among college-aged men (largely of the Ivy League), the growing black middle class, as well as some "spunky" college-aged girls, the coat fell out of fashion until it was revived by Salzman between 1955 and 1956. Importantly, Lane's sudden awakening at the sight of Franny's raccoon coat is inspired by the coat's associations with 1920s excess.[22] Like Salzman's "true raccoon," Franny's signature, cliché garment calls to mind a subtext of opulence, recreation, and youthful frivolity. Franny's coat thus reads as "a complement" to her personality and wealth or, as Salinger describes Lane's affectionate kissing of the coat's lapel, "a perfectly desirable, organic extension of the person herself."[23]

Salinger's narrative voice in "Franny" frames his titular character in a manner that bears striking, discursive resemblance to the construction of leading ladies in women's film.[24] The utility of this anonymous narrative voice, McLuhan would argue, is well-known to advertising agencies and Hollywood, who address audiences as passive consumers of information and imagery.[25] Women's film often presented "an exaggerated [lead, woman] character, played by an extravagant beauty"; over the course of a film, this leading lady is galvanized in her dealings with "the emotional, social, and psychological problems that are specifically connected to the fact that she is a woman."[26]

Thus, Salinger's anonymous narrative voice communicates the values, expectations, and priorities of Franny's world using "folklore" (or, assumptions and stereotypes that append to clichés) that are familiar (drawn from various media) to Salinger's general American readership. This speaks to Salinger's narrative virtuosity, c. 1955, as the anonymous voice adopted in "Franny" appeals to a readership otherwise accustomed to receiving information from various media. In the Introduction to McLuhan's *Mechanical Bride: Folklore of Industrial Man* (1951), Philip B. Meggs sums up McLuhan's implicit relevance to Salinger's fiction, particularly *Franny and Zooey*:

> The rational world of print spawned by Gutenberg's invention of movable type around 1450, McLuhan thought, would yield to a new world of audiovisual sensation. [...] Generations who primarily received information from printed communications were influenced by this medium to sense things one at a time in the logical sequence found in a line of type, while those whose primary communications media are electronic discern multiple communications simultaneously, often through more than one sense.[27]

Salinger constructs his narrative voice in "Franny" to maximize the story's appeal to audiences who seek entertainment from not only books, but also other sources.

In a sly impersonation of Lane, Salinger informs readers that Franny is, not only "unimpeachably right-looking" and "extraordinarily pretty," but she is also "so much the better, not too categorically cashmere sweater and flannel skirt."[28] In terms of fashion, Salinger leaves less to the imagination (racoon coat, sans *categorical* "cashmere sweater and flannel skirt"), suggesting that there is *something extra* about Franny. Otherwise, descriptions of Franny's appearance are vague ("right-looking" and "pretty").[29] Communicating Lane's appraisal in comparison with other college girls' fashion sense, readers may gather that Franny's particular fashion operates as an agent of characterization, in addition to being a complement to her wealth. However, whatever it is about Franny that makes her *not too categorical* to Lane is left entirely to readers' imaginations. Via Salinger's brief impersonation, readers are encouraged to adopt Lane's positive opinion of Franny, but are nevertheless required to fill in the more vague contours of her personality and interiority on their own. Thus, "Franny" goads readers with the possibility of a new concept of American femininity just within reach—but essentially undefined. Furthermore, Salinger formulates his expression by weaving feminist critiques by McCarthy and Didion into Franny's story as part and parcel of the cliché-assemblage that constructs her identity.

The narrative blind spot that is Franny's interiority quickly becomes a motif, supporting a theme that is yet ambiguous to readers. When Salinger reports Franny noticing Lane's admiration of her appearance, her own feelings are omitted; instead, in response, "she elected to feel guilty for having seen it, caught it, and sentenced herself to listen to Lane's ensuing conversation with a special semblance of absorption."[30] This calls to mind the function of McLuhan's cultural cliché as a mode of awareness; as the wearer of the coat, Franny cannot acknowledge Lane's awareness of the coat's associations and familiarity—lest the garment's seduction is broken. She must deny her complicity, her choice of coat-via-association, in order to uphold Lane's fantasy of she and the coat's linked meanings.

This split-second process narrated by Salinger harkens to a piece written by Mary McCarthy for *The Reporter* in 1950, which examines the complex and cliché operations of fashion media discourses. McCarthy notes that women (like Franny) are enticed into acquiring specific garments through advertising media's use of extremely tactile and sensuous language (fashion's "erotic element"), and its associated promises of "fun" and "pleasure" to be experienced in fashions that "plunge," "bind," and "hug."[31] The associations which make Franny's coat cliché are heightened through the garment's further associations with fashion's evocative, mass discourse. When Salinger narrates that Franny experiences guilt at Lane's taking notice of her coat, he adds an important, McLuhanian extension to McCarthy's critique of fashion discourse: the fashionable subject's (Franny's) socialization, via the clichés and folklore surrounding women's fashion.

Here, Salinger's narrative strikes another uncanny resemblance to a common convention in popular women's films from the time of "Franny" and *Franny and Zooey*'s publication. Behind Salinger's narration of Franny looms an additional, unwritten rule book of behavior, according to which Franny must conduct herself if she wishes to advance among company like Lane.[32] Early on in *Franny and Zooey*, Salinger hints at Franny's struggle with these rules. Not only does this cliché-as-social register require Franny to turn a blind eye to Lane's sizing her up, but it also encourages her (and readers) to "ignore the question of [her] identity" and instead, formulate a persona through her garments.[33] Similarly, in *Mechanical Bride* (1951), McLuhan argues that fashion and related media encourage (both men and) women to ignore their human qualities and, instead, interact as mechanical and exchangeable components.[34] Franny's coat, and her guilt at noticing Lane's appreciation of it, illustrates this relation; the cliché not only overtakes Franny's interaction with Lane, but her environment as well.

As in women's films, Franny is faced with a choice while out to lunch at Sickler's—that is, whether or not to adhere to "good sportsmanship" in relation to Lane. In this context, "good sportsmanship" refers to a sacrificial ethos in behavior, attitude, and action, through which a leading lady—like Franny—should defer her desires "to those of the man or society."[35] Readers will see Franny's struggle with this crucial, cliché social value again, ironically dramatized, in "Zooey." However, through an impersonation of Franny (formulated as a letter that Lane keeps in his pocket), Salinger foreshadows her difficulties at lunch, teasing readers with the comic-ironic prospect of this fashionable young woman's social failure:

> I think I'm beginning to look down on all poets except Sappho. [...] I may even do my term thing on her if I decide to go out for honors and if I can get that moron they assigned me for an adviser to let me. [...] Do you love me? You didn't say once in your horrible letter. I hate you when your being hopelessly super-male and retiscent (sp.?). Not really hate you but am constitutionally against strong, silent men. Not that you aren't strong but you know what I mean. It's getting noisy in here and I can hardly hear myself think. [...]
> P.P.S. I sound so unintelligent and dimwitted when I write to you. Why? I give you my permission to analyze it. Let's just try to have a marvelous time this weekend. I mean not try to analyze everything to death for once, if possible, especially me. I love you.[36]

Franny's discourse hinges on her distaste for Lane's "super-male" tendencies; importantly however, Salinger's impersonation does not explicitly register this frustration. Rather, a pattern of intentional, semantic errors and calculated omissions appears in Franny's letter, softening its focus on her aversion to Lane's "super-male[ness]." Instead, Franny's aggravation is channeled into complaints about a "moron" adviser, noise in her dorm, and the "dimwitted" tone of her own letters. Salinger also omits the subjects from certain of her letter's sentences (e.g., "I" from, "but am constitutionally against strong, silent men"; and "you" from "I mean not try to analyze everything to death for once"). Through these rhetorical sleights of hand, Salinger directs Franny to first absolve herself, and then Lane, from connection to her complaints.

The socially savvy rhetoric and mechanics of Franny's letter suggest an acute self-awareness in its presumed writer: at only twenty, Franny is caught between teen-aged and adult worlds, but Salinger's impersonation credits her with a sharp ability to diplomatically navigate her world's social expectations (here, gender politics) via discourse. However, Franny's skill in diplomatic communication (she notes in dialogue) is a "strain."[37] Communicating with Lane is not comfortable for Franny; in this way, Salinger further teases readers with Franny's vulnerable position, which manifests as her reticence against cliché (e.g., her coat's perceivable associations). The veiled impatience of the letter reemerges in Franny's environment through dialogue, particularly when Lane scolds her for calling him a "section man": "You've got a goddamned bug today—you know that? [...] Your letter didn't sound so goddamn destructive."[38]

Lane's remediation alerts Franny to her conversational deviation from "good sportsmanship," as it ironically alerts readers to Lane's obliviousness to her feelings expressed in the letter. The subtle, comic irony of their exchange is carried through Franny's "solemn nod" in agreement with Lane; however, as with her guilt at Lane's arousal by her coat, Franny's ironic nod likely signals further guilt over (or refusal to acknowledge) Lane's obliviousness to her feelings. This seemingly inconspicuous exchange narratively reinforces the important social choices that underlie "Franny," particularly concerning good sportsmanship. Cliché envelops Franny's environment, and her relation to that environment (like the coat on the back of her vacated chair) is revealed as "somewhat askew," as revealed in and after her ladies room breakdown.[39]

Readers observe Franny's impulse toward "good sportsmanship," combined with her disconnection to Lane, suggesting that her relationship with him must be managed according to specific, if strenuous, rules of engagement. When Franny departs for the restroom, for instance, Salinger signals the apparent subversiveness of this move through Lane's reaction:

> It was very clear that the sense of well-being he had felt, a half hour earlier, at being in the right place with the right, or right-looking, girl was now totally gone. [...] the same coat that had excited him at the station, by virtue of his singular familiarity with it—and he examined it now with all but an unqualified disaffection. The wrinkles in the silk lining seemed, for some reason, to annoy him.[40]

On her way to the ladies room, Franny indecorously abandons her coat via inadvertent strip tease.[41] Without its wearer, the garment is not exciting to Lane; he looks away from it "feeling vaguely, unfairly conspired against" and as though the "weekend was certainly getting off to a goddamn peculiar start."[42] Rid of her exciting, initial cliché, Franny is suddenly strange, no longer "right-looking"; instead, she is suspicious, perhaps "vaguely" conspiratorial, to the annoyed Lane. His reaction also illuminates Franny's desire to flee, suggesting in the protagonist a kind of performance anxiety, or unwillingness to continue in her role as the "right-looking girl" in the raccoon coat.

During her date with Lane, Franny is overwhelmed by a network of clichés—in discourse, costume, behavior—that she must uphold to maintain her social environment. Similarly, Salinger confronts readers with the realization that Franny has no escape from the cliché of her characterization. This expression culminates in Salinger's depiction of the ladies room at Sickler's restaurant, furnishing a glimpse into Franny's turmoil. The space itself is vast, "almost as large as the dining room proper"; but luckily for the distraught Franny, the room is also empty, releasing her from the space's social obligations. However, in his construction of Franny's escape, Salinger retains the initial cliché's parameters in suspension. As Franny retreats to "the most anonymous looking" of the restroom stalls to cry, Salinger's rendering ironically heightens the alienation constructed through his impersonations of Lane in the previous scenes:

> Without any apparent regard to the suchness of her environment she sat down. She brought her knees together very firmly, as if to make herself a smaller, more compact unit. Then she placed her hands vertically, over her eyes and pressed the heels hard, as though to paralyze the optic nerve and drown all images into a voidlike black. Her extended fingers, though trembling, or because they were trembling, looked oddly graceful and pretty. She held that tense, almost fetal position for a suspensory moment—then she broke down.[43]

The moments of Franny's "outburst-inburst" again withhold insight into Franny's interiority, extending the story's pervasive, narrative blind spot.[44] Salinger's methodical description of Franny's lapse replaces emotion's heuristic place of priority with awe or voyeuristic pleasure; favoring visible procedure over emotional interest, Salinger's descriptions prompt readers (not to empathy, but) to wonder over—indeed, to question—Franny's expression of turmoil.

Further emphasizing the scene's prioritization of the visible over the emotional and encouraging skepticism toward the restroom foray, Franny's gust of feeling abruptly recedes, "without the painful, knifelike intakes of breath that usually follow a violent outburst-inburst." Salinger shifts narrative focus from the methodical process of Franny's "outburst" to a nondescript image of Franny's "expressionless, almost vacuous face."[45] However, this simulation of physical closeness is not applied to emphasize the protagonist's state or to clarify plot. Rather, Salinger uses Franny's face (along with her vague, physical descriptions) to draw attention, again, to her absent interiority—a compelling reversal of the close-up's conventional use in film and television. Franny's instant recovery from her breakdown thus reads as jarring, particularly alongside descriptions of its process. Here, the wondering and skepticism effected toward Franny are crucial, echoing Lane's vague sense of being "unfairly conspired against"; and her quick recovery suggests the "outburst-inburst" is a potentially occasional, disingenuous means by which Franny copes with the myriad associations of the raccoon coat.[46] The sum of Salinger's bathroom scene is the provocative suggestion that Franny has made her choice (however deceptive it requires her to be), concerning her identity within the parameters of cliché.

In the 1950s American academy, some feminist sociologists questioned cultural and institutional sexism in areas like mass media, advertising, and traditional cultural practices. In a 1956 work, *Women's Two Roles: Home and Work*, Alva Myrdal and Viola Klein anticipated Betty Friedan's 1963 discussion of female malaise and the feminine mystique. Myrdal and Klein assert that American society's limited social and professional possibilities for women led to their living in "degrading" states of dependence upon men.[47] As a result, many "intelligent, lively, and educated" women became intellectually "stultified" in various American institutions, particularly marriage.[48] Such ideas are also echoed by Joan Didion and Mary McCarthy in many of their non-literary articles. For instance, in a 1960 piece for *National Review*, "Marriage a la Mode," Didion critiques the brand of marital advice dispensed by "women's 'service' magazines," like *Ladies' Home Journal*.[49] She refers to the *Journal*'s expert "know-how" as merely temporary, superficial solutions to women's problems in marriage.[50] Thus, the advice dispensed by magazines like *Ladies' Home Journal* often addresses husbands' desires, expectations, or anxieties, rather than wives' (i.e., the *Journal*'s readership), alluding to potential for future troubles.[51] Betty Friedan would make a similar claim in *The Feminine Mystique* only a few years later (1963), noting "to women born after 1920, feminism was dead history"; American media's lack of interest in issues around women's rights in the 1950s, Friedan claimed, was transforming feminism into a "mystique" of "man-hating" and toxic ambition.[52]

Salinger's ladies room breakdown is crucial for its sly reinstatement of the narrative's initial cliché, the "right-looking girl" in the raccoon coat. By way of her escape and subsequent "outburst," Franny reifies the initial cliché's authority in formulating and stabilizing her characterization and, therefore, identity. Little changes for Franny in the dining room scene that follows; she faints and awakens on the restaurant manager's office couch; however, "Franny's" seemingly inconclusive ending is more calculated than it appears. With Franny helpless, in the absence of her interiority, Salinger leaves much to readers' imaginations concerning his protagonist; this ending plots an important transition to "Zooey," where the myriad clichés of this story are probed. Given "Franny's" internal pattern of mass cultural references, one may easily read Franny as defiant or immature at the close of her titular narrative: this develops into an important, driving theme in "Zooey." At the end of "Franny," she is left in need of help that Lane cannot provide (beyond a glass of water); Franny is alienated, not only from the social and cultural factors contributing to her crisis, but also from herself. Unable to reconcile cause or cure for Franny's condition, Salinger relegates this responsibility to the writer, Buddy Glass.

"Zooey's" (False) Alternative

By reassigning the story of Franny's crisis to his alter-ego, Buddy Glass, Salinger narratively admits that a resolution to Franny's problems cannot be obtained through the characterizing and atmospheric shorthand of cliché. However, in "Zooey," Franny falls sharply out of narrative focus, and brother Zooey Glass is suddenly positioned as the text's new protagonist.[53] This shift in focus reads as a shift in narrative voice and style; from "Franny's" anonymous voice, Salinger shifts to a voice that implies long familiarity with both Franny's and

Salinger's readers. In 1957 and 1961, readers would have been familiar with Buddy as a fixture of Salinger's fiction, and therefore less likely to passively accept information from him: he is protagonist in both *Raise High the Roof Beam, Carpenters* (1955) and *Seymour: An Introduction* (1959), where he also self-identifies as author of Salinger's "A Perfect Day for Bananafish" (1948), "Down in the Dinghy" (1949), and "Teddy" (1953).[54] This comprises the sort of prankish misdirection by Salinger about which critics like Alfred Kazin would have once complained. Salinger knows that Buddy possesses scant means to resolve Franny's crisis (they are the same man, after all), beyond his protagonist Zooey's talent for repartée. And Salinger initially alerts readers to this through "Zooey's" inward-looking narrative voice and cantankerous dialogue.

Salinger highlights Buddy's writerly shortfalls via his reflections on literary critics and unflattering depictions of the story's cast, the Glasses. Although absent from the Glasses' Manhattan home, for his own part, Buddy bemoans critics' appraisals of his stories.[55] And rather than depicting characters through familiar, cliché markers as in "Franny," Buddy initially depicts Zooey arguing with his mother while he is in the bathtub; confused mother Bessie peskily urges him to counsel Franny.[56] Compared to "Franny," Buddy's narration reads as familiar and self-conscious; this amplified self-consciousness signals his potential inability to address Franny's problems in this "prose home movie."[57] As David Seed has noted, the story's introverted language and subject-matter run the risk of the narrative's tone (unfocused, unhappy) overtaking its expression.[58] I agree with Seed, but rather, I read Buddy's tone as indicating the entire Glass family's inability to help Franny, despite his claim that his story hinges on the Glasses' "pure and complicated" love for their youngest sibling.[59] Buddy's unfocused, unhappy tone is discursive effect; for all the story's Eastern philosophical and literary references, and all the family's previous adventures, no precedent exists in which a young woman achieves "en*light*enment or *peace*" (which Franny claims to desire) without either first obtaining a career or marriage.[60]

In 1955 (when *Franny and Zooey* is set), the Glasses' lack of a model for Franny to follow was not uncommon.[61] Similarly, in women's films of the 1950s and 1960s, rules of behavior dictated that women may either marry or go "out among mankind and [do] good instead"; beyond these "domestic" or "noble" models, women were given few additional examples to follow.[62] This is a point Friedan also notes, claiming that American women "are sorely in need of a new image to help them find their identity":

> Many of us knew that we did not want to be like our mothers [...] Strangely, many mothers [...] did not want their daughters to grow up like them either. [...] [E]ven if they urged, insisted, fought to help us educate ourselves, even if they talked with yearning of careers that were not open to them, they could not give us an image of what we could be.[63]

Friedan identified American women in the early 1960s as inundated with "public" images of beauty and femininity from mass culture, but nevertheless lacking "private" images of women "to tell her who she is, or can be, or wants to be."[64] The atmosphere cast by Buddy's representation resonates with this cultural concern, as Bessie is depicted as the opposite of that to which Franny should aspire.[65]

Buddy anticipates Friedan; Bessie is a housewife, having retired from being a vaudeville dancer in 1925, about nine years before Franny was born.[66] Little on Bessie's career in show business is developed in "Zooey"; instead, via narration and dialogue she is depicted as a "stupid" and "impenetrable mass of prejudices, clichés, and bromides."[67] Buddy references "clichés" in negative association with his mother, registering an attitude toward these cultural indicators that sharply contrasts with Salinger's narration in "Franny." Instead of applying cliché to characterization, situation, or description, cliché specifies the nature of Bessie's ineffectualness: stubbornly observant of essentialist, standardizing typologies, like *proper diet*—which, she surmises, may be troubling Franny.[68] Buddy's reduction of Bessie to a denigrating image not only anticipates Friedan's concern with women's shortage of private images, but his depiction also echoes a related matter concerning women's portrayals in literature at this time.

In *On the Contrary* (1961), Mary McCarthy records struggling to find a work of American fiction that "best represented the modern American woman."[69] She mentions *Madame Bovary* (1856) and Henry James's *A Portrait of a Lady* (1881);

But since then? It was like leafing through a photograph album and coming, midway, on a sheaf of black, blank pages. Was it possible that for twenty-five years no American woman had had her likeness taken?[70]

McCarthy locates the most modern depictions of women in the 1930s, by William Faulkner and John Dos Passos, and traces this dearth to "narrative experiments of the twentieth century."[71] These experiments, McCarthy explains, reflect writers' (including Salinger's) declining interest in the social sphere, and therefore in character invention. However, this disinterest reads as culturally tone-deaf, she notes, emerging in the midst of a boom in influential sociological studies, including *The Lonely Crowd* (1950) and *The Organization Man* (1956).[72] Despite the new "array of social types" created by America's postwar "institutions," "bureaucracies," and "regimented 'schools' and systems," creative writers did little toward extrapolating characters from them: "It is as though a whole 'culture' of plants and organisms had sprung into being and there were no scientists or latter-day Adams to name them."[73] While Bessie is narratively dismissed as "an impenetrable mass" of "clichés," Buddy cannot similarly dismiss Franny. This may signal a sensitivity in Buddy (similar to McCarthy's), concerning her difference in "social type" from Bessie; but his depiction of Franny may be read as a dismissal of a different kind, on the basis of her perceived, social immaturity.[74]

When Franny awakes on the family couch, she describes a complex, unsettling dream to Zooey. However, Buddy's narration defers engagement with the dream, offering a portrait-in-prose of Franny:

There were half-circles under her eyes, and other, subtler signs that mark an acutely troubled young girl, but nonetheless no one could have missed seeing that she was a first-class beauty. Her skin was lovely, and her features were delicate and most distinctive. Her eyes were very nearly the same quite astonishing shade of blue as Zooey's, but were set farther apart, as a sister's eyes no doubt should be—and they were not, so to speak, a day's work to look into, as Zooey's were. Some four years earlier, at her graduation from boarding school, her brother Buddy had morbidly prophesized to himself, as she grinned at him from the graduates' platform, that she would in all probability one day marry a man with a hacking cough. So there was *that* in her face, too.[75]

As McCarthy notes, Buddy's depiction registers difficulty articulating Franny in the context of social life; her "features" and "first-class beauty" are vaguely defined and no reference is made to her personality. The sole indicator of Franny's social relationality lies in Buddy's ominous reference to a "man with a hacking cough," whom Franny may marry one day. This remark does not elucidate Franny's grin, but on the heels of her faintly praised physical beauty, this reflection reads as an oblique judgment against Franny.

Assuming that she wants to get married (there is no evidence in the text to support this), Buddy suggests a threatening inevitability regarding Franny's oncoming adulthood. The "man with a hacking cough" suggests a pollution or contamination that Franny will overlook and bring into her life. This logic reflects the dictum of "rules of behavior": "Those who do not become good sports but who fight circumstances (and many films show us that behavior choice) will suffer the consequence."[76] The fate that Buddy prophesizes for Franny is one that she will suffer due to her tendency to struggle with self-sacrificial "good sportsmanship"; because "at twenty," Franny is willing "to check herself back into the mute, fishy defenses of the nursery" (i.e., the Glass family home), she will inevitably suffer an uncomfortable future.[77] Thus, Buddy elides his narrative inability to understand Franny's crisis and instead frames her condition as a manifestation of immaturity and self-indulgence in having her breakdown, of all places, in the Glass family home; this places Franny and her crisis in full light of the fact that the clichés encoding her identity cannot be resolved, even outside the social realm.

Once readers perceive Buddy's resorting to cliché in representing Franny, his depiction begins to uncannily resonate with the title character of "Franny." While Buddy's stylistic difference from "Franny's" anonymous narrator is meant to reflect the precision of familiarity's rendering, Salinger's impersonation (while amusing) is incomplete. This impersonation highlights an important narrative shortfall in "Zooey," revealed through the story's dialogic dominance by Zooey, Buddy's protagonist. While Buddy frequently blends and veils his opinions with Zooey's point of view, Buddy's narrative limits are not ameliorated in dialogue. Consider Franny's account of her bad dream, which Zooey jokingly volunteers to interpret:

It was just hideous. I was at a *swim*ming pool somewhere, and a whole bunch of people kept making me dive for a can of Medaglia d'Oro coffee that was on the bottom. Every time I'd come up, they'd make me go down again. I was crying, and I kept saying to everybody, "*You* have your bathing suits on. Why don't you do a little diving, too?," but they'd all just laugh and make these terribly snide little remarks, and down I'd go again. […]

These two girls that are in my dorm were there. […] They had a big oar, and they kept trying to *hit* me with it every time I'd surface. […] The only person who made any *sense* was Professor Tupper. I mean he was the only person that was there that I *know* really detests me.[78]

In the dream, Professor Tupper, a religion instructor at her college, does "absolutely nothing" to help Franny, and her peers work against her gaining ground. However, Zooey never "interprets" Franny's dream, signaling that "good sportsmanship" is not a rule of behavior to which he must adhere. Buddy reveals his unwillingness or inability to engage his sister's interiority, represented by the dream and constituting a disquieting similitude with Franny's absent interiority in "Franny."

Buddy defers readers' empathic relation to Franny and disallows access to her interiority through Zooey's dismissal of the dream: "You look like hell. You know that?"[79] This brief, early exchange sets the tone for the remainder of the siblings' dialogue, constructing a discursive pattern in which Franny's problems and desires are dialogically reframed and re-directed by Zooey. In lieu of interpreting Franny's dream, Zooey "holds forth" for several pages on his distaste for the television industry (where he works as a "young leading man") and a lunch meeting for which he is late.[80] When Franny attempts to draw a comparison ("Everything you're saying brings back everything I was trying to say to Lane on Saturday") between her pre-breakdown experiences and Zooey's opinions, he interjects, refusing her comparison.[81] Through this dialogue, Buddy's representation resonates with Salinger's in "Franny": Franny and her crisis, Lucinda Rosenfeld has noted, are presented as readers are "meant to think" of them.[82] Buddy's self-conscious narration performs the very descriptive block that McCarthy describes, illustrating women's shortage of "modern," aspirational, positive social and private images. "Zooey" shows readers that "Franny's" anonymous narrator is similarly limited by faulty methods of "impersonation" via cliché.[83]

Buddy's depiction recalls a still darker thematic among many American intellectuals, such as Daniel Bell. Bell skeptically framed expressions of revolt, such as Franny's crisis (and linked recitations of the "Jesus Prayer") as signs of "regress," typical of her generation.[84] Recalled in Zooey's dismissals are several of Bell's claims concerning "expressions of revolt" in America "today."[85] Zooey, like Bell, is bored with crises like Franny's, perceiving such breakdowns as distortions of earlier eras' sociological concerns into personal ones. In a multi-page critique of her crisis, Zooey accuses Franny of "trying to lay up" some kind of "spiritual treasure" through the "Jesus Prayer" and retreat to their family home, framing her frustrations with the prevalence of "ego" among her peers and instructors as only a thin veil for her own self-interests—no better than the "section men" at school, whom she claims to despise.[86] As to her fixation on *The Way of the Pilgrim*'s "Jesus Prayer," Zooey reaches back to "a little apostasy" Franny had at ten years old and shames her for eliding religious figures and ideas she "constitutionally" rejects—for example, a "God who says a human being, *any* human being [...] is more valuable to God than any soft, helpless Easter chick."[87] Assessing her doctrinal cherry-picking, along with her crisis, as examples of "tenth-rate thinking," Zooey chides Franny for having "bother[ed] to pick and choose the place" where she has her breakdown (his own domestic turf). Yet, Zooey/Buddy's discourse recalls a compelling issue raised by Betty Friedan, concerning sociological models' negligence of women's changing social and private roles over time, particularly following the Second World War.[88]

At first, Franny rails against Zooey's Bell-reminiscent incredulity, asserting that she is aware of being "as egotistical and self-seeking as everybody else" and "what kind of imbecile do you think I am?"[89] Through her early objections, Franny attempts to tell Zooey that his critique misses the point; he ignores her, however, and only when he renders Franny "prostrate, face down [...] on the couch" does Zooey take his cue to exit.[90] Zooey's overriding discourse constructs a set of conditions in which Franny becomes an "unwilling audience of one" to her brothers' "interminable home movie."[91] Sociological models that are structured like Bell's (e.g., studying the "postwar mood" of "The Mood of Three Generations"), Friedan explains, do not see women differently than men, in the grand scheme.[92] Such models "assume an endless present, and base their reasoning on denying the possibility of a future different from the past."[93] Women's destinies in American society have historically been defined by anatomy, Friedan asserts; and as long as sociological theory looks to *society* for definitions of women, these models will be unlikely sources for new, transcendent roles or images for women. Whether a woman comes of age in the 1930s (e.g., Bell's "twice-born" generation) or in the 1950s ("after-born"), theories like Bell's cannot account for cultural and social changes that are inspired, as McLuhan points out, by the expansion of mass cultural media.[94]

A further difficulty that opens through Buddy's representation concerns the differences in temperament Bell assumed between Buddy's "twice-born," and Franny's "after-born" generations. In "The Mood of Three Generations," quoting Norman Podhoretz, Bell asserts that the twice-born generation's problem

> is less [...] the "fear of experience" [or, immaturity] than an inability to define an enemy. One can have causes and passions only when one knows against whom to fight. The writers of the twenties—Dadaist, Menckenian, and nihilist—scorned bourgeois mores. The radicals of the thirties fought "capitalism," and later, fascism, and for some, Stalinism. Today, intellectually, emotionally, who is the enemy that one can fight?[95]

Bell's "twice-borns," however, found success in this milieu by adopting a "sober, matter-of-fact, 'mature' acceptance of the complexities of politics and existence" that helped many (like Dos Passos and Podhoretz) to become cultural movers via adaptation and compromise, rejecting the idea that they needed an "enemy" at all. Bell continues: "Political intellectuals became absorbed in the New Deal. The papier-mache proletarian novelists went on to become Hollywood hacks"; and by Bell's logic, other "twice-born" aesthetes like Buddy (b. 1919) likely went on to become writing instructors at women's colleges.[96] However, Franny belongs to Bell's "after-born" generation, coming of age in the 1950s during the time Bell wrote.[97] Unlike the "twice-born," Franny's generation is assessed by Bell as incapable of attaining a level of maturity similar to Buddy's. However, Bell's reading of the postwar mood does not account for women of *any* generation, blending in his portrait of Franny's "college" demographic both men's and women's experiences.

Recalling Bell's critique of the "after-born" generation's tendency to misconstrue psychological discomfort for personal enmity in others, Zooey encourages Franny to identify her enemies based on characteristics that transcend their "hairdo" or "goddamn necktie" (Salinger 161). To follow Zooey/Buddy's and Bell's logic: Franny's only perceivable "enemy" is herself—this, Zooey reasons, is the cause of her "tenth-rate nervous breakdown."[98] This harkens to McCarthy's and Friedan's concerns regarding the paucity of new public and private images of women; but a more interesting resonance comes to the fore through Zooey/Buddy's distaste toward Franny and her crisis. In his attempt to understand Franny's struggle through his own discourse and understanding of mature social acceptance, Zooey/Buddy continues to rely on various cultural clichés linked to "rules of behavior," in the final scene's darkly humorous attempt to resolve Franny's crisis via "the kind of low-grade spiritual counsel" to which, according to Zooey/Buddy, Franny is "entitled."[99]

Zooey's final attempt to counsel Franny in *Franny and Zooey* comprises Salinger's final signal to readers that his representations possess no language by which to account for, or resolve, Franny's crisis. Indeed, although "Zooey" does not rely on the cultural cliché in the same way as "Franny," Buddy's narration nevertheless overflows with symbols (particularly religious ones) and seemingly significant references presumed to aid interpretation. The operation of the cliché in "Zooey" emerges as the narrator's and protagonist's discursive dissonance with Franny, a clash between medium and subject. Frequently in "Zooey" the protagonist's evaluations do not match Franny's own self-expressions; and the "spiritual counsel" offered in the closing scene is no exception. Operating under the assumption that Franny's recitations of the "Jesus Prayer" indicate her admiration of religious faith (or, as Zooey puts it, her desire for a "religious life") Zooey tells his sister: "The only thing you can do now, the only re*lig*ious thing you can do, is *act*. […] [B]e God's actress, if you want to. What could be prettier?"[100] Zooey's appeal is wholly predicated on Franny's presumed faith in the importance of demonstrating faith. Furthermore, in this appeal's direct address to: first, Franny's presumed vanity ("What could be prettier?"); her presumed desire for a "religious life" ("be God's actress"); and finally, her desire for self-fulfillment ("the only re*lig*ious thing you can do, is *act*"), Zooey's statements are also *structured* to appeal to Franny's "faith in faith," to use Amy Hungerford's terminology.[101]

In the context of "Zooey," however, these religious signs mean little for Franny. Buddy's narrative stylization, and its supporting discourses, is questionable in their relevance to a treatment of her crisis, as Franny herself does not report the serious, religiously or sociologically oriented foci that her brother(s) propound(s). Franny only reports desiring "en*light*enment, or peace."[102] Thus, in a manner uncannily similar to the formulaic conclusions of women's film, Zooey's final "spiritual counsel" attempts to provide Franny with what she does *not* have (morality and responsibility), via means relevant to what she *does* have (presumably, some grasp of religious faith and acting ability); therefore, as an implied "reconciliation between the two," Zooey advises Franny to become "God's actress."[103] Couched in moral discourse, Zooey's appeal endeavors to redirect Franny's focus toward the socially acceptable, productive work of acting (in lieu of her unproductive prayer recitations) in the interest of her achieving self-fulfillment via responsible means. In a moment of 1950s mass cultural and intellectual discursive consensus, the tough-love idiom that Buddy imparts to Zooey wryly recalls women's film, positing Franny's crisis as an inevitability and implying her irresponsibility (as critics have noted since *Franny and Zooey*'s publication) in having her "little nervous breakdown" at home.[104]

Zooey's advice further implies specific rules of behavior that Franny will have to follow when or if she becomes "God's actress." Zooey advises Franny against upsetting herself with acting's infuriating details, such as artless "Fat Ladies" who are present in all audiences, or the "goddamn 'unskilled laughter' coming from the fifth row."[105] To this end, he asserts: "An artist's only concern [should be] to shoot for some kind of perfection, and *on his own terms*, not anyone else's."[106] While this idealistic sentiment may seem encouraging, it is at best misleading; structured to appeal to Franny's presumed immaturity and vanity, Zooey instructs Franny to serve her own ideals in acting. However, Zooey's statements also critique Franny's presumed self-centeredness as a characteristic that "God's actress" should not possess; thus, Zooey subtly notes that an audience's artlessness does not condition their unworthiness of art, or at the very least, entertainment. As a popular "leading man" in television himself, the behavioral subtext of Zooey's appeal means to name the conditions of his own (and Franny's prospective) employment: that is, achieving one's own sense of perfection. By Zooey's logic, becoming "God's actress" is not merely the "only re*lig*ious" (or, moral) thing that Franny can do, but it also becomes the only responsible thing that she can do. Zooey's "second-rate spiritual counsel" attempts to offer Franny a moral and responsible route to self-fulfillment (conditioned on her following these rules of behavior) via her continued work in acting. This advice overlooks Franny's desire to quit acting, as she informs Lane in "Franny."[107]

Zooey's morally inflected career advice is deeply flawed, misidentifying the conditions of the work he encourages Franny to pursue. As a professional television actor, Zooey is aware that if Franny pursues a performance career, she will be required to perform to *others'* standards of perfection (e.g., directors', producers', sponsors') if she wishes to gain and retain employment and presumed fulfillment. This is an inconvenient fact about which Zooey himself complains in his early tirade on the television industry. Following Zooey's advice would likely result in Franny's exclusion from the mainstream entertainment industry; if she were to pursue a professional acting career, this result would likely not resonate with her actual interests.[108] By glibly asserting that Franny "has no right to think about" things like her audiences' artlessness, Zooey's apparent support of idealism actually reframes and redirects Franny's concerns—away from others' perceivable flaws, and toward her own—furthering the narrator's interest in a neat, narrative reconciliation for her crisis.

"Zooey" grapples with sociological idioms concerning civic maturity versus immaturity, and the detached performativity required for maintaining a mature social status.[109] Indeed, Buddy's narrative inability to represent either Franny or her crisis (and to remain unnoticed in this) reveals a compelling, historically significant intellectual and creative block that is confronted in *Franny and Zooey*. All told, "Franny's" liberal use of cultural clichés in characterization, juxtaposed with "Zooey's" wry tone of inevitability, positions the composite *Franny and Zooey* as a reflexive satire; in Salinger's dark burlesque, the Glasses emblematize the ways 1950s intellectual and mainstream discourses on women and maturity constructed self-deceptive understandings of identity, along with acceptable models for how that identity may interact with society. Taken together, the stories comprising *Franny and Zooey* not only posit Franny as extremely vulnerable, they provide unsettling insights into her family's limited understandings of themselves and the effects of the outside world on their siloed clan. Indeed, while many have read Salinger's Glass children as portraying the agony intrinsic to seeking depth in American culture and society, few have considered whether Salinger imparts his Glasses with the capacities they require to attain (or understand) what they seek. He does not; and that is the point.

At the conclusion of *Franny and Zooey*, Franny does not fall asleep in her parents' bed because she is relieved or because it is bedtime; Franny falls asleep because she is disappointed, having received no relevant counsel from *any* of the leading men in her life. Indeed, this ending may be more tragic than the reassertion of the status quo that was, as Basinger has noted, so frequently referenced in women's film. Although leading ladies of the genre were generally re-absorbed into their society's various paternalistic systems, these characters were also depicted as *accepting* this resolution of youth toward mature womanhood. But Franny simply wants "en*light*enment or *peace*." As for the "Jesus Prayer," *The Way of the Pilgrim*'s theology of ceaseless prayer only serves as a distraction for Franny, deployed to subvert the causes of her actual, inner crisis: that is, rehearsing and repeating cliché's discursive and behavioral patterns, which repress and defer her honesty and self-interest. Franny cannot help, it seems, but to cooperate with some of the rules, however fed up she may be—just as she cannot help but repeat the prayer. The complex relationality featured in *Franny and Zooey*, between discourse and its effects, is a feature of Salinger's text that distinguishes it from the populist, middlebrow aesthetic into which it was sometimes lumped by critics of its time. Looking closely at Salinger's text, readers find that social concerns and mass cultural formulations resonate within *Franny and Zooey*; however, the contribution they make to the work resides (not with the models, forms, or debates they pursue, but) with the darkly comic and subtly tragic textures that their frameworks (and blind spots) impart to narrative discourse.

Franny and Zooey's resonances with social concerns (e.g., gender politics), mass cultural formulations (e.g., interwoven cultural clichés), and dominating narratives of historical progress link Salinger's composite novel to important aspects of *mood* within the recuperative, post-Second World War decade in which it is set. With regards to Franny, readers may perceive the receptive and recitative manner in which she is expected to behave; and in the absence of recourse to her own interiority, Franny's various resistances to and questions about her prescribed place in the world are easily read (or, dismissed) as desubliminized, aesthetic stands against her brothers' well-meaning assessments and "spiritual counsel." To readers' knowledge, Franny does not clearly envision or define what she desires for herself or her future after college; she claims to wish for "en*light*enment or *peace*," as well as distance from the egomaniacal tendencies of her peers. But essentially, Franny is not quite sure of what she wants—or what she needs. Furthermore, she rebuffs consideration of either, in favor of Seymour Glass's copy of *The Way of the Pilgrim*. As the member of the Glass family most well-known for his violent suicide at the end of "A Perfect Day for Bananafish," Salinger's readers may find it difficult to square this behavior (particularly at the end of "Franny" and through "Zooey") with the "en*light*enment or *peace*" Franny claims to seek. Furthermore, as she is conspicuously inarticulate about her desires, it is also difficult to read Franny as either enlightened or peaceful at any point in the text. After all, her "inburst-outburst" in the ladies room of Sickler's restaurant catalyzes the remainder (and majority) of the text.

In prankish response to both Trilling's asserted death of longform American fiction and McCarthy's ironic mourning of character innovation amid postwar progress, *Franny and Zooey* provides readers with a paradoxically faithful (or, wryly sur-*realistic*) image of modern womanhood via Franny Glass. Salinger's composite text shows readers precisely *how* dominant social models' theoretical and analytical omissions not only curtail women's real options in life, but demonstrate that little (particularly in social and professional realms) seems to have *actually* changed for many American women with the "end" of ideology. Betty Friedan would make similar claims only a few years later. For instance, while Franny Glass pursues a higher education in 1955, this was nowhere near the norm for a majority of American women at the time. In the 1940s, only about 30 percent of American women who graduated high school would attend college; by 1958, that number would rise to only 40 percent, and then to 45 percent by 1963.¹¹⁰ Yet, by illuminating the scene of struggle into which Franny's college football weekend devolves, the text's study in contrast brings readers' attention to *its own omissions*: Franny manifests as *act* (or, cultural cliché) in the absence, or negation, of her interiority (echoing women's absence in theories like Bell's). Importantly, she is not quite a realistically drawn character, not quite a full person, yet extraordinarily valuable to grasping the totemic ideas (symbolic or representative of particular qualities or concepts) that have defined and qualified young, privileged white American womanhood since at least the Second World War.

Yet while totemic, cultural clichés and convenient theoretical omissions do amount to arguably stifling, if not oppressive, circumstances for women like Franny Glass, Salinger's text also offers readers occasion to critically consider the issue of Franny's privilege, particularly as compared to other American women (fictional and actual) of her generation. Particularly interesting in the case of *Franny and Zooey*, for instance, in sharp contrast with Carlene Hatcher Polite's *The Flagellants* (1967), is that much of Franny's privilege (transcending any financial considerations) resides with her appearance: she is the "right-looking girl" of the Yale football weekend; and to narrator Buddy, she is a "first-class beauty," even in the throes of her crisis. Franny's appearance is deployed to align her character, her breakdown at Sickler's, and her protracted crisis in "Zooey" with *acting* (consciously playing a role, an aesthetic set of moves) and therefore *not* actual concerns or threats to Franny or those who bear witness to her crisis. Only Franny's maligned mother, Bessie, is alert to the potential that her daughter's health and well-being may be in danger. Importantly, Franny is also *not* perceived as dangerous for feeling sensitive to her environment at college; and she is not regarded with suspicion or fear for her complaints against contemporary poetry or college instructors. In this way, Franny is granted protection via a rhetoric of idealized femininity—protections, importantly, that are withheld from Polite's African American woman progatonist, Ideal, in *The Flagellants*. This aspect of *Franny and Zooey*'s narrative texture, in combination with its protagonists' clear positions of privilege, further enlarges its place in mid-century longform fiction and fashions it a useful, comparative link to a crucial literary wave that was on the horizon of early-1960s American culture: the Black Arts Movement.

2

Ideology and Nostalgist Aesthetics: Carlene Hatcher Polite's *The Flagellants*

In the Prologue of Carlene Hatcher Polite's first novel, *The Flagellants* (1967), protagonist Ideal is introduced to readers as a small girl, who is much younger than Franny Glass and living in an impoverished, regional town called Black Bottom. Black Bottom is described by Polite as a brutal place where children like Ideal are frequently left unsupervised, and belligerent adults openly nurture their vices; in the Bottom, social survival strictly concerns one's willingness to acquiesce to the workaday cruelties and contradictions of poverty's lived experiences. In sharp contrast to Franny Glass' family background, one must be tough to survive Black Bottom. And Polite's Ideal is anything but tough, finding herself often frustrated and frightened in Black Bottom; *The Flagellants*' Prologue offers troubling images and events that depict her being "bullied for her cowardice" and "chastised for being softhearted" frequently, among other offenses.[1] Ideal is black and is described as a very beautiful, but "unusual" child—"unusual," that is because she is terrified by the mundane sights and sounds of her hometown.

One local woman, for instance, who "enjoyed the reputation of being down to earth, filled with motherwit," resents Ideal's fearfulness and regularly torments her by playing jokes on the child.[2] This woman deduces that the girl's "high-strung and willful nature would be her ruination," unless her mother (who does not appear in the novel) "lay down the law, demand that she walk a chalked line." This woman interprets Ideal's sensitivity and apprehension as a mark of "the devil"—the Bottom's term for unruliness and unpredictability— and advises her mother to "watch every move" that Ideal makes.[3] To "control a child of Ideal's looks and temperament," the woman instructs, Ideal needs "the devil beaten out of her constantly"—and Polite's third-person narrator implies that Ideal's mother follows this instruction: "The applied advice sprouted a self-destroying root at the bottom of the poor child's free heart."[4]

Ideal's sensitivity is construed by her fellow Bottom-dwellers according to their unwritten, and often unspoken, rules for Black Bottom life. Rules, of course, that appear to vary widely from the expectations of "good sportsmanship" placed on Franny Glass in *Franny and Zooey*. Unlike Franny, whose fainting and depressive crisis are *not* perceived by others as threatening or dangerous, adults (as well as other children) around Ideal instinctively and aggressively force back the child's perceived protests to everyday life in Black Bottom. More troubling, while Franny's physical beauty is presented to readers by Salinger's narrators as a sign of the young woman's inherent innocence or faulted good nature (i.e., denoting her membership in a sorority of American mid-century *true womanhood*), by contrast, Ideal's beauty is read in the context of *The Flagellants* as a serious potential problem for her in adulthood (unless she has "the devil beaten out of her constantly," as a child). By contrast, Franny's emotional reactions are seen as benign (or are dismissed as foolish) by others *and* her beauty is not explicitly framed as problematic. Ideal, on the other hand, is depicted intermittently as a nuisance and an offense to her fellow Bottom-dwellers; she is openly bullied for her sensitive temperament, her peers revel in making a fool of her, and her beauty is perceived as a liability. Within the first pages of *The Flagellants*, readers may begin to sense a broader message by Polite, concerning the operations and purposes of ideology, particularly in the decades after its purported demise.

Like Franny (and contradictory to her peers' perceptions), Ideal's personal emotions can and do not constitute a true resistance against Black Bottom's dogma, despite what her fellows might appear to assume. Like Franny, the child Ideal is unable to precisely establish or articulate a problem with her environment. Therefore, the unusualness that Ideal's fellows perceive in her becomes a rationalization, that is, a descriptive play of contrasts, embodied in Ideal and poised against their conception of "Bottom thought": that is, that "God was vengeful, night was steaming with witches [...] the devil walked the land, [and] good feelings were the result of listening to his charm."[5] Thus, Ideal's emotional reactions may not constitute revolt, *but they do* create space for Bottom ideology to dominate her, flattening her to meld with these community values. And indeed, in a manner that echoes Franny's resigned lying back on her parents' bed at the end of *Franny and Zooey*, Polite depicts Ideal's domination through the child's sudden obedience toward the end of *The Flagellants*' Prologue. This encompasses Ideal's ultimate experience of her environment: beyond an act of will, Ideal obeys, for the sake of survival, the command of the Bottom's ideology of acquiescence. A much more brutal and severe rendition of Franny's prescribed "good sportsmanship," the acquiescence expected of Ideal (and at a much younger age) subverts her personal interest and sense of self while *further* entailing that she *also* suppress her emotions (particularly "good feelings" and fear). The rules—or ideology—that Ideal is forced to live by in Black Bottom require her to toughen up and bury her responses.

As *The Flagellants*' remaining chapters unfold, readers may note that Ideal retains this concept of "Bottom thought" into her adulthood; as the narrator states, Ideal "would remember [the] sounds and images" of Black Bottom "for the rest of her life."[6] The resonances of Ideal's early experiences name the conditions of her later life: as a child, she is consistently treated as a problematic object to be acted upon; and in adulthood, she expects to be, and is, treated just the same. Rather than primed to become the tough, "iron-willed, effectual" matriarch, who is "treacherous toward and contemptuous of Black men" (akin to accusations made by her partner, Jimson), Ideal learns to accept disorienting circumstances in which she has no control as a norm.[7] Polite's Prologue is a key element to understanding *The Flagellants*' expression, particularly concerning the complex historical moment, and intersecting cultural debates, with which this experimental novel engages (and in which it was embedded) at the time of its American release. *The Flagellants*' temporal structure can be difficult to follow; its characters are flat; and it offers a stark, often brutal, treatment of the nature of intra-racial American communities and relationships. Polite's *The Flagellants* was published in America at the height of the Black Arts Movement (BAM); and surprising many readers at the time, its form and style were rather out of step with the movement's aesthetic values.

For reviewers of the 1960s, a time when the non-integrationist BAM was in its heyday, Polite's narrative style and mode of characterization in *The*

Flagellants were certainly "strange."[8] Closely linked with the philosophy of Black Power, the movement's aims were nationalist, demanding that black art should serve and empower the African American community. Proponents of the movement did not express interest in collaborating with or assimilating into the predominantly white publishing mainstream, seeing it as irrelevant to black community life; instead, writers were expected to create in order to promote the brotherhood of all African Americans via African American cultural autonomy. Of these aims, Malcolm X asserts that black American writers should seek to "launch a cultural revolution to unbrainwash an entire people" whom he felt remained stripped of their African cultural identities since slavery.[9] Thus, the BAM advanced the artistic urgency of dissolving the separation between art and ideology; in contrast to the New Critics and the New York Intellectuals of the same time, movement thinkers conceived literature as a *direct reflection* of social experience, and the novel form, as a *transparent medium* for ideological meaning. In order to break down the division between ideology and art, and to clarify how these divisions may be deployed toward racist ends, black artists were encouraged to discard aspirations for being accepted by America at large.

Polite's novel, however, seemed not to "address itself to the mythology" (e.g., problematic literary tropes that BAM writers would have been encouraged to critique or omit in their own work) and/or concretely link itself to the struggles of black American communities, in tandem with the movement's injunctions; primarily, the BAM's supportive, cultural-specific micro-nation is nowhere to be found in Polite's novel.[10] Although Polite's protagonists suffer, they read as rather withdrawn, even isolated, from any conceived (or imaginary) African American community in the city where they live together as adults. In fact, this sense of disconnection pervades the novel by way of the protagonists' (and especially Jimson's) paranoid and melancholic relation to the world. Polite's two main characters dwell in the past, judge other black Americans' (particularly their elders') ways of life, and they are highly suspicious of the motivations of other black, and white, people alike.

In 1976, Noel Schraufnagel denigrated the novel for this negative, self-defeating aspect of its protagonists, claiming that their ostensible strife is merely a figuration of their respective, misguided senses of "martyrdom."[11]

Jimson's and Ideal's attitudes, Schraufnagel asserted, are the result of their various unsuccessful efforts to "accommodate" American society's "white-is-right" doctrine.[12] By contrast, BAM artists were expected to write from the place of their systemic misrecognition. This radical self-alienation aided artists' efforts in distinguishing themselves *both* from white American cultures and from other contemporaneous, anti-establishment (also predominantly white) cultural circles (e.g., the Beats, the New Left, the New American Poetry). This cultural nationalism emphasized and reflected the misrecognition of African Americans in the predominantly white, American public sphere.

However, what Schraufnagel overlooks in his assessment of Polite's novel is its purposeful, experimental cooptation of various troubling literary tropes toward revelatory ends—that is, toward efforts to reveal how neither Jimson nor Ideal has been equipped to help themselves (either in childhood or in adulthood) toward self-realization, a sense of purpose, or stability (whether emotional, economic, or otherwise) in their lives. Rather, Polite illustrates, both have, in their respective ways, been hobbled: first, by the beliefs of the flawed adults who reared them under flawed conditions; and second, by the wider society that offers them little opportunity (particularly Jimson, who struggles to retain work), but much friction. Polite's characters are not drawn, and do not function, to "accommodate" any particularly clear, ideological position—and this is precisely the point. Polite's refusal to depict her primary African American characters with clear and effectual political or social stances comprises an important layer of the critique that, I claim, *The Flagellants*' levels against the BAM's aesthetic values (as well as those of its eventual, feminist heirs).

In his study of black nationalism, Alphonso Pinkney distinguishes Black Power's revolutionary, *political* nationalism as "a combination of Black nationalism and Marxism-Leninism"; however, an important distinction must be made, with respect to the BAM's *cultural* nationalism.[13] While Black Power's politics underscored class oppression over racial oppression, the BAM's cultural nationalism gave priority to racial oppression, based on the principle that African Americans constituted a distinct cultural nation within the United States, who required a distinct aesthetic framework developed apart from any surrounding white cultures. Despite the dispersed and occasionally factional nature of the BAM, a common theme among the movement's groups was "a belief that African Americans were a people, a nation, entitled to (needing, really) self-determination of its own destiny."[14] Distinguishing itself from the legacies of previous black nationalisms and the predominantly white, middle-class American New Left of the day, the exercise of self-determination was a central feature of the movement's cultural activity across the United States; therefore, the BAM underscored the need for artists to strive toward the development of a distinct African American culture that would be distinguished from predominantly white American cultures. Being black, the BAM maintained, was central to the experiences of African American artists, and this should be reflected in one's art; as black identity was posited as communal, it thus became the responsibility of black artists to speak "directly to black people" from this position.[15] Perhaps more than the Harlem Renaissance, the BAM saw such artistic activity as a necessary component to, and a political priority toward, the advancement of self-determination for African Americans and their communities across the United States.[16]

Origins and inspiration for the formation of the BAM may be traced to both global and domestic sources. The Cold War, Civil Rights, and America's involvement in international politics fashioned a complex matrix of colliding interests that contributed significant influence to the development of the movement. Following the Second World War, for example, the defeat of German National Socialism named the victory of universal principles of democracy over and above eugenic myths of a superior race; as a result, in much of the world an idea of the impropriety of unabashed, institutionalized implementations of racism began to evolve.[17] And as the years following the Second World War were also marked by significant strides in decolonization, an international atmosphere emerged that placed the United States under significant pressure. Extant, domestic demands for the dismantling of Jim Crow and the end of segregation were increased by this comparably progressive, international environment.[18]

One domestic result of this growing global attitude was the desegregation of the American military in 1948; with Executive Order No. 9981, President Truman ended racial segregation in all branches of the armed forces. However, as Smethurst has pointed out, the desegregation of the American military did not prevent internal, more underhanded, discriminatory practices and power struggles within the ranks of the armed forces themselves. The continuation of discrimination in the US military, notwithstanding its official desegregation, is a fact that would resonate with many black American men; pointing up a link between ideology and racism, these internal, social contradictions would influence those who went on to become BAM thinkers, leaders, and its reading public.[19]

With much of the BAM's developmental influence growing out of men's experiences in Truman's Cold War military, along with their attendant feelings of alienation from the federal government, African American women's own experiences of oppression in this complex moment in American history arguably became subsumed. As Madhu Dubey points out, in the context of Black Power and the BAM, African American women were often framed as reminders of America's legacy of slavery, and represented (in literature, speeches, and depictions of everyday life at the time) as obstacles for black men in their efforts toward revolutionary freedom.[20] Within 1960s nationalist discourses, black women were posited as links to the past, to white values—to that from which black nationalism strove to separate itself. In this way, while distinguishing themselves from both predominantly white American culture *and* various, predominantly white anti-establishment literary circles, the artists and intellectuals of Black Power and BAM *also* unfortunately succeeded in largely separating themselves from black *women* writers and intellectuals. Most disconcertingly, black nationalist discourses incorporated elements of 1960s federal rhetoric on the black family; and black nationalist writers (in concert with the contentious Moynihan Report, for instance) named black men as *the* primary victims of American racism.[21]

Against discursive tendencies (perpetrated by both black and white intellectuals) to "homogenize and essentialize black women," new feminist discourses began to develop in opposition to the BAM (as well as in opposition to the predominantly white Women's Liberation Movement of the 1970s) in order to explore the ways black women were hemmed in by their ideological position at the interstices of race, class, and gender discourses.[22] Women began "forming work-study groups, discussion clubs [...] women's workshops on the campuses, women's caucuses within existing organizations, [and]

Afro-American women's magazines," contributing critical inquiry into the role of black women in nationalist discourses *and* American society at large.[23] During the 1970s, black women voiced analytical responses to the BAM's nationalist program in essays and anthologies; and in their creative literary pursuits, women writers responded to the BAM's urban, northern, masculinist literary culture via new paradigms that emphasized rural folk aesthetics—reclaiming for themselves the stigmatizing past with which they had been associated by the BAM.

The Flagellants also disagreed with the BAM's values concerning black identity, racial oppression, and the role of ideology in literary production; and as the novel's Prologue deploys a folk aesthetic, the text appeared even more out-of-step with BAM-era theorists' and artists' values. Yet, Polite's text also disagreed with literary modes that would eventually become valuable archetypes for many black *women* writers from the 1970s onward. The late 1970s and 1980s brought more overtly academic critiques of the BAM and black nationalist literary values; and with the consolidation of black feminist literary criticism in the 1980s and 1990s, projects reclaiming black women writers of Polite's time (i.e., the 1960s and 1970s) became prevalent as well. Thus, writers who deployed the feminist, contra-BAM, folk aesthetic in their work eventually went on to become those who were recovered and acclaimed by these projects in the 1980s and 1990s; by extension, these writers would become those who are recognized, studied, and taught today in many American universities. Authors such as Toni Morrison, Gayl Jones, Alice Walker, and the recovered works of Zora Neal Hurston are perhaps some of the most well-known for deploying this aesthetic in their work. However, Carlene Hatcher Polite was not included in these feminist literary reclamation efforts—and this is not because she did not engage a folk aesthetic in her first novel. Indeed, Polite deployed this model in *The Flagellants* more than a decade before the folk aesthetic, associated with writers such as Walker et al., would emerge in African American women's literature. However, while Polite's novel impressively anticipates this paradigm, *The Flagellants*' Prologue also proposes a starkly critical take on folk aesthetics, which I explore in the next section of this chapter.[24]

In further contrast with her BAM counterparts, Polite's *The Flagellants* does not clearly prioritize racial oppression and unidirectional misrecognition in its expression of black lives in 1960s America. In fact, race relations and specifically named racial experiences are relatively irrelevant to her narrative. Rather, the novel's salient conflicts and controversies are generated within intra-racial relations, such as in the respective childhoods of Jimson and Ideal, or within their romantic relationship. These depictions challenge and destabilize, not only the BAM's notion of communal identity, but also the idea that African Americans constitute a distinct cultural nation apart from the rest of America. These identitarian distinctions, Polite points out, are not so clear as the BAM believes. According to *The Flagellants*, since no one is exempt from ideological imbrication and collusion, no individual, collective, or school of thought may be wholly innocent when it comes to the perpetuation of racism and racial oppression. In contrast to Polite's BAM contemporaries, *The Flagellants* demonstrates how literary aesthetics are not necessarily the ideological product of predominantly white American culture and systemic, racist misrecognition. Through Jimson and Ideal's relationship, which preoccupies the bulk of the novel, Polite illustrates how ideology's subtle transfer of oppressive values forms (not only destructive forces against black solidarity, but also) complex, social relationships between consent and ideological operations that are perpetuated through everyday routines; this, the novel alludes, is how ideology ultimately goes unnoticed and unchallenged, even decades after its supposed demise following the Second World War.

Carrying the critiques generated by *Franny and Zooey* to arguably more entrenched, intersectional dimensions of American life, *The Flagellants* illustrates how the exercise of self-determination (in art as well as in life) is not so clear a process as the BAM would have it; in fact, as exemplified through Jimson and Ideal, Polite's characters do not necessarily struggle with distinguishing between ideology and reality—but rather, with choosing between competing, similarly ideological *iterations of reality*. Polite presents her two main characters via a projective mode of characterization; this enables her to showcase processes of ideological inscription that seriously compromise the characters' abilities to be read as autonomous subjects bestowed with agency. In this way, Polite shows, the problem of self-determination does not lie solely with pointing out the issue of white Americans' proposed misrecognition of black lives (whether in art or actuality), but also with black men and women misrecognizing themselves *and* each other. And this is a burden, Polite contends, caused not only by ideological white racism, but also by similarly ideological black sexism. To understand the novel's depiction of ideology's effects on black American communities, I first turn readers' attention to *The Flagellants*' Prologue. This brief, conceptually dense section outlines the novel's (arguably bleak) interpretation of community solidarity.

Polite's Organic Community

In the 1970s and 1980s, black women artists gave voice to their experiences of racism, sexism, and class oppression by offering their critical responses to the cultural and aesthetic paradigms that had been adopted by the BAM. Although black women suffered an absence in the discourses of Black Power and the BAM, in their later literature, this absence would be injected with an understanding of it as imposed by American culture. Several African American writers have been credited with achieving this effect in their fiction, including Gayl Jones and Toni Morrison.[25] Jones' work has been further credited with unabashedly depicting traditionalism and dogmatism as limiting conceptions of black femininity to reproduction and domestic labor. However, while the contra-BAM, folk aesthetic in African American women's literature would not emerge in critical discourses until the 1970s and 1980s, Polite's 1967 novel anticipates the dawning of this paradigm, *while also* rigorously questioning whether images of impoverished, rural communities should be considered an authentic (i.e., productive, empowering) source of African American culture. A similar critique would not appear again until 1990, when Hazel V. Carby would publish "The Politics of Fiction, Anthropology, and the Folk: Zora Neal Hurston." In this essay, Carby offers a critique of the turn to folk aesthetics, which had been largely inspired by the recovery of Zora Neal Hurston's fiction, in African American literature and criticism.[26] Yet, decades before Carby's piece, *The Flagellants*' Prologue prophetically inculcates black women in the continuance of both the silencing *and* dogmatism for which such (often segregated) rural communities have been criticized.

Although Ideal's childhood is infused with Christian morals, Black Bottom, the narrator relates, is a place where "the devil [is] a permanent resident walking, talking, visiting freely among the dwellers."[27] This affects Ideal for life and consequently, the Prologue unfurls as a register of images and scenes that haunt her for the rest of the novel. *The Flagellants'* Prologue thus operates as a site of synthesis and distribution, prefiguring Ideal's later emotional state. Take, for instance, the jarring opening scene of *The Flagellants'* Prologue; here, readers are introduced to Ideal, who is apparently trapped at an adults' jazz party. She is detained atop a bed, where grotesque, "Matisse-like" adults revel in the dark and "implore" the child to dance for them.[28] Although the narrator does not mention any physical harm being perpetrated against Ideal, this scene indicates her anxiety, revealing her experience as akin to a nightmare:

> One of her hands grasped and held together the woman's nightgown that she wore. A black bird in snow tracks the same patterns as she did atop the big brass bed that night. Every color within the room hurled challenges across the bed. Every moan and coaxing cheer whirled through the confines of the room. The stationary form could no longer contain the strain of the child's protest or the noise of the scene.[29]

Ideal reacts to this Dionysian revelry by crying and hollering, "I want to go home." Her anxiety may be sensed through her posture on the bed, described as "fixed in an arc," as he skips among the sheets like a snow-bound blackbird (to avoid encroaching "Black Cats"). However, the narrator does not directly communicate this information; as little Ideal clutches the over-sized nightgown that she wears, readers only sense that she is being exploited by adults who should be her protectors—but this scene is *not* directly invested with this significance. Instead, Ideal's shame and fear are projected, by way of the narrator's use of a metaphor-punctuated image. This absence of compassion is key to the remainder of the Prologue's expression, as well as its effects in Ideal's later life.

The narrator's dispassion implies that there is a difference between Ideal and her environment; moreover, neither the party's boisterous atmosphere nor the child's negative reaction is bound by any valuation by Polite's narrator. This very subtle move reveals that the party's paralyzing condition is a norm in

Black Bottom for Ideal. As such, this sense of paralysis mutates and migrates among the Prologue's scenes. Throughout the rest of the Prologue, additional scenes are offered, reiterating Ideal's informal education in Bottom norms and values. In these scenes of miseducation, however, Ideal's reactions to the Bottom's ideology are shown as merely evidence of her inscription within it:

> The tones [Ideal] heard [as a child] became her mother language. The beliefs she overheard became her first fear. She would remember these sounds and images for the rest of her life. They were her roots. She would retain this life in that part of her mind that dwelled deep within her eyes—behind a frown. The images would become less distinct with time, but she would be colored by them until her dying day.[30]

One such scene comes in the form of advice that Ideal's great-grandmother offers on their walk home from the nightmare-like party: "Remember what I tell you, Ideal. Always walk tall. Never bow down to anything or anyone; unless, of course, you feel like bowing—quite *naturally*, you will then."[31] This contradictory advice is offered without explanation, unsettling the young Ideal.

This rendition of elder authority presents another layer of Black Bottom's condition to readers, further informing this early depiction of Ideal; that is, the great-grandmother asserts that Ideal should "always walk tall," but stipulates this decree of self-preservation with an illusion of choice: "unless, of course, you feel like bowing." The great-grandmother encourages Ideal to "walk tall," presumably unashamed of reactions she may have to disagreeable conditions (such as the party); but then tells the child that she should "*naturally*" expect herself to *also* "feel like bowing" on occasion. She never tells Ideal *when* she should "bow." Ideal's inability to understand her great-grandmother's abstract advice renders it useless and frustrating to the child; the narrator mediates:

> What did walking tall mean? What did bowing have to do with feeling? What would bowing before something or someone do to the heart of the bower? The great-grandmother's heart had answered these questions long ago.[32]

Rather than asking these questions, the child lets go off the old woman's hand and runs ahead, "trying to outdo her own shadow"; and the great-grandmother (in an ironic, symbolic moment) chastises Ideal for this. Ideal cannot connect her "fearfulness" and "cowardice"—the things for which she is bullied—to the act of "walking tall." In the characterization of the great-grandmother, Polite evokes a model of cultural and familial connection that posits a mother-figure as the root of black women writers' art—a model of literary origins for which *later* writers, like Alice Walker, would become famous. Anticipating this model, Polite appraises the gesture of imparting a mother-figure as the authoritative medium for a younger female generation's access to history; Ideal's great-grandmother, a former slave, is an agent of historical preservation, supporting the past and its transmission to a new generation. As a result, despite her great-grandmother's advice, Ideal is consistently made to perceive her emotions and reactions as problematic aspects of her character that must be controlled. This ironic appeal to cultural and familial connection demonstrates how advice by elders—rather than inspiring—will inhibit Ideal's ability to create a new narrative for herself as the novel progresses.

And indeed, as the Prologue draws toward its close, Ideal does learn to find it "natural" to bow in most instances—particularly if she wishes to avoid frightening situations, as experienced at the party, or via her "down to earth" tormenter. For instance, the strict treatment that Ideal receives, as a result of her tormenter's motherly advice, is not relayed to readers as particularly distressing to the child. In fact, in the latter part of the Prologue, Ideal's fears appear to diminish to something like resignation—or, "bowing." The contradictions Ideal faces are thus framed for her as part of normal life— "one's nature" *should*, in this way, fall in line with Black Bottom (18). With the cessation of her emotional reactions, Ideal learns to perform bowing as if it were natural; and with this, her individuality and experiences are subsumed. Through Ideal's resigned bowing, Polite imparts an important commentary upon how class oppression and patriarchal ideology have been unwittingly adapted and normalized by her literary forebears—and thus, are at risk for similar normalization by writers yet to come (e.g., Walker, Morrison). Polite challenges this forthcoming aesthetic's avoidance of cultural conflicts with urbanization, using her Prologue to call attention to potential sources of these conflicts. Indeed, Polite's prophetic commentary was correct: more than a decade after *The Flagellants*' publication, Alice Walker's recovery of Zora Neal

Hurston's 1930s fiction revealed an aesthetic marked by the association of genuine, black experiences with folk culture and the impoverished, provincial life of the segregated South.

Walker's 1974 essay "In Search of Our Mothers' Gardens" inaugurated the reclamation of this folk aesthetic.[33] This work by Walker during the 1970s marked the emergence of the folk aesthetic in black feminist literary criticism. Polite's Prologue questions whether such aesthetic nostalgia may harbor dangerous social ramifications, particularly if black writers are meant to authenticate the social purpose of literature in their work's narrative style.[34] This point becomes particularly significant as Ideal eventually moves away from Black Bottom to New York City, where she will meet Jimson. On the Prologue's final page, as she prepares to leave the small town behind, one of her fellow Bottom-dwellers warns her: "Where you are going now, Ideal, you will have to act and talk just like white folks; because if you don't, God will strike you dead."[35] Punctuating the close of the Prologue, Polite's narrative voice intervenes to mediate naïve Ideal's response to her fellow's warning:

> Staying next door to white people was the same as staying next door to black people, yellow people, brown people, any people. They cried the same blues, the same joys, ate, slept, had babies and funerals, went their merry and tragic ways.[36]

Here, Ideal is faced with a new, and totally alien, concern; issues such as racial relations or the negotiation of racial dynamics are completely irrelevant in Black Bottom—poverty binds everyone together. In the city, however, it is apparently different—pressures will compound, Ideal is told. This forms the outset of Ideal's emotional genealogy, paralleling the novel's significant chronicle of her misrecognition by Jimson as a castrating matriarch.

Cyclical Aesthetics and Ideological Operations

The Flagellants' aesthetic enacts a complex relation to BAM values and critical strategies concerning the division between art and ideology. The BAM's critical context emanates from various local responses to more general developments within American culture of the 1950s and 1960s and *The Flagellants* fashions a dark satire of these responses. In contrast with her contemporaries, Polite's novel demonstrates how ideology shapes human experiences by defining acceptable modes of thought and practices; and particularly in American following the Second World War, ideology does this very subtly, interweaving its values through political and social realms so that it becomes familiar and therefore goes unchallenged. As such, the novel shows, any resonances between polarized ideologies (such as black nationalism and American mass culture) warrant exploration. Thus, rather than reflecting only one ideology, *The Flagellants* reveals the subtlety with which ideologies operate, how they blend and recombine, and how they are perpetuated through routines that organize human life. Through its thematic and ideological ambivalence, *The Flagellants* performs precisely how—as Jean Cary Bond and Patricia Peery would later write—the transference of oppressive values (which work for the oppressor) fashions dysfunctional and particularly destructive forces against black community solidarity.[37] To enunciate precisely how the experiences of Polite's main characters occur as a result of their unknowing consent to racist patriarchal ideologies, *The Flagellants* proceeds to enact complex relationships between consent and ideological operations.

Of course, Polite's novel resists straightforward interpretation, such as thematic or character analysis; despite the time of its publication, New Critical close reading methods may not so easily be applied here. *The Flagellants'* main theme is misrecognition—a burden that is imposed by the ideological, "structural constraints of white racism" and the "restrictions of black sexism."[38] This theme is served through the novel's structure and style, rather than illustrated in its form or content. Other content, such as Polite's mode of characterization, is also constructed in service of the novel's style. In the novel, Ideal and Jimson do not learn or grow; the text's minor characters operate as talismans (whether from childhood or depicted as part of adulthood), significant only for how they affect the ways Ideal and Jimson perpetuate their tumultuous relationship. Ideal's and Jimson's stasis (whether together or apart) is important because this allows the novel's structure to play out as a process in and of itself. Rather than functioning in service of character growth, the structure of *The Flagellants* operates similarly to ideology itself—providing a rhythm, or a current, by which the characters are moved.

For example, *The Flagellants'* first two chapters offer a snapshot of Ideal's and Jimson's everyday interactions, offering a sense (however disorienting) of their characterizations and relationship. *The Flagellants'* Chapters 1 and 2 open on the present state of Jimson and Ideal's romantic relationship, which is dissolving toward a violent turning point. By contrast, Chapters 3 through 10 take readers back in time, to happier days of their romance; however, in these chapters, pacing gradually intensifies and events grow increasingly extreme. This development reveals that the novel's chapters operate as a metaphor for a vicious cycle: the process of Jimson and Ideal's relationship toward its inevitable end. Finally, Chapters 11 and 12 present events that immediately follow those of Chapters 1 and 2—the consequences of this vicious cycle.

The sweep of fantasy and resentment intrinsic to Chapters 1 and 2 is meant to disorient readers, particularly following the Prologue. In the first chapter, through a rare moment of first-person narration, a now-adult Ideal contemplates her unhappiness and waits in the bedroom of her small apartment for Jimson to come home:

> Jimson, you beautiful black man, we cannot stay it. It is so much more natural being ignorant and forsaken, deceived and handicapped, poetic and slobbering […] Crusts of substandard life refuse to budge from under my toenails. I feel the sunlight and imagine one day I will wheel us out into the just life. Then this incarnation can be exploited as soul, as a past, as something to be thankful for, as a gauge toward attainment, as the surmounted obstacle.[39]

Ideal's interior monologue lasts for a little over six pages and, in this span, her thoughts continually shift between anticipating escape from and resigned acceptance of her "substandard life." Polite's presentation of this self-deprecating, static Ideal is a significant departure from realist, BAM assumptions concerning the existence of a whole, authentic character. On the one hand, Ideal imagines escape from her current conditions, convincing herself that the sum of these circumstances will result in vindication. Yet, she is resigned to the notion that it is more "natural" for her to remain "ignorant" and "handicapped" by her circumstances. Uncannily similar to her great-grandmother's advice about bowing, Ideal is not aware of the contradictory nature of her thoughts.

Significantly, Ideal is re-introduced to readers in an apparently gut-wrenching state: "going mad waiting for rebirth"—but really, just waiting for Jimson to come home.[40] She does not offer readers a self-determined or hopeful performance. Instead, Ideal is presented as shut in her dirty apartment, powerless against her own thoughts until her man returns; in both body and mind, Ideal is at once split and contained. Recalling Cynthia Washington's 1964 piece in *Southern Exposure*, this extreme initial depiction questions where black women might fit into a paradigm such as the BAM's defining blackness as naturalistic and bodily. Ideal's thoughts reveal that she does not recognize herself within a revolutionary model of black beauty and vitality; she understands "bowing," as well as being "forsaken" and "deceived," to be her "natural" states of existence. The hopelessness of this scene calls to mind how the BAM's essentialist model of black identity subsumes gender differences and black feminine consciousness. As such, women's experiences of racism and sexism are given no voice or critical inquiry; they are presented as natural, which Polite emphasizes in this scene. The first chapter's scene, formed entirely of Ideal's interiority, recalls that black women's complex inner lives are erased or absorbed in much of the nationalist discourses of the 1960s.

When Jimson arrives home, narrative tone shifts as Ideal quickly disposes of her maudlin mood and they go out for a drink. At the bar, Jimson's anger is triggered by Ideal's reminiscences on their happier, earlier days as a couple. The scene dissolves into exchanges of character judgments, insults concerning former lovers, and racial epithets; Jimson alludes to Ideal being a Jezebel and a Sapphire, and Ideal retorts calling Jimson a "black dog."[41] Their row spills into the street where Jimson leaves Ideal to an accumulating crowd of onlookers. Soon thereafter, the couple carries on insulting one another at home; here, narrative pace slows back down as their fight takes a more methodical form. Instead of merely hurling insults, the couple exchanges stories about the shameful dispositions of two men they each once knew; comparing one another to these disreputable men, Ideal and Jimson accuse each other of perpetuating the past's oppressive cycles that propagate racism. For instance, Ideal invokes Booker Shad, a stubborn bluesman who descended into madness when his musical gifts were not properly appreciated. With this yarn, Ideal reproaches Jimson for adhering to a "school" of thought which believes "the more one suffers, the deeper the soul."[42] At this point in the novel, Polite's narrator has offered no evidence as to whether Ideal's judgment against Jimson is correct; however, Jimson's dismissal of the sketch is revealing, as he states, "I said I wanted to talk to you. I did not say that I wanted to hear your Jimson critique."[43]

Through Jimson's anecdotal rebuttal, insight may be gained into both his characterization and their relationship. Jimson tells of an old man from his childhood, Papa Boo, former slave and a boarder in Jimson's middle-class, childhood home. Papa Boo was a "miserable old Uncle Tom," a "creature who knew his assigned place," and possessed "only that intelligence which was the effect of the emulation of the white man."[44] To Jimson, Papa Boo was a disgraceful figure because of how he performed racial identity. According to Jimson, because Papa Boo wanted so badly to be accepted by white people, he grew to hate other black people. He would berate the young Jimson, telling him that he was "the Prince of Darkness, a shame before God, [and] the ugliest child in the world."[45] "I was the reason my people were kept down; anything that looked like me had to be kept back," Jimson recounts. Papa Boo's presence in young Jimson's life fashions an environment of stigmatizing shame, positioning the boy as a malignancy, based not upon his actual behaviors, but upon his physical characteristics, such as his skin tone. To Jimson, Papa Boo represented "the spikes of tradition and absurdity" that oppress black Americans with feelings of "persecution" and "ineptitude"; such feelings led Papa Boo—and others like Ideal, Jimson contends—to think they are able to create safe spaces for themselves by performing racial stereotypes and shaming those who do not conform.[46] For Jimson, this malignant shaming is a form of accommodationism (ironically recalling Schraufnagel's complaints) and individuals, such as himself, must "save" themselves by removing these interactions and influences from their lives. This reminiscence of Papa Boo is thus deployed to point out Jimson's own generation's denial of their elders' "innate feeling of ineptitude" and "contempt" for youthful naiveté; he recalls Papa Boo in order to suggest to Ideal that she, too, suffers from harmful idealism and unacknowledged persecution by her elders.[47]

However, Jimson's yarn about Papa Boo has a second function, as well: that is, shaming Ideal for calling Jimson a "black dog." Problematically, Jimson shames Ideal for shaming him in the very manner that Papa Boo once had. At once, Ideal is compared to the ignorant oppressor, Papa Boo; and she is reduced to the defenseless position Jimson had been forced to assume under Papa Boo's torment (and it is not mentioned that Jimson had first insulted Ideal, in Chapter 1, with Jezebel and Sapphire commentary). By the end of Jimson's story, the narrator relates, Ideal had lost "her three dimensional being," becoming a "flattened symbol."[48] Jimson's means for putting Ideal in her place erase her experience of his sexist insults in Chapter 1; the story of Papa Boo negates her interiority and personhood and, instead, demands that she recognize Jimson's. His story reduces Ideal to a stereotype—and one that neither fits her experiences nor precisely accounts for why she insulted Jimson in the manner that she had. The result of this scene is twofold: Jimson's story inadvertently casts himself as the "hypocritical flunky" (rather than Ideal), as he blindly perpetrates the shaming he once endured by Papa Boo. And Jimson's yarn, however unfitting to her experiences, does affect silencing shame in Ideal: she is aware that apologizing would just "give her the appearance of a well-disciplined child," so she says nothing.[49] Instead, Ideal "bows"—or, ruminates on the pain that Jimson's childhood experiences must cause him.

As the novel continues, more information is offered, concerning how Jimson and Ideal arrived at this punishing point in their relationship. From Chapters 5 through 8, narrative pace shifts frequently to highlight the increasingly antagonistic relation between the couple. The bulk of this section is punctuated by Jimson's repetitive lectures to Ideal on the overbearing nature of black women. In Chapter 6, Jimson (who is unemployed from Chapters 3 through 5) announces that he has found a job—which he agrees to keep on one condition:

> He was going to work; but the decision did not cause Ideal to jump up and dance, grab him around his neck [...]; since the announcement, naturally, was accompanied by an infernal red tape sealing the condition with, "Stay home, Ideal, and just be my wife." Any man deserving the name wanted his wife to do just that—stay at home and be his mistress-mother.[50]

Ideal's displeasure with Jimson's "natural" condition for keeping his new job is not stated by Ideal herself, rather it is mediated by Polite's third-person narrator. Ideal offers no testament to her actual feelings about becoming a housewife; in fact, she does not speak in Chapter 6 at all.

Instead, Polite's narrator relays Jimson's presumptions concerning Ideal's feelings about becoming his "mistress-mother"; her disapproval is assumed by Jimson/the narrator. For instance, when Jimson tells Ideal the news, the narrator states: "What was her contention this evening? Why no cheers and buying spree?"[51] This is swiftly followed by a lecture from Jimson; with wry consideration for the reader, the narrator summarizes:

> If Jimson went to work, she would criticize, see the nest for what it barely was. If he stayed at home, she bitched, blessed him out. Jimson had several favorite lectures. One began, "I will teach you to take care of yourself"— the liberal's world-wide doctrine of local assistance. You are not prepared to manage yourself. You need our help; so that we are assured that you will govern your affairs in the right white way, my way. [...] The lecture did Ideal no good.[52]

Through the narrator's synopsis of Jimson's "favorite lecture," Polite expresses a problematic reliance upon white institutions—not only for gainful employment, but also—for models to structure one's personal affairs.

Before Toni Cade Bambara's essay "On the Issue of Roles" (1970) publicly discussed interpersonal conflicts between black men and women, *The Flagellants* elucidated the nationalist collusion with Daniel Patrick Moynihan's 1965 policy document, *The Negro Family: The Case for National Action*— also known as the Moynihan Report. Moynihan Report "designated black matriarchy as the principle cause of a culture of pathology that kept black people from achieving equality"; this purported model, where women made household decisions and were the primary income earners, posited the black woman as controlling, emasculating her male partner and destroying her children's hope of future opportunities.[53] Claiming that black communities could be strengthened if black women assumed a subordinate position and allowed men to lead, Moynihan reported on the alleged deviance of black American families, rather than "identifying the structural barriers facing

African American communities."⁵⁴ Although black men initially railed against the report's claims, several critics have pointed out how the movement adopted Moynihan's construction of black womanhood.

Within the "natural" model that Jimson proposes, his commitment to a patriarchal family system like the one suggested in the Moynihan Report is implied; and his annoyance with Ideal's presumed disapproval mirrors black nationalism's investment in a model of patriarchal masculinity. This reveals, as bell hooks has argued, the way that white oppressors are "able to establish a bond of solidarity with Black men based on mutual sexism," drawing readers' attention to Jimson's collusion in oppression through his willingness to assume an antagonistic relation to his partner, Ideal.⁵⁵ The lack of masculine privilege that Jimson feels as a result of Ideal's (he imagines) "chronic dispraise" displaces onto Ideal his oppression and disenfranchisement in the labor market.⁵⁶ This, of course, also directs attention back to an important aspect of the novel's critical context, in which African American men felt alienated from the federal government, as well. Thus, Jimson may be read as summoning patriarchal values in order to obtain a sense of normalcy— in order to allay, however misguidedly—the "chronic dispraise" he feels from his social experiences in America at large (particularly in light of his difficulty retaining employment). Summonsing echoes of Moynihan in this scene through Jimson's speech and Ideal's silence, Polite reveals how the myth of the black matriarch opposes (not only the nationalist assertion of essential difference from the decadent, ineffectual white middle class, but also) the movement's promise to rouse a new black consciousness from accommodationism.

Through the narrator's mediation of Ideal's thoughts and feelings, Chapter 6 also demonstrates how black feminine consciousness is subsumed within both American cultural and nationalist patriarchal models. Jimson becomes an excessive supplement to Polite's narrator in the latter half of the novel. This is key to Polite's expression via Jimson, who is unwittingly caught in an interminable feedback loop: he is unaware of how he has been hobbled by racism and malignant shaming since childhood. At the end of Chapter 6, Jimson quits his new job (he believes his white female boss sexually desires him) and, at the beginning of Chapter 7, he walks home imagining the quarrel that may catalyze with Ideal. When he arrives home, he is ready to argue. Before he tells Ideal he has quit, he presents a litany of questions:

> Can you tell that I have paralyzed myself? [...] Can you tell me why you need to castrate me? Why I need to be castrated? [...] Can you tell what is fact about me and what is fancy? Can you tell what I want?[57]

Jimson's interrogation demands that Ideal tell him whether or not she knows him, or is able to recognize him, for who he is. However, Jimson himself may not know the answers to these questions; he cannot perceive how he is inscribed within ideology. His questions are merely dissemblance, protecting him against the onslaught he imagines Ideal will give.

If Ideal is able to perceive Jimson's ideological inscription and/or dissemblance, she does not testify to it. She is speechless, calculating her reaction so as not to further hurt Jimson. She tries to placate him, asking him to explain what is wrong, hoping he does not misidentify his pain as being her fault. Up to this point in the novel (despite Jimson's allegations), Ideal has been reticent in the face of Jimson's tirades, sustaining herself on imaginative escapism and obeisance. In Chapter 7, however, Jimson does not allow this. He responds to her pacification with violence; he exploits her obedience and demands she physically engage him. Polite's narrator mediates:

> If this is what Jimson needed in order to calm down, take away his throw, Ideal would respond. [...] [S]he bit, clawed, kicked, and held on with her not-too-dear life to any part of his wailing body that extended itself. Why did she do as she was told, Lord?[58]

In this instant, a crucial shift takes place in Ideal and Jimson's relationship. Ideal reacts, flinging "her whole body against him, flailing" obediently fighting Jimson "like a man," as he requests.[59] Until now, Ideal has not been violent, nor has she perpetrated the "never-ending tirade," "chronic dispraise," or "bitching" that is suggested by the narrator in Chapter 6. This moment in Chapter 7 marks an important change because it is here that Ideal at last enacts (if only by direction) the bullying expected of her by Jimson. However, Ideal's fighting "like a man" does not pacify Jimson. The narrator relates, "he trounced upon her as if she were original sin, the cause of all suffering, the original slave trader."[60] Ideal's engagement permits Jimson's physical violence, but also Ideal's fighting back validates the shame planted in Jimson by Papa Boo.

By demanding Ideal beat him, Jimson validates the shame he feels for quitting his job, once again demonstrating his inability to conform to Papa Boo's mold; and simultaneously, Jimson is ashamed of the idea that he must have a job in order for Ideal to respect him (or so he believes). In the same way that Jimson tells a story of his own experience of shaming in an effort to inspire shame in Ideal, here, Jimson feels shame for failing to adhere to a particular interpretation of blackness, while he is also ashamed at the (mistaken) idea that he has no choice but to adhere to this image. While he is intellectually aware of his subjugation within society, as well as the origins of both racial stratification and intra-group injustices, Jimson cannot extricate himself from the forces he points out. In the argument that he imagines on his walk home, Jimson reveals the actual cause of his quitting his job: by quitting, he believes he is rejecting his white supervisor's expectation that he conform to a particular image of the perfect black man. In so doing, however, he merely enacts an inverse image—irresponsible, unreliable—which is the interpretation that he (and the narrator) accuses Ideal of harboring. Jimson's sense of himself is forged in his relationships with Papa Boo and Ideal, and these relationships are weighted by numerous vectors of identification that are propagated in both white- and black-coded ideological systems. Thus, the relationship with Ideal illustrates the inseparability of African American racial and gendered trauma via the complex emotional states that play out in their interactions.

The Problem of Inscription

Jimson's blindness to his collusion via patriarchal ideology is importantly reflected in Ideal's pacification and obedience. While Polite's narrator is aware of Ideal's internal states, mediating her ruminations, more frequently, the narrator reflects Jimson's perspective. This becomes more apparent when Jimson projects his interpretations of Ideal as an emasculating matriarch; as the novel progresses, this repetition results in an increasingly controlled, normalized view of Ideal-as-matriarch—despite there being no cause or evidence for this interpretation. Ideal's experiences of misrecognition thus seem to foreclose any hope of productive debate with Jimson; throughout the novel, she absorbs Jimson's tirades with Black Bottom resignation. Until finally, in Chapter 11, following one of Jimson's last tirades, she speaks out against him:

> Do you ever stop and think about what comes out of your mouth? Do you wonder why it is that you have given the history of your people, the black people in America, such a negative, lascivious, unintelligent depiction? [...] You mean what you say about being out here by yourself, the social anchorite detached from life, don't you? [...] It would be a pitiful sight to behold hearing you preach this doctrine from a black church's pulpit some Sunday morning, or [...] before the good brothers of any fraternity. You name the group. The people would massacre you."[61]

Ideal's monologue extends for several pages, revealing an alternate perception of race. In this key scene, Ideal shifts the narrative focus onto Jimson's negativity toward race, forcing him to face his contingency. Ideal addresses Jimson's unconstructive relation to society in his own idiom and, for the first time, Polite's narrator is silent as she speaks.

Of course, Ideal's Chapter 11 monologue should not be read as decoupling her from this relationship's dysfunction. At the beginning of *The Flagellants'* final chapter, another disorienting moment emerges much like that which opened Chapter 1. Here, Ideal's inner monologue fuses with Polite's narrative voice; however, unlike Chapter 1, instead of a depressed, resigned Ideal, the character becomes abruptly aware of her ideological inscription as matriarch. Ideal sees how her thoughts and practices feed into both Jimson's misrecognition of her and her own misrecognition of Jimson:

> Out of accident, the chaos was borne along, so that now, evil has emerged. Evil accepts as its guise self-pity. [...]
>
> Why could we have not made of our ideals something constructive, taking from our experiences its creative force to bring to the world our loving attitudes? Must we make of the soil a playground for our adult temper tantrums? If our original good intention is toward ourselves, and proceeding in its normal, changing order toward mother, father, our brothers and sisters, must we employ our most evil force to gain that good intention?[62]

In this two-page inner monologue, Ideal acknowledges her awareness of ideology and how her resignation has perpetuated the "substandard" conditions readers find her bemoaning in Chapter 1. She notes this very sensation as that which holds her and Jimson back from self-fulfillment. Yet, while the narrative work of Chapters 11 and 12 may be read as either hopeful or scathing, the function of these chapters is merely descriptive, leading readers to a rather flat ending at the close of *The Flagellants*.

At novel's end, Ideal and Jimson part ways: Ideal is tired and she asks Jimson to leave. The novel's imagistic model for subject formation enables a complex understanding of ideology's work; Jimson and Ideal are faced (not with the problem of distinguishing the ideological from the actual, but) with the problem of choosing between competing versions of actuality. A consequence of this is that conventional conception of character as Self is replaced by the ideologically inscribed, or positioned, subject. The conventional, autonomous subject marks the condition for historical progress, which is generated by rational subjects who scrutinize social and cultural norms. Yet, Jimson's and Ideal's static characterizations frame the blind spot of this rational subject: that is, the belief that a subject may be a fully developed, self-reflective individual who harnesses reason toward overcoming oppression. In Polite's model, the unique voice of this autonomous agent is revealed as merely ideology speaking through a subject position. Thus, Polite presents a rigid subject, overdetermined and interpreted by ideology—paralyzed, and without space for either resistance or agency.

Historicizing *The Flagellants*' context through examinations of cultural, political, and social influences begins to reveal how the novel became so obscure. In a time when African American men vied for a portion of American political patriarchy, when African American women voiced to their intersectional experiences in narrative, and at a time when the American academy (the New Critics, the New York Intellectuals) insisted that social experiences and ideological apparatuses had no role in literary production, scholarship, or criticism, *The Flagellants* simply did not fit into any interpretive model. In Polite's novel, no individual, collective, or ideological school is innocent when it comes to the perpetuation of racism. And every character, every idea—however flat or magnified—has a hand in contributing to the novel's culminating atmosphere of resignation: mass culture holds as much responsibility as nationalist discourse; women and men are culpable; the city is just as dangerous a space as rural Black Bottom; and elders are just as misguided and flawed as the youth. And perhaps most interesting, issues of specifically named, racial experiences fall to the background in *The Flagellants*; in the novel, it is a rare occasion when black and white Americans cross paths, and although these rare interactions are generally negative, all human interactions in the world of the novel are equally so.

Amid a variety of critical contexts that asserted particular, separatist paradigms for art, criticism, and the role of the artist, *The Flagellants* (a novel that simply refuses to choose a side) was a book about which one could barely write during the late 1960s, the discursive operations simply did not exist. This point may explain its near-absence from BAM-era scholarship. And this perhaps also accounts for how other (predominantly white) American academic reviewers, if they noted anything positive about the text, could only speak to its emotional depth. Polite's *The Flagellants* is a text that insists the reader assume a self-reflexive, auto-critical attitude toward long-form fiction; it demands a certain analytical creativity, historical awareness, and even a kind of fearlessness. This may explain how, as a rediscovered text in the early 1990s, the novel was poised as little more than a biographical analogy, stripped (along with Polite) of its innovation and masterful interpretation of its late 1960s audiences, and the means by which they made meaning from expressive art.

The Flagellants encourages readers to unmake the (often ideological) organizing principles through which literary meaning is created via interpretation; such all-encompassing models cannot lead to liberation nor can they sustain life, particularly where freedom of expression is concerned. The distress and eventual resignation to "Bottom thought" endured by a young, sensitive (and, importantly, beautiful) Ideal, for instance, at once conditions her adult life and readers' understandings of her misguided resilience in relation to Jimson. Problematically, "Bottom thought" becomes an organizing principle for their cyclical, dysfunctional relationship; and within this model, neither character is permitted agency to grow or change. Without reasonable, alternative models (an even sharper dearth than readers might claim for Franny, a decade earlier) in either private or public spheres,

"Bottom thought" subtly becomes the only sustainable perspective through which Ideal relates to (i.e., misrecognizes) either Jimson or herself. Brutal and often suspicious words and actions become their style of relating (even to those outside their relationship); and this style, of course, not only tints their projective characterizations, but also illustrates the novel's primary theme of misrecognition. *The Flagellants* enacts not only various means and forms by which ideology persists after the Second World War, but the subtle ways by which even its resistant strains (e.g., BAM, Black Power) are able to be partially coopted in public (and private) arenas toward counterintuitively sustaining a competing, unsettlingly discriminatory, status quo. In fact, *The Flagellants* shows, whether or not Ideal and Jimson hurl insults, Jimson still struggles to retain employment and Ideal still feels unfulfilled; the drudgery of their years-long routines has taught them to perceive these conditions as "natural."

Polite's *The Flagellants* offers readers a layered cautionary tale concerning the role and impacts of ideology in American conceptions and depictions of race, as well as in the formation of literary traditions and communities in the United States. The novel offers competing and disorienting iterations of reality, formulated via ideology's revenant echoes through art, politics, and society in the world of the novel; the result of this non-realist cacophony is an uncomfortable, if not jarring, story of sexism and racist ideology's ghoulish persistence in mid-Cold War America. Central to this expression is *The Flagellants*' entreaty to question the apparently accidental (yet "natural") scenes where its characters must dispense with personal interests in order to survive, as they nevertheless complicate this survival via the painful, selective memories (i.e., nostalgist aesthetics of a personal variety) with which they identify. As Jimson's and Ideal's cyclically impoverished and tortured states are at once of their own making and far beyond their control to change, like *Franny and Zooey*, *The Flagellants* also seems to narratively grope, or hope, for some beyond—that is, some point in the historical future where antithetical, contradictory views have been overcome, and ideology's "end" is accepted as (not its wholesale disappearance, but) its transformation into innumerable, malleable schemas by which citizens may make and remake meaning in their lives according to personal interest. As *The Flagellants*' reminiscences suggest, if Ideal's critical impulses and confidence had not been so violently dampened from such an early age, she might have become a dancer as she had originally planned; and Jimson might have become a poet. The hopelessness showcased via the limitations of Polite's (as well as Salinger's) characters signals a need for new models—in literary study, public discourse, and contemporary actuality—toward deriving meaning from cultural productions, as well as from life in contemporary America.

3

"Sorcery" and Historical Narrative: Leslie Marmon Silko's *Almanac of the Dead*

In claiming the "end of history" in 1989, Francis Fukuyama inserted himself into an extant narrative, or a lineage of others, claiming history's end—G.W.F. Hegel, Karl Marx, and Alexander Kojeve, specifically. Fukuyama imagined the end of the Cold War, and the coming end of the twentieth century, as not only marking the end of "history" as bloody ideological struggle, but as also precipitating the end of "man" (or, humanity), properly speaking. Adapting Kojeve's interpretation of Marx in the context of his *Introduction to the Reading of Hegel*, Fukuyama imagines this finite conception of humanity as fighting against itself for recognition and against nature, or the natural order, for work and profit.[1] After the Cold War, Fukuyama asserts, on the shoulders of Western democratic equality, liberty, and bolstered by capitalism's engines of profit, humanity looks forward to sharply reduced warfare, free work (i.e., not-necessary, or creative and self-expressive), and mutual recognition among all (if only in the realm of ideas; Fukuyama admitted this victory incomplete in the real world, *c.* 1989).[2] Fukuyama's predictive claims read as optimistic as America moved closer to the twenty-first century; however, as Leslie Marmon Silko's *Almanac of the Dead* (1991) attests, the art of divination makes an uncomfortable bedfellow to the sorcery of historical narrative.

Enticed with the possibility of existential and ideational boredom after the end of history, Fukuyama leaves open the potential for history to begin again in the post-historical age—just as all classical ideologies' ends construct their very renaissance or reincarnation through alternative organizations and structures. In his thinking, Fukuyama poises himself as following the legacy of nineteenth century, post-Kantian conceptual ontologist, Georg Wilhelm

Friedrich Hegel, and one of Hegel's most well-known twentieth-century interpreters, Alexander Kojeve. Fukuyama asserts the Cold War as denoting a continuation of a presumed "end" to history that Hegel (according to Kojeve) defined in 1806—that is, with the collapse of the Prussian monarchy at the hands of Napoleon, and the assertion of the French Revolution's principles of liberty and equality. With no improvements presumably left to be made on the principles of the "liberal democratic state," Fukuyama reasons, the end of the Second World War (in Kojeve's time) and his own contemporaneous end of the Cold War succeeded in spatially, and therefore globally, extending the "vanguard of humanity" borne within Hegel's early-nineteenth-century Europe.[3] With considerable work done in the interest of liberal democratic principles since 1806, including, Fukuyama notes, the abolition of slavery and the enfranchisement of women and minorities, by the end of the Cold War, "history" as such (i.e., a series of real struggles for recognition) was well on its way to a final end and/or another beginning.

Fukuyama's logic is compelling, idealistic, and optimistic, periodizing nearly 200 years of human history prior to the late 1980s as a deep level convergence of political, social, and cultural systems on a global scale, and all in the direction of humanity's (or, Marx's presumed) eventual achievement of "universal homogeneity" in the "realm of freedom" (*Reich de Freiheit*).[4] I claim that Leslie Marmon Silko's second novel, a hotly debated text titled *Almanac of the Dead* (1991), not only anticipates, but offers an interestingly anti-Hegelian-Hegelian supplement to Fukuyama's triumphant idealism, concerning the global "ends" of "history," the twentieth century, and humanity. In *Almanac*'s expression (i.e., non-linear, contradictory, multi-vocal, and temporally ungrounded), capitalist democracy is not imagined as history and humanity's *last* suitable form of government, as it is in Fukuyama; rather, capitalism and democracy alike are de-prioritized as so many stories (among many possibilities and perspectives).

By contrast, Fukuyama's "end of history" via global democratization and capitalistic enfranchisement does not account for this condition as theoretical, as it was originally imagined by G. W. F. Hegel.[5] Instead, in his Introduction to *The End of History* (1992), Fukuyama defines the "old question" with which his project engages: "Whether, at the end of the twentieth century, it makes sense for us once again to speak of a coherent and directional History of mankind that will eventually lead the greater part of humanity to liberal democracy?" A theoretical (or, metaphysical) account of history's *Jenseits* (i.e., Marx and Hegel's German; the *hereafter*, or *great beyond*), or "end" (Fukuyama's preference), would explore whether humanity's trials of wage labor, consumerist accumulation, and violence *could ever* resolve into globally unopposed, "universal homogeneity" in the realm of ideas *or* the material world.[6] In this account, Hegel's "realm of freedom" (beyond Marx's "realm of necessity") is akin to a theoretical, processual afterlife (translating *Jenseits* as a metaphysical state) or *history's* great hereafter.

The material conditions of history's great hereafter, then, might be alternatively translated, or imagined as (not triumphant, as in Fukuyama, but) rife with frustration, unmet expectations, unfulfilled promises, and unfinished business. In this formulation, work is *meant* to be fulfilling and creative, but it does not meet the mark, or certainly not all the time.[7] Leslie Marmon Silko's *Almanac of the Dead* offers several such alternatives to reading this stage of history. *Almanac* reflects on the last 500 years of human history and re-imagines Fukuyama's triumphalism at the beginning of the 1990s as, in some cases, harmless and generally accurate and, in other cases, as desperate, insincere, or otherwise destructive. That is, *Almanac* re-imagines deadlocks like those closing the stories of Franny and Ideal (i.e., inalterable, deterministic circumstances contextualizing existentially delimited characters) as conditions that are immanent to life in the *world*—not as conditions which infringe upon or befall life, as Salinger and Polite posit. In *Almanac of the Dead*, characters have access to veritable markets of alternatives through which they may make and re-make their lives, and ranges of beliefs and histories to which they may prescribe; only a select few identify with Fukuyama's privileged democratic capitalist, as characters' options in *Almanac*, rather uncannily, are as limited as their imaginations and wealth.

Where Fukuyama locates assurance in the Cold War's end, *Almanac of the Dead* suggests that such assurances (in any historical context) merely stem from stories, specific narrative positioning and framing, of world-historical events. Silko's second novel suggests a post–Cold War world, but more broadly envisions a pre-apocalyptic, post-historical United States and post-industrial globe on the brink of people's revolution, rebellions by the homeless, and the disappearance of "all things European" from the American continents.[8] However, by novel's end, nothing that is set in motion is completed, no ancient prophesies are fulfilled. This is paradoxically because, *Almanac* suggests, *history's great hereafter* is a theoretical condition (not unlike Fukuyama's triumphalism) that, as such, clashes with the conditions and distinctions that authorize, administer, and define the marketized and material realm from which it emerges.

In this way, *Almanac's* reconceptualization of Fukuyama's "end of history" begins with its framing of the 1960s as instilling a promise, or a hope, that *someday* humanity will shrug off the prescriptive social and political remainders of bygone ages, and enjoy concrete alternatives to existential circumscription. Indeed, beyond Silko's novel and within the broader context of my study, the 1960s' resurgence of various American feminisms, the advent of Black Power, and Americans' invigorated attention to politics' influence on racial and gendered discourse may bolster readers' own visualization of the decade as assuring that *someday* tragically determined destinies like those of Franny, Ideal, and Jimson will be avoided via humanity's homogenous attainment of agency.[9] By contrast, *Almanac of the Dead* suggests that this promise, or hope, of *someday* only amounts to *one story* that may be told of the American 1960s; that is, amid early-1990s triumphalism, Silko reminds readers that the 1960s' proverbial *someday* does not specify the 1990s as its destination. Thus, *Almanac* suggests, the 1990s' own assured mood merely mirrors (or, derives elements of its form from) the 1960s' assurances, which do not encompass a promise of a finished political, social, or economic condition. *Almanac's* expression thus emerges from its depiction of a post-1960s America (and wider world) in which the 1960s' revolutionary ideas, existential rebellions, and Marxist critiques—particularly regarding sexuality, gender, and racial equality—have been marketized and, as a result, fatally neutralized. That is, revolutionary ideas, existential rebellions, and Marxist critiques are reduced to official *styles* of (or, false alternatives within) capitalism; engendered by the very system they profess to overthrow, the various *styles* from which characters choose can never be politically productive, nor can their commodified pseudo-critiques encapsulate the totality of anything they approach.

For instance, in *Almanac of the Dead*, the Cuban government runs a school in Mexico City, comic-ironically called the "Freedom School"; native American tribes in the area are actively encouraged to attend classes in Marxism here, in exchange for free arms and other supplies at the expense of the Cuban government.[10] A local native woman, Angelita (nicknamed "La Escapia," the Meat Hook) is a top student at the school and a great admirer of Marx (although she is certain he "stole" his ideas about egalitarianism from indigenous peoples).[11] However, like her tribesmen, Angelita does not care for the Cubans' interpretation of Marx, or her instructor, a handsome Cuban named Bartolomeo; but she is invested in protecting her tribe's interest in taking back their land from the federal government. So, Angelita diligently attends the Marxism classes, stockpiles her free supplies, and initiates an affair with Bartolomeo to gather intelligence on the Cuban government's intentions with the natives.

In *Almanac of the Dead*'s universe, ideology's relevance and productivity are solely defined by its alignment with material motives and forces that inspire characters to either mobilize against or defend a (historical, ideological, and essentially narrative) status quo. Angelita carries on her affair with Bartolomeo, and proverbially *buys into* the Cubans' particular, Marxist status quo insofar as she continues to stockpile munitions, funding, and supplies from them; however, in the course of her affair, Angelita realizes that the Cubans' interpretation of Marx omits indigenous issues (including the loss of land), despite her understanding of colonial history's prevalence in Marx's manuscripts. Angelita cites this omission as evidence of the Cubans' imperial interests and ultimate desire to erase her tribe's histories of resistance against colonial powers—just as they erased the native Cubans' extensive histories, including stories of "the great Cuban Indian rebel leader Hateuy," before the instatement of Fidel Castro.[12]

The Cubans' ideological status quo, their interpretation of Marxism (and therefore, their material aid), is suddenly undesirable in its denial of tribal stories of colonial exploitation and native rebellion. In response, Angelita and her associates establish a trans-partisan, global support network (comically named), the "Friends of the Indians," through which they stockpile enough munitions and funding to avenge their stories via Bartolomeo's execution for "crimes against certain tribal histories"; through these material and symbolic acts of rebellion, Angelita and her people seem to free themselves from reliance on Cuban government aid in their project against the federal government, just as their ancestors had supposedly done for generations before.[13] Problematically, however, in placing Bartolomeo on trial and eventually executing him, Angelita and her people effectively place "more than five hundred years of white men in Indian jurisdiction […] on trial with Bartolomeo"—Bartolomeo himself, as well as his death, is reduced to symbols, or totems, for the tribes' historical resistance against ideological and historical oppression.[14] While this underground coup is cathartic for Angelita and her people (as it is for tribal people elsewhere, who view the revolution on local television), it does not lead to the redistribution or restoration of Mexico's tribal lands to its tribal people. Nothing happens. Angelita eventually splinters from the company of the native American and Mexican revolutionaries she leads, in order to attend an "International Healers Convention" in Tucson, Arizona; by novel's end, readers are left to guess what becomes of the Meat Hook—as with the majority of the novel's cast of nearly eighty similarly self-interested characters.

It is likely no surprise, then, that Silko's *Almanac*, like Angelita's revolution, ends in a stalemate. However, the deadlocks which accumulate within, and finally conclude, Silko's *Almanac of the Dead* are not the results of personal circumscription via gender and race, as with Franny Glass, Ideal, and Jimson; rather, *Almanac*'s stalemates derive from radical ideologies' neutralization via marketization and characters' personal interests. Capital itself keeps interest groups, like Angelita's would-be "all-tribal people's army," locked into impotent pantomimes, or dramata, of humanity's immemorial struggles for recognition.[15] The differences between Fukuyama's and *Almanac*'s portraits of a post–Cold War world may become clear, beginning with their diverse understandings of reality: the former, propositional and de facto; the latter, conceptual. *Almanac*'s conception of reality accounts for the inevitability of change within the material realm (e.g., birth, death, social reorganization, economic flux), as in the philosophy of Hegel; that is, *Almanac* reveals (e.g., via characters' interminable, if pointless struggles for recognition) that nothing is fixed in a world of change, including reality. Thus, in this concrete world of change, reality is not a meaningless fact that is opposite to non-Being (or death, as in the work of Kant), but a dynamic construction consisting of the real *and* ideal, existence and essence (or, Being and non-Being, life and death). And interestingly, much as in Hegel, *Almanac of the Dead* envisions *history's great beyond* as imminent to (i.e., part of, but also created by) the actual, material world. However, *Almanac*'s expression (unlike Kojeve or Fukuyama) meditates on the weight of the ideal (or, "the weight of ghosts," as the novel puts it) on the material realm *and* the concurrent, reductionist danger of imagining humanity as incapable of effecting an ultimate end (such as freedom) within history's uncannily purgatorial *hereafter*.[16]

Thus, although *Almanac*'s dramata neither are materially necessary nor offer lasting, spiritual fulfillment to characters, these dramata nevertheless have very concrete consequences. Unlike the psychological distress and cognitive dissonance demonstrated in Franny's, Ideal's, and Jimson's characterizations (although the same, disingenuously totalizing systems still exist), in *Almanac*, characters do not experience such ethical or existential crises. *Almanac* contains no protagonist; and although Silko's characters (like Salinger's and Polite's) are aware of the ineffectuality and destructiveness of the systems in which they are situated, they remain unbothered by this fact. If they are bothered, they simply select another path, another set of stories, toward fulfilling their personal interests. For instance, prior to becoming involved with either Bartolomeo or the Cuban Marxists, Angelita lived unhappily with (and similarly supported her people through) a missionary group of strict Catholic nuns. However, she eventually abandons them when she realizes the nuns' maligned "Marx the Devil" may be a friend to her people in taking back their land from the government:

> The old Castilian nuns at the mission school had called Marx the Devil. The nuns had trotted out the bogeyman Marx to scare the students if the older students refused after school work assignments, free labor for the Catholic Church. [...] [E]nemy of all missionaries, this Marx *had to be* Angelita's ally! She had understood instinctively [...] Marx the tribal man understood [...] Generation after generation, individuals were born, then after eighty years, disappeared into dust, but in the stories, the people lived on in the imaginations and hearts of their descendants. Wherever their stories were told, the spirits of the ancestors were present and their power was alive.[17]

In Angelita's reading of *Das Kapital* (the volume of which is not specified in *Almanac*), Marx accommodates stories like those of her tribe. Thus, as Angelita is invested, first, in her own interpretation of Marx and, next, in her tribe's interest in reclaiming their land from the government, she quickly abandons the Cuban Marxists, like the nuns, when she realizes *their* reading of Marx does not include indigenous peoples' stories of exploitation and resistance.

However, the difference between Angelita's continual slippage among interest groups, and Fukuyama's portrait of humanity at the end of history is Angelita's dangerous inability to perceive her work as non-necessary, due to her problematically near-religious reverence of Marx. As she exclaims prior to Bartolomeo's execution, "Marxism is one thing! Marx *the man* is another!" (original emphasis):

> Screw the police and army. Angelita didn't care. They would not take her alive. Before she died, she must explain to the village people about Marx, who was unlike any white man since Jesus. For now—screw Cuban Marxists and their European totalitarianism![18]

In her appeal's dangerous cocktail of vengeance, self-interest, and nationalistic pride, Angelita distorts Cuba's history in a manner similar to the Cuban Marxists' refusal to acknowledge her own tribal stories. And worse, she does so to violent ends (Bartolomeo's execution), recalling European settlers' violent offenses against the Cuban natives; Angelita omits Marxism's legacy in Cuba as linked to the newly independent nation's early-twentieth-century attempts to garner munitions and monetary aid from Russia. The country had no actual political affiliation with Western European governments since the late-nineteenth century. By perpetrating the very historical offenses for which she accuses Bartolomeo, Angelita ironically reveals her leadership of the "all tribal people's army" as non-necessary. The people's revolution never amounts to anything, after all.

In *Almanac of the Dead*, revolutionary, nationalist, and democratic ideologies alike (along with native histories) are absorbed by the same forces that, on the one hand, drive native tribes to (and then against) the Cuban Marxists and, on the other hand, which allow governments to retain tribal lands: vested material interests and forces, thinly veiled by ideological (or, historical) motivations.

Indeed, to many in Silko and Fukuyama's time (in light the fall of the Soviet Union and the Berlin Wall), the idea of *ideology* became synonymous with insincerity—carrying connotations of "mere rhetoric."[19] Importantly, however, for others in this moment, ideology (particularly in the form of nationalism, as in the 1960s) was still very relevant. Similar to Eastern Europe during and just after the Cold War, the homelessness and other economic hardships which *Almanac* depicts in Arizona, New Mexico, and just over the Mexican border "generate social discontent, demands, and mobilization" that find expression in institutional bodies, causes, and rebellions like those by Angelita La Escapia and her tribesmen, as well as Bartolomeo.[20]

Similar to during and just after the Cold War, in *Almanac*, readers observe an ideological divide between communism (illustrated by chapters set in Mexico and South America) and capitalism (largely represented by chapters based in Tucson, Arizona)—a divide, for example, expressed in one incarnation as a contest between ancient prophecy and "all things European" (to be discussed in the next section of this chapter). However, as Andre Gunter Frank argues in "No End to History! History to No End?" against Fukuyama (published less than a year before *Almanac*), the true contests of the Cold War—just as in *Almanac*'s world—are *not* the ideological distinctions between the communist Soviet Union and the democratic capitalist United States. Rather, the true contests are immanent to the struggles taking place in the world economy during and after the Cold War.[21] As readers see in the novel's resonances between otherwise diverse characters, economic forces beyond anyone's control shape the political relations and social movements that are illustrated in *Almanac*.

Silko's *Almanac of the Dead* comprises countless other distortions of stories, or historical narratives, similar to those of Angelita's tribesmen and the native Cubans. This is because the ideal causes and/or noble interests for which characters work in the novel (in lieu of conventional jobs or careers) are non-necessary, or free; it is done, in other words, because characters believe these pursuits—which include vocations such as drug dealing, weapons smuggling, snuff film distribution, and so on—will fulfill their personal interests (which are often vengeful) and their material desires (which are often vast).[22] In contrast to Fukuyama's optimism, then, non-mundane work in *Almanac* constitutes characters' impotent struggles for recognition. Because characters' beliefs (e.g., Angelita's, regarding tribal sovereignty) are marketized as their *works* in the material world, this seemingly self-interested work becomes the force driving human competition and struggles for recognition. Paradoxically, characters' ideals can thus never be fully realized in an essential, total form—material existence will not allow this, *Almanac* emphasizes, because it is always in flux. As a result, the interminable, various narratives through which characters rationalize their work generate illusions (for both themselves and readers) that victory, fulfillment, freedom, and so on are just on the horizon—though they never arrive.

Almanac of the Dead offers conceptual expressions of both a dynamic real world's effects on the static ideals of characters, *and* essential and existential conditions under which ideals may burden or destroy those who seek spiritual fulfillment in the real world. Reality's continual shuttling between the ideal and the real (i.e., the *illusory*, temporary ability of ideals to exist, for better or worse, in the material realm) is referred to as "sorcery" in the novel.[23] In fact, *Almanac*'s number of echoing plotlines and stories correspond through the generality of sorcery's influence, as a seemingly omnipresent social and political force, over all of the characters in the novel; the novel's massive, 500-year timeframe is disconcertingly exemplified by its reliance on "sorcery." Through Silko's large cast of projective characters, the complex structure of *Almanac* is thus permitted to swell and magnify as a process in itself, with the characters' resonant stories and values forming the basis of the novel's broader portrait of ideological work within *history's hereafter*. In this way, Silko depicts *history's hereafter* as a process and a goal (similar to Hegel's and Gilles Deleuze's concepts of becoming) through which characters (and readers) exist at once in the past and the present, in the realms of reality and myth.

Characters' senses of reality are thus multiple, inducing disequilibrium (as well as shocking moments of *Unheimliche*) among the novel's various narrative registers (e.g., mythical, historical, expository). Sorcery's bewitching, distorting influence on characters and their senses of reality thus generates a negative portrait (in the manner of photography) of Fukuyama's "coherent and directional History of mankind": that is, a depiction of humanity's path through *history's hereafter* as paved by *accident*, immanent to the compounding effects of projective humanity's self-interested pursuits under sorcery's distorting influence.[24] Thus, seeming ideological distinctions among the novel's large cast of characters *are part and parcel* of "sorcery," which operates as a distortion of characters' material conditions of existence—driving much of the novel's action, but ultimately coming to little concrete effect in favor of any of its constituents.[25]

A Glyphic Grundrisse: The "Five Hundred Year Map"

In *Almanac of the Dead*, "sorcery" manifests as an immaterial, political, and social force that is out-of-joint with time and place, possessing no particular origin or progenitor beyond human action; as such, this concept is deployed in various forms throughout *Almanac*, calling readers' attention to the varied means by which individuals, groups, and systems (methodically *and* unwittingly) sanction their own (and allies') irrational desires for position and power (or, *megalothymia*). Thus, gradually and insidiously, sorcery swells throughout the novel's many narratives, geographies, and temporalities, generating hegemonic distinctions between self and Other, manifesting fear, hatred, and suspicion between groups and individuals. Once again, these distortions blind the novel's many characters (and readers) to the problematic similarities that inhere in their real conditions of existence and the generalized dissatisfaction they *all* feel—regardless of their race, ethnicity, or economic status. Sorcery operates to divide individuals and communities in *Almanac*, creating illusory barriers to understanding and the perception of common experiences (particularly at economic and social levels). Because of sorcery's irresistible influence over humanity, and subtly diverging from Hegel, Marx, and Fukuyama, *Almanac of the Dead* depicts human history (i.e., memories of agency) and its associated beliefs (individual and collective) as assemblages of inconsistent, unreliable narratives that are always in flux—that is, imperfect human creations offering limited perspectives on history's totality vis-à-vis ideological values, economics, cultural practices, and so on. Thus, through its reconceptualization of history, *Almanac* compels readers to attend to its many, uncanny moments of sorcery's resonance.

By contrast, as Hegel's philosophy of history conceives world events (e.g., Napoleon's victory over Prussia) as contributing to humanity's progress toward ultimate freedom, the ideal realm is imagined as immanent to, and developing within, the material realm. Similarly, via Kojeve, Fukuyama's "last man" envisions humanity rapidly approaching "universal homogeneity" by way of democracy and capitalism, positing these ideals (i.e., as worldwide liberty, equality, and global enfranchisement) as developing within the material or real world. In Fukuyama's narrative, there are no alternatives to democracy and capitalism; these forms are framed as the sole governing forces that satisfy humanity's desire for recognition (or, *thymos*). Central to this proposition is a conception of humanity as non-opposing: that is, abandoning all pretentions of inventing forms of human society that are *higher* than democracy and capitalism. The effect of this brand of literalized, reductively constructed notion of culture is philosophies of history that reflect developmental, linear progressions of ages or eras (despite Fukuyama's claims otherwise) that encapsulate humanity's *progress* within inevitable waves toward some ultimate end—such as Fukuyama's "universal homogeneity," or democratic and capitalist forms of government. Yet, bound up in such theories of history, *Almanac* teaches, is a literalization of the differences among cultures (whether religious, ethnic, geographic, etc.) as a feature that is *immanent to* culture itself; that is, differences among cultures are imagined as part of their *essence*, or essential to culture as such. *Almanac of the Dead*, nevertheless, imagines several alternatives to this form of historical philosophy and narrative.

Almanac of the Dead conceptualizes history as a variety of discourses, or forms of communication. Some of these discourses, readers find, are real, or expository, while others figure as mythical, sacred, and so on; interestingly, in this formulation, the primary equivalency among these discourses is *not* a single, "homogenizing" or "ultimate" discourse, as readers find in Hegel, for instance. Instead, in *Almanac* historical discourses proceed from the potentially unfamiliar, cyclical coordinates of sorcery. For its part, the Five Hundred Year Map initiates the novel's complex consideration of historical narrative, simultaneously abstracting and epitomizing the predominating influence of sorcery over the novel's characters, their beliefs, and conceptualizations of self.[26]

Following *Almanac*'s extensive table of contents and preceding its body text, a pictograph appears, titled with a text box—"ALMANAC OF THE DEAD Five Hundred Year Map."[27] In the context of the novel itself, the Five Hundred Year Map is never mentioned; therefore, within the world of *Almanac*, neither the Map's source nor its creator can be verified. Indeed, the Map's unverifiability and seemingly incomplete character comprise an important theme linked to the partial historical narratives that irrupt within the novel; and although fundamentally incomplete and un-interpretable, such narratives are nevertheless key to (readers' and characters') understandings of indigenous identities and cosmologies, such as the lost stories of the Native Cuban, Hateuy.

Beginning with the Map, then, *Almanac* questions whether human history's *progress* really ought to be conceived in relation to *thymos*; after all, events such as Napoleon's Prussian victory and the fall of the Berlin Wall are conceived as inherent to progress because of how they have been narratively framed (i.e., in relation to relevant values)—that is, as *privileging and preferring* certain forms of government and/or economic systems. Troublingly, in the universe of *Almanac of the Dead*, on the other hand, such preferences and privileges are equated with certain *categories* of people, cultures, ideas, work, and so on. Thus, beginning with the Five Hundred Year Map, *Almanac* reconsiders Fukuyama's essential *thymos* as, in reality, a human desire for recognition on the basis of imagined superiority (i.e., *megalothymia*), rather than a benign desire for recognition on the basis of humanity or consciousness alone (or, *isothymia*). In this way, *Almanac* prompts readers to consider the troubling similarities between the (frequently championed, democratic ideals of the) Enlightenment and the (more oft-maligned, imperial conquests of the) Age of Discovery. That is, whether Hegel's Napoleonic Battle of Jena, the Spanish naming of New Mexico's Pueblo peoples, or the American Revolution, *Almanac* expresses the importance of acknowledging historical (and therefore ideological) work as traditionally having hinged on imagined superiority, in means as well as ends. And perhaps most importantly, as *Almanac*'s Five Hundred Year Map makes clear, in the context of human history thus far (as in the writing of Hegel, Fukuyama, and others), only *certain* ideological struggles are valorized and recognized with labels and titles such as, "Battle of Y" or "X Revolution," much as only *certain* monuments and other defining cultural structures are depicted on maps.

Almanac and the Five Hundred Year Map's inquiry into *thymos* and the triumphalism of its context is most prominently expressed by the Five Hundred Year Map's title: that is, labeling the Map's representation as linked to a broad sample of historical time (500 years). Of course, conventional cartography generally does not plot sweeping tracts of *time*, but more often delineates the parameters of a territory or locality at a specific *moment in time*. Emerging concurrently with the Columbiad quincentennial and a rise in academic critiques linked to "mapping as a signifying practice across historical time," the Five Hundred Year Map highlights an important, internal layer of meaning within cartography, by which it has historically exerted power.[28] Interestingly, this was also a claim propounded in the late 1980s and early 1990s by historians researching new considerations within cartography's representational techniques. In *The New Nature of Maps: Essays in the History of Cartography*, for instance, J. B. Harley theorized that cartography has historically exerted powers of social and political categorization, division and organization through its standardized visual techniques, which simultaneously highlight authority, and silence (for example) Native populations. Indeed, similar to Fukuyama's essentialist narrative of historical progress, Harley contends that ideas which claim

> that maps can produce a truly "scientific" image of the world, in which factual information is represented without favor, is a view well embedded in our [Western] mythology.[29]

Defenses of maps' objectivity, like claims that the form is scientific, are part and parcel of the craft's lore; that is, these ideas are immanent to (created by, or inhere to) cartography itself (perhaps in the interest of its preservation)—in the world of *Almanac*, this qualifies as "sorcery." Thus, newer scholarship in cartographic history emerging in the early-1990s (alongside *Almanac of the Dead* and Fukuyama) worked to academically normalize an updated understanding of cartography as historically operating as "an intricate, controlled *fiction*" that forges *symbolic* associations among "geography, history, colonialism, and modernity"—implying and generating *real* political and social consequences.[30]

The Five Hundred Year Map first contributes to this historical and existential series of examinations by emphasizing its own negative space, drawing attention to the conventionally blank or blurred spaces that would otherwise surround a map's primary subject(s). The Map's adaptation of negative space as visual subject matter begins with its title; the apparent subject, or title, of *Almanac*'s Five Hundred Year Map (500 years) itself constitutes a proverbial *negative space* within conventional cartography. In addition, the Map's rendering of what appear to be parts of California, Arizona, New Mexico, New Jersey, and Mexico is likely not what readers would expect, given experience with conventional maps of the Southwestern US and Mexican border region. For example, there are no roads marked on the Five Hundred Year Map, there are no state borders, and the United States is not labeled. The city of Tucson, Arizona, serves as the Map's visual *heart* (i.e., its subject) as it is nearly centered on the Map and punctuated by an encircled black dot. Besides Tucson, however, the Map only demarcates a limited selection of localities across its otherwise vast land area, including the Laguna Pueblo Reservation, Phoenix, and Cuba. Moreover, land area on the Five Hundred Year Map appears oddly condensed, as these locations (and others) are depicted as much more close together than readers may know them to be: for instance, the Laguna Reservation appears very nearby to Tucson, though the two locations are a few hundred miles apart, and in different states; further, Tucson is depicted as extremely close to Mexico—which itself figures as a more prominent focal point on the Map than this city-center itself. Traditionally, cartography sacrifices geographic scale (ironically, often in educational materials) in order to highlight a specific relationship across a broad territory, for instance, like North America.

However, instead of establishing common ownership, highlighting natural resource diversity, or elucidating some other relationship among its locations, scale is sacrificed in the Five Hundred Year Map to emphasize a commonality among its locations (and associated lists of character names) that it does *not* otherwise visually elucidate. Thus, without altered scale's associated, standardized visual codes and insignia such as borders, roads, or other clues of territorial ownership, the Five Hundred Year Map's play with scale cannot complete the visual circuit by which conventional, cartographic techniques assemble a reflection of dominant social and political configurations.[31] The Map's focus on *space*, then, in lieu of *territory*, is expressed through its combined emphasis on adapting conventional cartography's *negative spaces* (i.e., information omitted or blurred so as to foreground a primary subject) for representational use and then, inserting within this space pointed, cartographic "silences"—to adapt a term from Harley's scholarship. According to Harley, cartographic "silence" conventionally refers to mapmakers' omissions of topics or considerations from maps that are generally unpopular among (or irrelevant to) the ruling class or government commissioning the image, such as poverty. One example of the Five Hundred Year Map's unique applications of silence comes through its omission of detail, or clear relational coordinates, that associates its claustrophobically depicted localities. Historically, through the use of cartographic silence, specific groups have been geopolitically ignored, deleted, or muted via the visual omission of their monuments and other defining cultural structures.[32] By contrast, *Almanac's* Map emphasizes cartographic silence as a provocative vehicle of meaning, rather than hegemonic gaps in information. In this way, the Five Hundred Year Map draws readers' attention to its enticing, almost vexing, omission of information, which blends with its unique plays on cartography's standard techniques.

As the Five Hundred Year Map is virtually devoid of conventionally applied qualifiers for territory, ownership, and boundary, it reads as taking very literally cartography's broad definition: delimiting an environment and depicting human interactions within it. For instance, in addition to the Map's compression of distance among its locations, it also features various lists of characters which seem to accompany the locations; these lists appear along arrowed, dotted lines that all radiate toward Tucson, Arizona. Conventionally, Harley teaches, particularly in empires' cartographic representations of overseas colonies, "the map served as a graphic inventory, a codification of information about ownership, tenancy, rentable values."[33] In an interesting deviation from this conventional manner of inventory, there are no dates or other data that would clarify either the lines, lists of character names, or the consequence of their presumably common destination of Tucson; further, only character *names* appear in the Map's inventories, not illustrations. This visual omission erases distinctions among the novel's characters along lines of race, origins, or economic difference.[34] In an important reversal, rather than the Five Hundred Year Map's inventories symbolically reflecting territory, ownership, and so on (i.e., borders), it presents inventories of names that suggest their listed characters—whether dead, legendary, or living—*belong* to the land on which their names appear, *rather than* the land belonging to any of them. Like the Map's condensation of space, its lists of characters detract from their ostensible differences, not only anticipating the novel's narrative resonances among them (particularly concerning the effects of sorcery), but also unsettling the perspectivist function of conventional cartography.

There are over a dozen lists of character names on the Five Hundred Year Map, scattered across the landscape. Several characters' names appear in more than one inventory list, reflecting their movement across the Map or geographic space, particularly in the context of the novel. However, more crucial to understanding the novel's alternative conceptualizations of history and historical narrative are certain other names which do *not* appear in more than one list. For example, characters who are deceased in *Almanac*'s narrative present (such as Yoeme) or who are figures out of historical legend or myth (e.g., Geronimo and "The First Black Indians") appear only once among the Map's lists. The Map's inclusion of these figures gestures to *Almanac*'s central emphasis on the unverifiability of *all* historical narratives. By associating the names of mythic and legendary figures to singular lists or locations, the Map demonstrates how the historical past is bound to symbolic, meaning-making associations. However, key to the Map's expression is its subtle acknowledgment of the diversity among various symbolic systems and the associations that may be made to certain historical figures. Within the novel itself, readers may perceive the dramata of historical symbolization play out through various narrative threads, such as Angelita's references to the lost stories of Hateuy (who is unnamed on the Map) or via the minor narrative of "The First Black Indians." As a child, one character, an African-American Vietnam veteran and Tucson local named Clinton, used to hear stories from "old granny women" in his family who would talk "about in-laws and all the branches of the family," including a "branch of the family that was Indian" and used to live in Tennessee.[35]

On the Five Hundred Year Map, the names of legendary or mythical people appear bound to the specific regions or locations that coincide with the stories (e.g., living characters' flashbacks, dreams, or formal tangents through myth) in which they are featured. Otherwise, the dead and legendary are indistinguishable from their living counterparts on the Map. As reflected on the Map, then, the novel's piecemeal recollections of Clinton's childhood conversations with "old grannies" locate the "very first black Indians" in Haiti.[36] However, this origin, and this family history, is not completely clear—to either readers or Clinton himself; other of Clinton's family members laughingly claimed that "[his family] had only meant they were [the] first black Indians in Tennessee," not in the world.

Nevertheless, Clinton is compelled by these childhood stories, and much like the deceased Yoeme (and several others in the novel), he keeps a notebook in which he records any information he finds that may verify the existence of his family's connection to "the first black Indians" of Haiti and Mexico. Keeping notes on "subjects that excited him" from his GI Bill-funded university courses, as well as transcriptions of his "old grannies'" stories on "the black Indians [and] the spirits of African people" in the United States, Clinton's notes are nevertheless composed of "fragments."[37] Like Yoeme's ancient almanac, for which *Almanac of the Dead* is named, Clinton's notes do not contain complete information on any African-descended peoples' histories before or within the United States. Importantly, however, despite the inconsistencies among his transcriptions, the notes that he keeps "never failed to make Clinton feel somehow hopeful and proud," particularly about his research on the African peoples' ancestral spirits, such as Damballah, "the pure and gentle."[38]

Indeed, Clinton takes his notebook's fragments of African histories with an air of gravity; like Angelita's advocacy for the stories of Hateuy and the interests of her tribe, Clinton's incomplete notes serve as a collection of stories that give his own, disenfranchised existence meaning. Clinton's stories of ancestral spirits help him to feel less lost in the United States, where, according to Clinton, the "people were all terrified" and had "forgotten" "the spirits of all their ancestors who had preceded them"; as a result, to Clinton, the ancestral "spirits seemed to be angry and whirling around and around themselves and the people to cause anger and fear."[39] Thus, even as his histories are not complete, and may not be entirely *true*, the stories nevertheless help to explain for Clinton the imperceptible, but deeply affecting, presence of sorcery (e.g., racism, intra-veteran tensions) in his everyday life. Furthermore, armed with stories of his people's history and some understanding of the fear-driven mechanisms behind African and Native Americans' historical oppression in the Americas, these stories give the otherwise marginalized Clinton a sense of control and hope for a better future—a kind of assurance, perhaps. And, if problematically (although not revealed on the Map), these stories *also* steel Clinton's resolve to—just like Angelita—form an "Army of the Homeless" with a fellow veteran associate, named Roy (or, "Rambo," to his familiars).[40] This is only one example by which *Almanac of the Dead* and the Five Hundred Year Map illustrate how stories of the past (however incomplete or unverifiable) hold as much, if not more, weight in the world of the novel (or, the realm depicted on the Map) than any present events or *real* living characters. That is, importantly, in *Almanac of the Dead*, the ideal realm—the metaphysical and spiritual—weighs heavily on actuality or the material realm.

Importantly, stories like Clinton's, Angelita's, and the often aggressive actions they precipitate, are part of sorcery, firing history's proverbial engines of *megalothymia* and misguided presumptions of essential difference, as noted by theorists such as Hegel, Fukuyama, and even Giorgio Agamben (whose work on the animal was gaining ground in Italy around the time of *Almanac*'s publication). In the novel, characters are united by the various ways their lives are touched by sorcery, or forces which *separate* (people, cultures, cosmologies, etc.) and distinguish from that which is otherwise encoded as welcome, relatable, or human. However, this crucial element of *Almanac of the Dead*'s reconceptualization of history is not clarified by the Map's use of space or its character inventories; in fact, these features of the Map function to *resist* this very type of interpretation. To better understand the unity among the novel's characters at the level of sorcery, look to the Five Hundred Year Map's sole illustration, a figure that is *not* a character in the novel, per se: the "*Giant stone snake*," labeled, "ancient spirit messenger."[41] Of course, without knowledge of contemporary and ancient Pueblo Laguna local stories and tribal histories, a solid familiarity with essays and interviews from across Leslie Marmon Silko's writing career, or reading *Almanac of the Dead* (i.e., initiating oneself into its universe), the *Giant stone snake* is nearly irrelevant to those who encounter *Almanac of the Dead*'s Five Hundred Year Map. Its location, for instance (apparently in New Mexico, just north of the Laguna Pueblo Reservation), as well as its relevance to various of the Map's listed names, holds little significance in the context of the Map alone. As Harley explains, such cartographic silences have historically been deployed as ideological filters that discriminated against native peoples.

The inclusion of the *Giant stone snake* on the Map thus signals an awareness of the privilege (or, implied power relations) that lies at the heart of conventional cartographic interpretation; in this instance, the inclusion of the *Giant stone snake* may be read as the Map's reincarnation of one of cartography's recognizable tools, the cartouche. As the Map's sole illustration, the *Giant stone snake* conjures the internal power of cartography's seemingly benign decorative techniques. Specifically, Harley points out, within the 500-year timeframe represented by the Map, a cartouche customarily served to frame or highlight a map's title, communicating through its use of ornate symbolism a sense of supremacy or religious right linked to the governing body and its associated territory on the map. Referred to by Harley as the "pictural loquens" (or, speaking pictures) of cartography, the cartouche pictorially represented the values of a governing body as "firmly tied to the soil" of a given territory or colony; thus, it stands to reason that cartouches on historical maps of North America (dating from the 500-year period of the Map, and commissioned in Western Europe) reified these power relations.[42] Furthermore, the religious and mythic associations that traditional Western European cartouches make rely on readers' familiarity with specific, values-laden (and often mythological) references for interpretation; in this way, the conventional cartouche is complicit in culturally hegemonic means through which knowledge is standardized. However, unlike the traditional garlands of laurels, allegorical Roman gods, cherubs, or the like, the Map's *Giant stone snake* does not incite conventional, iconographic interpretation; further, the Map's "*Giant stone snake*" does not resemble a biomorphically accurate creature, evading easy biblical associations. Moreover, the Map's *Giant stone snake* does not frame the Map's titular "*Five Hundred Year Map*" text panel on the verso page, nor does it portray a right to territory or clear power supremacy.

Unlike its European counterparts, the snake's function on the Map is not apparent as "decorative, illustrative, programmatical, doctrinal, or controversial."[43] The Five Hundred Year Map's particular deployment of the cartouche (in addition to its lists of character names and oddly compressed geographic space) transmutes the cartographic silence that its obscurity creates. That is, the Map's aesthetic (not unlike the novel's) functions to softly alienate, while also enticing, the casual glance to linger one reflective moment longer; thus, some may be left wondering (or questioning) the Map and/or the "*Giant stone snake*'s" glyphic relationship (if any) to the novel. And although it is not a large image, the snake figures prominently on the Five Hundred Year Map, facing the Map's primary, titular text panel. This placement gestures to the snake's significance—and the import of serpents, more broadly, in the novel. In this way, the *Giant stone snake*, in particular, reminds readers that non-European symbol systems and ways of understanding the land, religions, and millennia worth of historical narrative have always resided on the depicted land.[44] Readers, for instance, may be reminded of the ancient African gods studied by Clinton, such as "the Giant Serpent" spirit, "Damballah, the Gentle," whom he believes followed African slaves who were brought to the New World of the Americas.[45] Thus, difficulty encountered by readers in deciphering the message or significance of the Map's non-European *Giant stone snake* is part and parcel of the Five Hundred Year Map's aesthetic; this visualization is therefore reflected in the novel's more general expression, concerning the centrality (and paradoxical variance and unreliability) of narrative to historical *knowledge*, as well as the dangerous influences of sorcery thereto.

Take, for example, Menardo, a successful insurance company owner who resides in Mexico; Menardo is wryly described by Silko's narrator as a "self-made" man, that is, a mestizo "of darker skin and lower class who had managed to amass a large fortune."[46] Convinced that his native Mexican ancestry is a hindrance to his personal and corporate success, Menardo harbors deep shame for this background and distances himself from his family; when readers meet Menardo, ties with his indigenous roots are all but "nearly dissolved."[47] Yet, despite the geographic and emotional distance imposed by Menardo between himself and his family, his indigenous grandfather's apocalyptic stories haunt him. Much of Menardo's internal turmoil derives from one key story told to him by his grandfather, in which the colonists' religion is described as based on their being rejected by their God:

Their God had created them, but soon was furious with them, throwing them out of their birthplace, driving them away. The ancestors had called Europeans "the orphan people" and had noted that as with orphans taken by selfish or coldhearted clanspeople, few Europeans remained whole. They failed to recognize the earth was their mother.[48]

Menardo's grandfather relates the Europeans' legacy as revealing their *own* persecution by a world management system like the one to which they subject Native peoples of the Americas. Yet, notwithstanding the repression of his grandfather's memory and associated "pagan" meaning-making systems, echoes of the old man's stories foster an unsettling experience of vulnerability in Menardo, particularly linked to his constructed, non-native identity.[49]

Thus, recent political unrest in Mexico (Angelita's indigenous army) and America (Clinton's "Army of the Homeless") resurrects these stories for Menardo, leaving him feeling threatened—financially and personally.[50] Menardo becomes increasingly nervous about the possibility of an impending "Indian war," as he hears news of "agitators" and "Bolsheviks" communicating with the indigenous and working classes of Mexico. Driven by fear that his tactical affiliation with Mexico's wealthiest, European-descended citizens may prove problematic to his surviving an "Indian war," Menardo's narrative thread gradually dissolves into recurrent nightmares about snakes and his fruitless attempts at their interpretation.[51] This may recall for readers the interpretive impenetrability of the Five Hundred Year Map's *Giant stone snake*.

Interestingly, linked to Menardo's precarious relationship with his indigenous heritage and fear of coming "Indian war" is a deep-seated, irrational fear of snakes, as he vaguely associates the creatures with his grandfather's indigenous superstitions.[52] In light of local political tensions, Menardo's dreams are also disturbed by visions of snakes: pavement turns into "black serpent skin" and then a "giant silver rattlesnake"; in fact, Menardo is so troubled by these images, he desperately entreats his chauffeur, a native Mexican named Tacho, to interpret his recurrent nightmares.[53] Unfortunately, however, Menardo (like Silko's readers) never receives an interpretation of his serpent-saturated nightmares. Instead, Menardo dies in a "freak accident" at the hands of Tacho; the "accident" occurs as Menardo is wearing a bullet proof vest, through which he misguidedly feels protection from his immaterial, dream-based fears.[54]

Problematically, for Menardo, the vest represents a near-supernatural form of power and superiority (*megalothymia*), in which he invests all of his spiritual faith for the sake of association; this structure of thought is the work of sorcery.

Because Menardo's bullet proof vest is a commodity of the material world, the fear-negating faith which he places in it registers as absurd; that is, a bullet proof vest cannot withstand the "realm of spirits and dreams," such as the paranoiac grip induced by the serpents in Menardo's nightmares.[55] Thus, Menardo's turmoil and associated death reveal the work of sorcery through his mistaken investment of metaphysical value and faith in a material commodity. Menardo blindly makes these investments because he is similar in spirituality to the damaged "orphan people" described in his grandfather's stories; cast out by their "insane" God, the spiritually bankrupt characters of *Almanac*, such as Menardo and several others, are totally alienated from their ancestors' stories and values.

In the case of Menardo, much like Angelita La Escapia, as a result of colonial influence through institutionalized Christianity, any reassurances for the future that is associated with ancestors or their stories have been lost. Numerous iterations of this tragedy of cultural and spiritual loss appear again and again across *Almanac*, imagining various peoples—Western and indigenous alike—as alienated from their origins and ancestors. For instance, another of *Almanac*'s characters, a Laguna man named Sterling, describes those living in contemporary Mexico in a manner uncannily similar to the orphaned Westerners of Menardo's grandfather's stories:

> The people he had been used to calling "Mexicans" were really remnants of different kinds of Indians. But what had remained of what was Indian was in appearance only [...] They had lost contact with their tribes and their ancestors' worlds.[56]

Interestingly, however, in the context of *Almanac*, these origins do not represent a brand of authority or symbolic authenticity; rather, *Almanac* is clear that a connection to one's ancestors is crucial to comprehending (or at least finding a semblance of comfort in) one's present, as well as the course to one's future, where ever one might reside. This is why, for instance, serpents are able to fulfill an empowering and spiritual function in Clinton's life; whereas

Menardo's fear of these *superstitions* drives him to forsake these indigenous origin stories in favor of a bullet proof vest.

The *Giant stone snake*'s relevance to nearly all of the novel's characters, envisioned through its prominent position on the Map's recto page, recasts the novel's numerous spiritually and culturally "orphaned" characters as an uninterpretable visual cue. The alienating effect generated by the prominent *Giant stone snake*, combined with the Map's sweeping abstraction of territory (via lacunae where state borders, roads, or property boundaries might be expected), may be described as *Unheimlich*: that is, a sense of the uncanny or an unhomeliness that irrupts through the Map's apparent dissolution of standard cartographic norms and their expected modes of interpretation. An aesthetic effect of repressed knowledge—such as the repressed memory of Menardo's grandfather—the Five Hundred Year Map inspires unfamiliarity, even as readers might view their geographic home in its image. This aesthetic effect calls attention to a sense of not being at-home in one's self, a kind of cultural identity crisis (or a spiritual disembodiment) that renders one a psychological (or, at the very least, a spectatorial) refugee inside of one's own life.

This disorienting effect is echoed in Menardo's narrative, as well as in other characters'; in the world of *Almanac*, characters proceed through life (to varying degrees) operating as though everything is low stakes and temporary. For some, this existential freedom is exhilarating, but more often than not, as with Menardo, the epistemic and ideological flexibility (and thus, superficiality) for sale in this world leads to variously manifesting, but nevertheless profound, aimlessness and blindness—in characters' choices, the conditions they seek, and so on. Importantly, the Map's aesthetic effect, and the irrationality that resonates among *Almanac*'s characters (i.e., their reactions to sorcery), is generated by and inheres to the novel's contribution to examinations of historical narratives like those by Hegel, Marx, and Fukuyama: the concept of "sorcery."

One character whose name appears rather nearby to the *Giant stone snake* on the Five Hundred Year Map is an older, Laguna Pueblo man in his sixties, named Sterling; interestingly, Sterling's narrative within *Almanac of the Dead* features a stone snake that deeply impacts the course of his life. Much as on the Map, however, the link between the stone snake and the changes precipitated in Sterling's life is not made immediately apparent, even in the novel. However, Sterling is banished from the Laguna Pueblo Reservation in New Mexico, where he had recently returned to retire, for facilitating a Hollywood film crew's access to a giant, sacred stone snake located at a mine near the reservation. Several elders in the village decide that the crew's filming of the snake constitutes a desecration, or blasphemy, ultimately warranting Sterling's exile.[57] And indeed, Sterling is bewildered by the Tribal Council's near-unanimous decision to indefinitely expel him; he does not identify with the "old time ways" adhered to by many in his community, nor does he understand the contemporary relevance of his tribe's old stories. He does not understand, for instance, why the tribal elders equate his misstep with the film crew to the theft of two ancient stone idols (the tribe's sacred "Little Grandparents") by white anthropologists before the First World War. *Almanac*'s narrator relates:

> All that had happened [over] seventy years before, but Sterling knew that seventy years was nothing—a mere heartbeat at Laguna. As soon as the disaster had occurred with those Hollywood movie people, it was as if the stone figures had been stolen only yesterday. [...] There were hundreds of years of blame that needed to be taken by somebody, blame for other similar losses. And then there was the blame for the most recent incidents.[58]

Historical offenses and indignities suffered by the Laguna Pueblo at the hands of colonizers are likely behind Sterling's expulsion. However, while the "Little Grandparents" are *familiar* to Laguna, neither Sterling nor his elders comprehend the stone snake's apparently natural emergence around 1980, or what it means (if anything) for Laguna and the old mine by which it materialized; indeed, the rock formation is a topic of argument among the elders of Sterling's community.[59] Much as the Five Hundred Year Map's *Giant stone snake* resists interpretation according to European cartographic standards, the stone snake that materializes outside a mine near Laguna similarly resists comprehension—apparently even by the elders of the Tribal Council who, unlike Sterling, claim strong identification with the tribe's old-time ways.

Little by little, over the course of *Almanac*'s various diversions, readers begin to perceive several forces and feelings, *beyond* the indignity of the Hollywood film crew, that isolate Sterling within his community and fix his tribesmen in suspicious relation to non-Native people and societies, more generally (much as Menardo negatively fixes indigenous Mexican cultures in his mind). For example, jealousy toward Sterling among his family members, the bruised ego of his jilted lover, and his community's distaste for the federal agents with whom they must now interface (i.e., the FBI unexpectedly raids the Hollywood crew's drug supply) appear over the course of Sterling's storyline to be much more prescient of his exile than anything concerning the supposedly sacred stone snake at the controversial uranium mine.[60]

The decision of the Tribal Council to ultimately banish Sterling, then, is reasoned according to their belief in Sterling's intent to *conspire*, specifically, to assist the "Hollywood people" in stealing the stone snake:

> The Council had concluded that "conspirators" could not be permitted to live on the reservation because, in their opinion, all of the current ills facing people of Laguna could be traced back to "conspirators," legions of conspirators who had passed through the Laguna Pueblo since Coronado and his men first came through five hundred years ago. Sterling shook his head. This was terrible. They had probably confused "conspirator" with "conquistador."[61]

The stone snake near Laguna, in this way, appears in Sterling's storyline as a contingency by which his fate is arbitrarily decided; Sterling's punishment operates to satisfy the many resentments and generalized hatred held against, not only himself, but also "Hollywood people," white people more generally (recalling the "Little Grandparents") and the American government that opened the mine in 1949.[62] In a dark comic twist, like the standardized aesthetics and techniques of European cartography, the sorcery that bewitches the community against Sterling generates its causes and effects immaterially, via social and symbolic circuits. This is the same symbolic, socially based belief invested by Menardo in his deadly, bullet proof vest.

Through *Almanac*'s narrator, readers may glean evidence of the insidious divide that opens between Sterling and his people; in a humorous, if dark, moment from Sterling's point of view, the narrator relates his assumption that the Council must have meant to charge him with attempting to *conquer* ("conquistador") Laguna with the "Hollywood people," rather than attempting to *conspire* ("conspirator") against them.⁶³ The irony, of course, is that Sterling is not guilty of *either* potential crime; while he *is* guilty of blindness to the film crew's drug use, as well as to the fierceness of their intent to film and occupy "off-limits" parts of the reservation, he is culpable of little more.⁶⁴ Although Sterling's obliviousness is not a crime equal in severity to imperial conquest or conspiracy, it nevertheless renders him *criminal*, according to his community's standards; because he lived off the reservation for years, away from his indigenous origins much like Menardo, Sterling's tribesmen misguidedly assume his ability to *know*, and therefore predict and curtail, the problems that end up arising as a result of having the Hollywood film crew on their reservation. By the same token, however, because he lived away from the reservation for so long, Sterling *also* misguidedly presumes that his fellow, more "old-time" Lagunas merely wish to "expel Sterling from the village forever," for *any* reason they may be able to hold against him; without family, besides his "poor little decrepit auntie" Marie, Sterling feels himself an outsider within his own tribe.⁶⁵ Through the colliding array of events, as well as communal and individual emotions and memories that it sets in motion, the stone snake at Laguna stokes insidious powers of sorcery among the people; the community turns against Sterling, and bitter feelings toward his tribesmen awaken in Sterling as well. Similar to European cartography's "silencing" of certain cultural landmarks, the Laguna Tribal Council's verdict to banish Sterling evicts (or, *erases*) him from association with the tribe, its history, and values, based on their belief that Sterling wishes them harm.

Here, *Almanac of the Dead* presents one of its more subtle, if still pointed, critiques of linear forms of historical narration, such as those found in the works of Hegel, Marx, and Fukuyama; within the Council's verdict and Sterling's pitiable reaction, *Almanac* offers a consideration of human behavior within history, which, in the case of Sterling's narrative thread, is framed by the nebulously significant *Giant stone snake* which readers find on the Map. Through the events precipitating from Sterling's association with the stone snake at Laguna, *Almanac* questions whether human history has, for *all* human populations, actually been driven by *thymos*; or, if historical progress, and therefore the last 500 years of human history's *hereafter*, is not merely generated by tribes' and various other societies' survival-anxieties—like Menardo's attachment to his bullet proof vest. This would also account for the Council's decision to banish Sterling, as well as their positioning him as a "conspirator" with the "Hollywood people." If history progressed on the basis of *thymos*, or *isothymia*, as according to Hegel and Fukuyama, then Sterling's Tribal Council should have praised him for the *recognition* that the "Hollywood people's" film would bring to the reservation and therefore the tribe; however, their actual reaction challenges neat, linear historical narratives that encapsulate human cultural movement, change, and/or disappearance according to coordinates solely oriented toward "recognition." After sentencing, Sterling does not logically respond by rallying *recognition* of his innocence, so as to remain on the reservation to enjoy his retirement; instead, after pitiably accepting that he may no longer quietly retire at Laguna, Sterling arbitrarily decides to defect to Phoenix, because "he didn't know a soul there."[66] Interestingly, however, as the Five Hundred Year Map states (along the dotted arrow connecting Sterling's name to Tucson, Arizona): "*Sterling accidentally goes to Tucson.*"[67] Thus, beyond the Tribal Council's collective verdict, *Almanac* notes that even at the level of the individual, humanity's progress is generated, moved by and within, *accident* (much like Menardo's "freak accident") or *series of accidents* based on (not always rational) choices. *Almanac* and the Five Hundred Year Map thus suggest that it is only *in theory* (or, metaphysically, in an ideal sense), composed *after* real events, that history (or its *hereafter*) may be proposed otherwise.

In this way, the Five Hundred Year Map's suggestion that Sterling's travel to Tucson is *accidental* is correct, but may also be read as misleading. Although it is correct that the Tribal Council was mistaken in their verdict, and Sterling *did* "accidentally" miss his intended bus stop in Phoenix, the Five Hundred Year Map offers a paradox with its note concerning Sterling's travels. Sterling is displaced in the most conspicuously labeled location on the Map; moreover, Tucson is accompanied by a self-titled panel, which appears to be a cartographic key to understanding the location. It reads:

> Home to an assortment of speculators, confidence men, embezzlers, lawyers, judges, police and other criminals, as well as addicts and pushers, since the 1880s and the Apache Wars.[68]

In addition to its prominence on the Five Hundred Year Map, Tucson, Arizona, also figures as an initial, and primary, setting featured in the text of the novel. And although the Map is silent concerning what precisely its listed characters share in common, the proverbial character description offered in the "*Tucson, Arizona*" panel seems to begin to illuminate some possibilities. However, as Sterling ends up here "accidentally," in ironic faithfulness to the cartographic form, the Map's description of Tucson should also be read as misleading. Importantly, Sterling boards the bus to Phoenix in the first place because his community positions him as a *criminal*—an unwelcome "conspirator" against the tribe. According to the world of the novel, the world represented on the Map, Sterling *belongs in a place like* Tucson. In this way, the Five Hundred Year Map assembles an image of *Almanac*'s characters as *predominantly criminal*, according to this fictional world's visualization of (or the frame it places on) cities like Tucson.

However, in a comic extension of its ironic loyalty to cartographic form, the Five Hundred Year Map's definition of Tucson and its inhabitants are *also* not as they seem—much as the Map's evaluation of Sterling's trip is misleading. Playing on the convention of the cartographic key, the "*Tucson, Arizona*" text panel offers readers of *Almanac* important information on the temperament of the city's population, according to the world of the novel. Taken together with Tucson's visual prominence on the Map, the dotted arrows drawing the eye toward the city, *and* the Map's lack of additional detail on its listed characters, the "*Tucson, Arizona*" panel pulls a majority of the novel's cast into association with the city and its criminality. This association is supported by Sterling in the novel, who notes from his self-education in law (obtained by reading popular magazines such as *Police Gazette* and *True Detective*) that Tucson has "a notorious history" and is "a place founded mostly by criminals."[69]

Upon closer consideration, however, without clear city limits, definite state borders, or other visual assertions of geopolitical relation, the criminality claimed of Tucson and its population actually reads as arbitrary, or general to the region depicted, rather than specific to the city itself. Through the spatial and discursive distance created by this regional counter-mapping (or omission of borders), the Five Hundred Year Map implies that Tucson is an uncanny site around which the novel's characters orbit. That is, as a locality,

Tucson is specific to the 500 years of historical narratives that intersect on the Map via the novel's various storylines. However, it is not more unique than Tuxtla Gutierrez, Mexico, nearby to Angelita and Menardo. Indeed, as newly transplanted Tucson real estate developer, Leah Blue, points out, "It was ridiculous for longtime residents to try to pretend Tucson wasn't any different from Phoenix or Orange County."[70] People in all places, she reasons, want the same things; Tucson and its residents, therefore, are essentially no different than people of any other urban center in the Americas.

Although Leah's point, mediated by *Almanac*'s narrator, is linked to a claim regarding the propensity of desert-dwelling residents to want to "see water spewing around them," she nevertheless offers an illuminating account of the Map's "*Tucson, Arizona*" as solely occupied by "criminals."[71] As *Almanac*'s narrator points out earlier on, mediating the perspective of Zeta (a weapons and drug smuggler, living just outside Tucson):

> There was not, and there never had been, a legal government by Europeans anywhere in the Americas. Not by any definition, not even by the Europeans' own definitions and laws. Because no legal government could be established on stolen land.[72]

Referring in-kind to a vast area that spans much of the Southwestern United States, Leah's professional perspective on Tucson, like Zeta's cynicism toward the American federal government, converges on a common element of *irrationality*. This is a potentially dangerous reaction, generated in those under sorcery's influence, such as Sterling's tribesmen at Laguna and Menardo's fixation on his vest. Recalling Zeta's evaluation of European settlements in the Americas, Leah's work as a "speculator" and real estate developer flies in the face of her own "definitions" of rationality. She laughs to her husband, a retired mafia operative: "I didn't say human beings were rational," concerning residents' feeling "more confident and carefree around water in the desert."[73] Leah justifies her own corporations' potentially lucrative (but unethically executed and environmentally destructive) plans for a new luxury city, "Venice, Arizona," by assuming that in the future "science will solve the water problem of the West. New technology. They'll *have* to."[74] Ironically, "Venice" is designed to satisfy the unreasonable lifestyle preferences of wealthy corporate transplants that she mocks with her husband.⁷⁵ Although approaching concepts of the law, as well as avenues toward self-preservation, along very diverse trajectories, each of the characters explored—Angelita, Sterling, his Laguna tribesmen, Menardo, Leah, and Zeta—illustrates an array of potential human reactions to "sorcery," or symbolic events, objects, and/or ideas that dissemble an existence of the ideal, or metaphysical, realm in the real world.

For example, in efforts to maintain some semblance of the ideal or metaphysical within reality, individuals and societies since time immemorial, *Almanac* teaches, have gone to criminal lengths toward making, or re-making, their lives according to any one of a number of cosmologies, beliefs, or histories with which they identify. Consider, for instance, how Zeta's beliefs concerning the American government steel her resolve "to break as many of their laws as she could" for her own profit.⁷⁶ Looking back to the land area depicted on the Five Hundred Year Map, readers may note that the region (with few exceptions) covers the vast 120,000-square miles of the Sonora Desert, traditional home to Zeta's Yaqui origins. Moreover, the Five Hundred Year Map's distorted Mexican border, a comic straight line, reflects Zeta's cynical outlook toward borders' dividing influence on social and political definitions of space and territory; *Almanac*'s narrator lends additional support:

> The people had been free to go traveling north and south for a thousand years, traveling as they pleased, then suddenly white priests had announced smuggling a mortal sin because smuggling was stealing from the government.⁷⁷

Through the Five Hundred Year Map's omission of state and local borders, along with the narrator and Zeta, Mexico's border reads as arbitrary. After all, as depicted via the Map's dotted arrows, characters in the novel move freely about the areas surrounding Tucson; Zeta, the narrator, and the Map therefore all conceptualize the area labeled "MEXICO" as an irrationally constructed exception to this free movement, only functioning to compel American citizens' *recognition* of Mexico as a separate nation. Flying in the faces of Hegel, Marx, and Fukuyama, whose works diversely position humanity's attainment of *recognition* as the *raison d'etre* for history's end, the Five Hundred Year Map, several of *Almanac*'s characters, and (often) its narrator reduce Fukuyama's essential *thymos* (recognition) to merely *one* of humanity's potential reactions (along with survival anxiety) to its inevitable encounters with sorcery—but not a state either that has been (triumphantly) attained *or* which stands as humanity's universal, essential desire.

Relatedly, below the Mexican border on the Five Hundred Year Map, readers may begin to perceive crucial divisions among the novel's characters, particularly along the lines of their *de facto* reactions to sorcery in the novel. Below the Map's Mexican border, readers find two text panels, titled "*Prophecy*" and "*The Indian Connection*," respectively.[78] Here, the Map links its own internal story (or dramatization) of cartography's standardized distortions to the broader operations of storytelling and myth (or, historical narration) within *Almanac of the Dead* itself. The "*Prophecy*" panel, located just off of Mexico's west coast, relates:

> When Europeans arrived, the Maya, Azteca, Inca cultures had already built great cities and vast networks of roads. Ancient prophecies foretold the arrival of Europeans in the Americas. The ancient prophesies also foretell the disappearance of all things European.

Importantly, the "*Prophecy*" panel is situated right next to the traditional home of the Yaqui indigenous tribe (as well as other tribes, due to the Map's condensed space) of Mexico, which is a broad region of Mesoamerica from which several Tucson-area residents in the novel originally hail, such as Zeta, her psychic twin, Lecha, their deceased native grandmother, Yoeme, and numerous other of the Map's characters and/or their in-laws. However, according to *Almanac*'s reading of Western history, "the Europeans arrived" in the Sonora Desert region of Mexico with Cortes during the sixteenth century, generations before any of the "famous criminals" studied by Sterling ever arrived in Tucson; in this way, the "*Prophecy*" panel operates on the Map as a *source-legend*, or origin story, for the dire, *criminal* conditions described in the "*Tucson, Arizona*" panel, and which reign across the realm.[79]

An element of unique importance to the Five Hundred Year Map's overall aesthetic, particularly indicated by the "*Prophecy*" panel, is the link presented between stories (e.g., the Maya's, Aztec's, and Incas' foretellings) and various cultures' notions of identity, purpose, and their future on the planet. Calling readers' attention to complex, extant societies, and cosmologies that lived in the Americas before European explorers reached its shores, the "*Prophecy*" panel mentions that the Maya (and others) "had already built great cities and vast networks of roads"—yet these structures do not appear on the Map. Reflecting the hegemonic and oppressive forces exerted on indigenous populations through contact with European settlers, the Map's absence of all but two indigenous landmarks (the *Giant stone snake* and Laguna Reservation) serves to highlight the cost of lost stories, or in this instance, lost "prophecy." This is an important notion within *Almanac of the Dead*'s reconceptualization of human history and its *great hereafter*; one example comes through Angelita La Escapia's address to her people, just after Bartolomeo's execution: "The Cubans had lied [to Angelita's people] and distorted the words of Marx; worse, [the Cubans' European forefathers] had attempted to suppress the powerful warning Hateuy had sent to the people of the Americas."[80] And indeed, readers of *Almanac*, like Angelita's people, cannot verify the message of Hateuy; however, although stories like these may not have verifiable sources or authenticated origins, their loss is poised as a major threat to the livelihood and well-being of a people. In this way, the "*Prophecy*'s" foretelling the "disappearance of all things European" gestures to a breaking point like that which is demonstrated, for instance, through the execution of Bartolomeo or Menardo's death by "freak accident." After generations of cultural hegemony by European influences on the island of Cuba, the people's loss of their history should not be forever abided, Angelita asserts—eventually a reckoning will come, at least symbolically.[81]

This point is further magnified by the "*Prophecy*" panel's facing counter-key, titled "*The Indian Connection.*" Here, the Map uncovers further insight into the broader material contests, and ideological contexts, that otherwise structure Silko's *Almanac of the Dead*:

> Sixty million Native Americans died between 1500 and 1600. The defiance and resistance to things European continue unabated. The Indian Wars have never ended in the Americas. Native Americans acknowledge no borders; they seek nothing less than the return of all tribal lands.[82]

Recalling Zeta's qualms with United States' laws around border-crossing, the Map's "*Indian Connection*" presents an echo of the previous, "*Prophecy*" panel's reference to "the disappearance of all things European." Supporting this reference, however, the "*Indian Connection*" reaches beyond the Southern tribes' prophesies of colonization and pinpoints a major issue, in addition to loss of land, for the indigenous populations living in the area depicted: "borders." Interestingly, much like sorcery's immaterial influence within and across the Map (and novel), besides "borders," other European "things" prophesied to vanish are not specified; in the Map's lower two panels, the presence of "all things European" is thus framed as an apparently all-encompassing, or all-affecting, force against which "the Indian Wars" have waged for about half a millennium. In this way, it stands to reason that Menardo, adherent to Western capitalism and commodities in lieu of indigenous "superstitions," finds his "accidental" death at the hands of Tacho—whom he does not realize is an associate of Angelita's. Furthermore, recalling Sterling's reflections on the founding of Tucson by "criminals," the panels below Mexico's border together consolidate the character- and land-relations suggested in the "*Tucson, Arizona*" panel.

As Sterling informs Seese (a cocaine addict working with Zeta's twin, Lecha), Tucson's "fine old families" became that way by enriching themselves on work in bootlegging, mercantilism, and brothel-ownership during the Indian Wars of the eighteenth and nineteenth centuries. According to *Almanac*'s narrator, echoing both the Five Hundred Year Map and Sterling's point: "The old Tucson mansions along Main Street were proof that murderers of innocent Apache women and children had prospered"; and in most cases, these families of "government embezzlers, bootleggers, pimps, and murderers" increased their earnings by exploiting and encouraging intra- and inter-tribal warfare among the indigenous populations in the area. Sterling relates:

> I don't know if this was ever proven, but there was something here called the Indian Ring, [...] Tucson merchants who did not want to see the Apache wars end. So they paid off a whiskey peddler. They sent the whiskey peddler to get Geronimo and his men drunk. The peddler showed Geronimo and his men the headlines from Washington, D.C. and warned Geronimo if he and his men "came in," they'd all be hanged. [...] The Indian Ring in Tucson kept the Apache wars going for years that way.[83]

Plying Geronimo and his warriors with alcohol in order to cultivate in them fear and hatred of the American federal government, Sterling's reflection may recall the distrust of "all things European" (not only by Zeta and Menardo's grandfather, but also) by Sterling's Tribal Council. Through the discursive echoes among the Map's "Prophecy," "The Indian Connection," and "Tucson, Arizona" panels, readers may perceive the sharp polarization that begins to materialize on the Five Hundred Year Map between "all things European" and Native Americans including the "Maya, Aztec, Inca" and other tribes of Mesoamerica.

The Map's last and largest panel, labeled "ALMANC OF THE DEAD, *Five Hundred Year Map*," offers further evidence of the novel's precariously divided world.[84] Omitting any mention of "things European," the Map's titular panel relates:

> Through the decipherment of ancient tribal texts of the Americas the Almanac of the Dead foretells the future of all the Americas. The future is encoded in arcane symbols and old narratives.

Here, the Map brings into sharp relief *Almanac of the Dead*'s complex interplay between ancient and modern myths in its reconceptualization of human history; that is, shifting its focus from the sorcery inherent to cartography, to the role of sorcery in the novel, the Map introduces the idea that future knowledge lies in decoding "arcane symbols and old narratives" within the cited "Almanac of the Dead." This cartographic key obliquely gestures to an important legend reflected in one of the novel's initial narrative threads: the almanac (or, "old notebooks") belonging to Yoeme, Lecha, and Zeta's elderly Yaqui grandmother. Yoeme is deceased in the present of the novel, but visits Lecha's and Zeta's plotlines through stories and scenes that each sister recalls as they attempt to decipher their respective sections of the almanac, bestowed to them for safe keeping by Yoeme. However, like the Map's titular textual panel, in the novel's section titled "Yoeme's Old Notebooks," Zeta's efforts at interpreting her portion of the almanac are continually frustrated by "Yoeme's scrawls in misspelled Spanish"; although Zeta's allotment, the "notebook of the snakes," is "key to understanding the rest of [Yoeme's] old almanac" (which her sister Lecha possesses), she is nevertheless unable to decipher its passages.[85]

Later in the novel, as Zeta's sister, Lecha, works to decipher her own, larger section of the almanac, readers learn that portions of Yoeme's notebooks are missing. For example, *Almanac*'s narrator inserts bracketed lines reading, "Numbers nine and ten are illegible" and "Manuscript Incomplete," within passages of important information identifying the almanac's prophecy concerning "the future of all the Americas."[86] Moreover, like Zeta's notebook, Lecha's is not reproduced in the novel for readers, rendering the "decipherment" of this "ancient tribal text" still more difficult. Reminding readers of the Map's titular key, then, Yoeme's undecipherable "old notebooks" cannot form a stable platform (i.e., the *only* "ancient tribal text") on which to build an apprehension of the future. Distinguishing itself from modernity's concept of possessive individualism via accumulated capital and commodity forms (i.e., a diverse, if criminal, means for controlling the future), the Map's titular panel thus compels readers to guess which set of myths—ancient or modern—will come to be true or correct in its divination of "the future of all the Americas."

Troublingly, however, Yoeme's almanac proves interpretively impenetrable; and, much like the almanac, the Map (and novel's) meaning of "all things European" is not fully elucidated for readers, nor is the time or cause of their eventual disappearance. That is, in the world of *Almanac of the Dead*, as envisioned on the Five Hundred Year Map, there is no foundational, ancient, or modern myth (or narrative), by which the present or future may be apprehended. On the one hand, this may be read as the result of cultural and spiritual loss at the hands of colonialism's hegemony; on the other, the world of *Almanac*'s general lack of an ethical (or at least theoretical) center may also be read as the end result of a long-standing domination, by capital, of people's motivations and movements. In the world of *Almanac*, both readings are operatively true.

Take, for instance, a brief dialogue between Menardo's chauffeur, Tacho, and his psychic twin brother, El Feo, on the nature of sorcery and its function in the contemporary world. In this conversation, the spiritually skeptical Tacho asserts that "95 percent of supposed witchcraft and sorcery was superstition and puffed-up talk"—but El Feo laughs at his brother, seeming to know better.[87] As if on cue, *Almanac*'s narrator digresses to a fable about the bifurcated existence of sorcery in the seemingly mundane world:

> Someplaces there were entire villages populated by sorcerers, all living together by mutual pledge to prey only on *outsiders*. Their pledges were frequently broken, and they turned upon one another in the most bloodthirsty manner [...] [T]his sorcery, this witchcraft, occurred among all human beings. The killing and devouring occurred behind bedroom doors, inflicted by parents and relatives, and the village of sorcerers continues generation after generation without interruption.[88]

The fable's movement through unspecified, mythic time calls readers' attention to the novel's concept of human history's *present* as the result of a story that has gotten out of control—unmoored to any spiritual or ethical center (i.e., a purgatorial *hereafter*). The image of the sorcerers' broken "mutual pledge" (to harm "outsiders" with their magic) calls to mind the Western epistemological focus, asserted by Menardo and Fukuyama, for example, on the individual (and his welfare) over and above the community.

The brothers Tacho and El Feo, much like the fable's sorcerers, draw the curiosity and interest of hundreds; and like the sorcerers, this attraction is largely based on the brothers' obscure, indigenous heritage. Here, *Almanac* blurs the differences between the presumably *good* brothers, Tacho and El Feo, and the *evil* sorcerers of the narrator's digression; this presents to readers not only the problem of origins/authenticity with respect to linear historical narrative, but also the difficulties inherent to neatly separating good from evil, self from Other, when the linearity of historical narrative is abandoned. Thus, calling to mind Tacho's cynical reading of sorcery, the fable's "sorcerers" are as much resentful charlatans (like Lecha, Zeta, and Leah) profiting on others' ignorance as they are self-concerned capitalists (e.g., Menardo, Angelita, and Sterling)—and the brothers, Tacho and El Feo, themselves.

Through this digression to a mythical tale about sorcerers in the middle of the twin brothers' conversation, *Almanac*'s narrator reveals the brothers' (and other characters') embeddedness in historical processes that are as old as colonialism and the Five Hundred Year Map's envisioned region. Revealing the novel's narrative present as the assembled results of countless ethical failings via violence and cultural hegemony, the narrator's tangent into mythical time thus illustrates the perseverance of sorcery across human history. Problematically, separatist historical narratives of this kind elide links between all people, excusing harm done to "outsiders," much as contemporary, inward-turning forms of individualism (in the style of Menardo, Angelita, and others) foster a ritualistic form of isolation that also justifies harm to others on the basis of survival. In this way, sorcery enables the co-evolving project of linear and Western epistemological narratives of human history, which then permeates and standardizes nearly every aspect of (particularly social and economic) life within *Almanac of the Dead*'s universe. However, as embodied by the twin brothers, who are leaders in Angelita's indigenous army, the forces (or, "spirits") of resistance against Western epistemological standardization are agitated by the world's mounting climate of systematized racism and disenfranchisement. Thus, in spite of the sorcery which irrupts through the novel's indigenous, homeless, "criminal," and other disenfranchised characters' planned uprising against European ideas and "things," *Almanac of the Dead* nevertheless emphasizes people's willingness to go to inhumane lengths (not for the sake of *recognition* or *thymos*, but) in the hope of attaining a stable experience of their ideals and beliefs, their home and culture, in the *real world* of the Americas.

As El Feo points out, "The white man did not seem to understand he had no future [in the Americas] because he had no past, no spirits of ancestors here."[89] El Feo's point resonates with the Map's definition of the future (i.e., "encoded in arcane symbols and old narratives"), as well as Angelita's vision of revolution. Importantly, while European symbol systems *do* exist in the novel (e.g., Christianity, capitalism), they are *not* linked to ancestral values or *Almanac*'s sole given, in the context of human history: nature, or the earth. As Calabazas, an elderly Yaqui smuggler asserts, linear conceptions of time and historical progress that are reflected in Western European epistemologies stipulate a "sort of blindness to the world."[90] In this sense, the spiritual bankruptcy with which many of the novel's indigenous characters associate white people speaks to a colonial clash between diverse means by which people come to know themselves and the world around them, a concept first introduced to readers via the Five Hundred Year Map. Europeans constructed a claim to the land of the Americas based on their own religious rhetoric, visual symbolization via cartography, and linked cultural hegemony; thus bolstered by their owns values, the systems of land distribution established by European settlers alienated the indigenous peoples who already resided there.

In this way, certain characters, like the Yaqui-descended Calabazas, *know* that the location of Tucson's "sewage treatment" plant, for instance, "is no accident" in the city's infrastructural planning; located near the Santa Cruz River, the city's plant condemns the land, which has historically fed the Yaqui people's livestock "on the tall grass and willows" "since the days *before there was a city of Tucson* to condemn Yaqui land."[91] Importantly, however, Tucson's sewage plant does not appear on the Map; in *Almanac of the Dead*, Western symbols like Tucson's treatment plant and Menardo's vest function as mechanisms of control and standardization—or, "criminal" means for apprehending futures. Nevertheless, readers and characters alike are left to question whether the Map's and novel's projected "disappearance of all things European" may first stipulate the disappearance of everyone and everything else.

For instance, for Zeta and her twin, Lecha (a clairvoyant, like Tacho's twin, El Feo) "learned a strange story from [their] gardener, Sterling" about a "giant stone serpent that appeared overnight near a well-travelled road in New Mexico," the sisters rejoice as they seem to comprehend the significance of the Laguna Pueblo Reservation's *Giant stone snake*:

> According to the gardener, religious people from many places had brought offerings to the giant snake, but none had understood the meaning of the snake's reappearance; no one got the message. But when Lecha told Zeta, they both got tears in their eyes because old Yoeme had warned them about the cruel years that were to come once the great serpent had returned. Zeta was grateful for the years she had had to prepare a little. Now she had to begin the important work.[92]

This "important work" begins with her murder of Greenlee, a white arms and munitions shop owner in Tucson and close compatriot to Menardo. To the sisters, the giant stone serpent at Laguna is a foreboding sign of "cruel years to come," presumably requiring of them significant strength and resolve; however, following Greenlee's murder, the sisters only attend The International Holistic Healers Convention, held in Tucson, at which Angelita La Escapia is booked as a speaker.[93] And what is more, the *Giant stone snake*'s significance (like the countless other serpents populating the novel) and its message are never revealed to readers.

Thus, with the Five Hundred Year Map in mind, it stands to reason that snakes in the novel—whether real, mythical, or in dreams—constitute "ancient tribal texts" (in addition to Yoeme's almanac) that must be decoded if the future of the Americas is to be grasped. In this way, *Almanac*'s intertextual myths trouble the past's symbolization in the present, while this formal move also supports the novel's broader, continual narrative resistance against the idea that any historical past may be *known* in its totality and deemed unequivocally *true* (as readers might glean in the linear epochs defined by Hegel, Marx, or Fukuyama). By refusing to clarify the meanings or consequences of *either* ancient or modern myths and texts that preoccupy the novel, *Almanac* operates as a compendium of almanacs. As a collection of notebooks that are never complete, always in process, *Almanac of the Dead* (like the Five Hundred Year Map) resolves to leave the work of divination on the shoulders of its readers.

One World, Many Tribes

Human history's *hereafter*, as imagined in *Almanac of the Dead*, reflects capitalism's priority in the material realm, as forecast by Fukuyama; however, in a sharp departure from the triumphalism of contemporaries such as Fukuyama, *Almanac* asks readers to question capital's primacy in *both* material and ideal realms—as it distorts humanity's connection to reality's only given: the earth. In *The End of History and the Last Man*, Fukuyama forecasts that the decline in communal life hallmarked by post-historical peacetime will lead to existential unrest; as humanity's topics for protest become matters of mere indifference, humanity will reject, in its metaphorical wars, "life in a society where ideals had somehow become impossible."[94] People, Fukuyama claims, will crave warfare—not "for its own sake," but for its "intangible" and "secondary effects on character and community."[95] Within this formulation, the role of capital goes without saying—it is required to sponsor, promote, and grow any social or political cause. There is no alternative to capital in Fukuyama's formulation; no system or cause will function without it in any long-term capacity, let alone the 500-year timeframe that encompasses the novel's many storylines. By contrast, *Almanac of the Dead* begins with the "Five Hundred Year Map" to challenge the prearranged privilege of capital; then, through its vast cast of projective and self-interested characters, the novel introduces problems of *the commons* with which Fukuyama does not directly engage. Without explicitly offering stable, long-term alternatives to capitalism and capitalist networks of exchange (however unnecessary their associated labor), *Almanac of the Dead* highlights various problems with this capitalist-commons model, as well as the often tragic results of this system's blindness to people's interest in *common goods*.

In a dark comic twist, the characters of *Almanac* are united in their inculcation by, and implication in, sorcery—a condition achieved through their general lack of a sense (concrete or otherwise) of *common good*. Interestingly, rather than presenting a depiction of Hegel's image of post-historical society "degenerate[ing] into a morass of selfishness and community [...] ultimately dissolve[ing]," *Almanac of the Dead* instead depicts a brutally efficient form of Fukuyama's universal capitalism (excepting a few, pseudo-radical Marxists).[96] In fact, this *common capitalism* is so general and dominant, ruled by the powers of private properties, interests, and businesses, that it does not *need* democratic processes to function. Diverging from Fukuyama's necessary model of *democratic* capitalism, *Almanac*'s characters do not work (however unevenly) to fulfill the ancient almanac's prophecy in the name of virtue (as Fukuyama might imagine), but in order to protect (or co-opt someone else's) valued, omnipotent *capital* toward satisfying personal aims: that is, survival, enhanced status, and/or increased comfort. *Almanac*'s massive cast of characters do not protest or foment guerilla warfare in order to nurture "virtues and ambitions" that cannot "find expression in liberal democracy," as in Fukuyama's formulation. Where Fukuyama's post-historical "last men" "will want to risk their lives in a violent battle, and thereby prove beyond any shadow of a doubt to themselves and to their fellows that they are free," *Almanac*'s characters risk their lives, or take the lives of others, in the fundamental interest of amassing (or repairing lost) capital. As *Almanac*'s narrator puts it, shortly before the "accidental" death of the capitalist, Menardo, and execution of the Marxist, Bartolomeo: "The Indians couldn't care less about international Marxism; all they wanted was to retake their land from the white man."[97] With only scraps of ancestral histories, and long detached from cultural codes and origin stories, characters in *Almanac* are driven by inconsistent, unreliable stories and various forms of *capital*—not classic ideology, as such—through human history's *Jenseits*.

In this way, *Almanac of the Dead* incites readers to examine their assumptions and expectations regarding American literature, particularly in the context of the novel's narratively heterogeneous conception of history. *Almanac*'s formal intertextuality, multiple plotlines, and narrative multi-vocality gesture back to the Five Hundred Year Map's transmutation of cartographic silence into representational space; that is, the novel's multiple uses of narrative and narration echo the excessive means by which mere narratives (or stories, rhetoric) constitute the foundations of otherwise sweeping conceptions (or philosophies) of history and historical progress—however practically unproductive those narratives may otherwise prove in the material realm. Thus, distinguishing itself from claims like Fukuyama's, which position the discursive multi-vocality of the 1980s and 1990s as evidence of ideology's dissolution into countless, unproductive discourses, *Almanac of the Dead* shifts the focus off of ideology and reminds readers of the predominating influence of *narrative* (i.e., of theorization and formulation) on broad, often hegemonic understandings of history.

On this point, Yoeme's almanac relates:

> One day a story will arrive in your town. There will always be disagreement over direction—whether the story came from the southwest or the southeast. The story may arrive with a stranger, a traveler thrown out of his home country months ago. Or the story may be brought by an old friend, perhaps the parrot trader. But after you hear the story, you and the others prepare by the new moon to rise up against the slave masters.[98]

This excerpt appears in *Almanac* within a section titled "From the Ancient Almanac"; its author is not specified for readers. According to the model offered in this passage, the origin and destination, or "direction," of stories are significantly less important than the messages carried by them. Therefore, as long as a story's implied interests resonate with its audience, stories may hold revolutionary potential. The past and future may be excavated toward establishing mindfulness of identity's codification via experience, as well as broader understandings of time and place. By the same token, however, the passage from Yoeme's almanac also implies a warning: history is an imperfect human creation—a story passed from one person to the next—and is therefore insufficient material on which to base definitions of progress or identity.

Almanac of the Dead demands that the stories of the past, like expectations of the novel form (and ideology), are allowed to change; this point informs *Almanac*'s conception of time as cyclic within history. According to the novel, time understood in any other form necessitates a blindness to the connections between all peoples and times. A fragment from Zeta's portion of the almanac echoes this warning, as its message (from a Yaqui spirit) implies that "people" have not been mindful of the cyclic nature of time; in spite of warnings, people have not paid attention to the patterns unfolding across the last 500 years, and so cannot protect themselves from the impending ruin of the coming days:

> *I have been talking to you people from the beginning*
> *I have told you the names and identities of the*
> > *Days and Years.*
> *I have told you the stories on each day and year*
> > *so you could be prepared*
> *and protect yourselves.*
> *What I have told you has always been true.*
> *What I have to tell you now is that*
> *this world is about to end.*[99]

Interestingly, *Almanac*'s arguably cynical, darkly competent image of post-1960s American society is remarkably unprepared for the end of days and "disappearance of all things European."[100] This unpreparedness, as the almanac alludes, derives from humanity's long-standing focus on amassing and defending capital (whether economic, social, cultural) rather than working to understand the stories (of origins, utopia, etc.) with which they identify and for which they unnecessarily labor.

Thus, like the Five Hundred Year Map, the whole of Silko's *Almanac of the Dead* highlights through omitting (again, as in negative portraiture) acknowledgment of the tensions between color-blind (or, universalist) and race-conscious (e.g., nationalist) political models in America, particularly following the 1960s and the (un)official conclusion of the Civil Rights era.

These tensions have long thematized American political culture, but became particularly prescient in the years following the first election of Richard Nixon to the presidency in 1969. However, unlike the myopic, highly personal trajectories of *Franny and Zooey* and *The Flagellants'* narratives, *Almanac of the Dead* depicts characters with endless alternatives to their life circumstances, as they pick up and relocate, redefine, and reconfigure their lives (often accidentally) in the interest of their ambitions and intuitions.

The novel's illusory equality via freedom of movement (as well as the generalized criminality and pseudo-revolution) thus configures a metaphor for an important shift in American political foci following the 1960s: that is, off of relationships among policy, racism and capitalism in America, and instead onto cultural and rhetorical questions of race consciousness and color blindness.[101] Thus, just as in Salinger's and Polite's worlds, where readers find the normative denial of ideology's existence via its transmission through new models and forms (e.g., mass culture, advertising, nostalgia, nationalism), the characters of *Almanac* ironically find similar restlessness and confusion in their lives, despite their curated and customized nature. This dissatisfaction is rationalized in *Almanac of the Dead* as most of its characters are descended from "orphaned people"—that is, their families have long been divorced from ancestors and origins; characters amble through the world in a manner, the novel teaches, that is akin to being blind (regardless of wealth, social or political status, etc.).

At the dawn of the twenty-first century, however, *Almanac*'s (race-conscious) rebuttal to Fukuyama's (color-blind) triumphalism is further tested, I claim, in the fiction of Philip Roth. In *Franny and Zooey* and *The Flagellants*, ideology is transformed through new, life-shaping discourses and mass media that nevertheless fail to improve characters' "substandard" lives; in 1991, *Almanac* presents an illusory corrective, depicting the completion of ideology's denial (and any sense of common good) as occurring through characters' *preferences* to trade and exchange these values for material comfort and wealth. However, in *The Human Stain* (2000)—a narrative of passing that deploys passing as a narrative strategy—Philip Roth illustrates that identity of any kind cannot be understood through material formulas of recognition, including prestige or notoriety, physical appearance, or visible signs of wealth. Rather, *The Human*

Stain (appropriate to the era in which it was published) compels readers to reconsider the ideological, or abstract, dimensions of identity and racial identification, particularly in terms of understanding polarized political models like color-blindness and race-consciousness, as well as their respective, potential abilities (or inabilities) to address concrete questions of policy, politics, and power that define the courses of citizens' lives.

4

Color-Blindness and the Trouble of Depiction in Philip Roth's *The Human Stain*

The Human Stain (2001) is the third novel in Philip Roth's American trilogy; this broadly thematic series (attributed to Roth's ghost writer, Nathan Zuckerman) offers profiles of men with whom Zuckerman has been connected (by geography, often more than by much else) at various points in his life.[1] The trilogy's most ambitious project, *The Human Stain*, consists of the fictionalized biography of Coleman Silk—a recently deceased, retired (via resignation) dean and professor at Athena College in western Massachusetts. Zuckerman compiles *The Human Stain* from recollections of occasional cognacs enjoyed in Coleman's company; data on his subject's youth from commentary by Coleman's estranged sister, Ernestine Silk; and, of course, from Zuckerman's own imagination. However, writing this biographic memoir requires more of Zuckerman than the customary creative prowess needed for his series' previous profiles; unlike the other men on whom he has written, Coleman Silk is a black American who estranges his family during the early 1950s.

According to Zuckerman's account, Coleman disowns his birth family to fulfill personal and professional ambitions, choosing to pass for Jewish, or "white" (which he reportedly selects on his military enlistment forms).[2] Importantly, however, Zuckerman does not learn this information from his acquaintance during one of their occasional meetings; rather, Zuckerman learns of Coleman's heritage from Ernestine Silk. Coleman's sister appears very late in the novel, well after Zuckerman has unfurled his reconstruction of his subject's life; he meets Ernestine at Coleman's funeral where, in a moment of racial *faux-pas*, Zuckerman mistakenly assumes his acquaintance's sister is the wife of Coleman's former colleague, Professor Keble (who is also African

American).³ As Jonathan Freedman points out in *Klezmer America: Jewishness, Ethnicity, Modernity* (2008), Ernestine seems to appear at this point in the text to serve this gestural and explanatory purpose, providing authority (and also sentiment) for Zuckerman's rendering.⁴ By contrast, I argue, Ernestine's belated introduction begins to gesture toward the limitations exerted on Zuckerman's representation by his frames of reference. Indeed, during their conversation after Coleman's funeral, readers discover that Ernestine furnishes Zuckerman with significant details from Coleman's childhood and young adulthood, which the writer retains in his imaginative reconstruction.

Despite her late appearance in the text, readers are meant to encounter Zuckerman's meeting with Ernestine as revelatory; after all, he and Coleman were only acquainted for a few months prior Coleman's unexpected death, and the two men never became very close. Thus, toward formulating his new-found (and newly lost) acquaintance, Coleman, into a biographical protagonist, the writer architects a complex representation of racial passing in which the dynamics of crossing the color line are unstable, consistently shifting between body and psyche with the tides of circumstance. Zuckerman adopts this strategy, on the one hand, because he perceives secrecy to be central to Coleman's life as a Jewish classics professor at Athena; and on the other, to emphasize that Coleman's long survival on the other side of the color line has been due (*not* to his appearance, but) to his ability to *psychically* and *discursively* occupy predominantly (if not traditionally) white (and especially masculine) spaces like the boxing ring or the academy. Thus, whether Zuckerman sets the scene of Coleman's life in the academic, multicultural, late-1990s context of his elder years around Athena College, or during his youth in 1940s and 1950s New Jersey and New York, his subject's possibilities for social mobility are uncannily ideological.⁵

To execute his architecture, Zuckerman must construct a biography that *itself* passes, as the passing narrative originates within African American literary traditions of the late-nineteenth to early-twentieth centuries, and Zuckerman is not an African American writer. Accordingly, Zuckerman transfigures the central, if taboo, topic of Coleman's story into narrative strategy. This includes Zuckerman's withholding important information from readers (such as the identity of his informant, Ernestine) until the end of the novel; his careful maneuvering of the structure of Coleman's memoir; and his manipulation of other characters' perspectives toward expressing his own opinions (or those he imagines for Coleman).[6] Zuckerman's narration in *The Human Stain* depicts Coleman indirectly, via the writer's imagination, along with partially lost and likely distorted memories of his and Ernestine's. This strategy allows the writer to place his subject's "gift to be secretive" at the center of his story, while also structuring the text to follow Zuckerman's (albeit limited) experiences of Coleman, interspersed with imaginative vignettes from Coleman's youth.[7]

Problematically, however, Zuckerman's focus on character motivation and self-invention all but ignores the material circumstances of Coleman's life as *either* an African American or a white American. For instance, Zuckerman's rendition of Coleman's life does not explore the fact that his subject estranges himself from a black family who is invested in the Civil Rights Movement and its economic goals for racial justice. In fact, in their late conversation, Ernestine tells Zuckerman that Coleman's abandonment of the Silk family was made permanent by their brother Walter, an activist and educator who fought relentlessly "for the integration of schools in New Jersey."[8] Ernestine reports that Walter (who believes that "what you do, you do to advance the race") was so angry over Coleman's decision to live as a white man that he forbade their mother from ever speaking to him.[9] The logic of Civil Rights, broadly conceived, is based on concrete outcomes that resonate with Walter's activism: given equal education (but not solely this equality), Civil Rights sought for equal and unbiased access to employment at all income levels; the Movement was also invested in labor unions and the retention of workers' pensions; the opening of historically white neighborhoods to families of color; the integration of America's Third-World Left into mainstream politics; and so on.

As the Silk family's pain and burden of loss are linked to the material and economic circumstances of their racial identity (as well as their activism toward changing those circumstances), these points are unexplored by Zuckerman, appearing only at the end of the novel (along with Ernestine) for readers' briefest reflection. While some scholars have attributed this omission to Roth's "attempts to move through and beyond the passing narrative," I claim that in omitting consideration of the economic and material dimensions of Coleman's life/lives, Zuckerman reveals the ideological limits and contradictions of the historical context(s) in and about which he writes, particularly where discourses on race and racism are concerned.[10] Roth's self-conscious narrator may be read as expressing suspicion of racial essentialism by limiting discussion of material and economic dimensions of racialized life, focusing instead on Coleman's individuality within his family and Athena College; however, through Zuckerman's simultaneous emphasis on the trickily atmospheric and ideological parameters of (not only Coleman's race travel, but) his professional ruin in the late 1990s, the writer *still* involves his biography of Coleman Silk in the drama of fixing racial meaning and making known the identities of characters. This is a central difficulty of Zuckerman's expression in *The Human Stain* (i.e., not *really* moving past the genre's formulas, so to speak). Embedded in history with his subject, Zuckerman recreates Coleman's life through the filters of *his* experiences, difficulties, and perceptions. This is not without consequence, I argue, particularly as Zuckerman shapes Coleman's experiences through the frames of *his* consciousness, which is affected by the racial discourses of his and Coleman's late-1990s context.

Although diverse in its representational techniques from Silko's *Almanac of the Dead*, Zuckerman's text reminds readers that history and identity are, often problematically, molded by consciousness and language. In *The Human Stain*, the narrator's consciousness and use of language highlight the problem of storytelling in connection with the narrator's central role in shaping narrative form; in *The Human* Stain, race is central to Zuckerman's representation of Coleman's passing, which he (not Coleman) shapes, along with *how* passing functions and takes form in the text as strategy and structuring agent. For instance, Zuckerman's teenaged Coleman, a quick-witted amateur boxer, carries his ability to be "neither one thing nor the other" (i.e., neither black nor white) into a career in academe, where he becomes "the first and only Jew to serve as dean of faculty" at Athena College.[11] However, Zuckerman alludes, this passing is ultimately achieved via Coleman's consistency in *psychically* occupying (e.g., as self-confidence, poise) and *discursively* deploying himself in ways that signal awareness of privilege (e.g., casual racism). As a consequence (Zuckerman sanctimoniously, if implicitly, alludes), Coleman's continued passage and tenure at Athena are thrown off course in March of 1996 (according to the writer's timeline). In reference to two regularly absent students in one of his classes, Coleman says: "Does anyone know these students? Are they real or are they spooks?"[12] Although he claims to have uttered "spooks" in reference to the students' "possibly ectoplasmic character" and not as the derogatory term for which it was taken, Coleman's absent students are black; when they learn what was said during class, they take offense, and the 71-year-old Coleman angrily resigns from Athena under accusations of racism.[13] Coleman's reputation is further sullied when a former colleague, Delphine Roux, apparently discovers his surreptitious affair with one Faunia Farley, a 34-year-old janitor at Athena College: "Everyone knows you're sexually exploiting an abused, illiterate woman half your age," reads an anonymous letter that arrives at Coleman's house, which he believes the antagonistic Delphine has penned.[14]

The Human Stain is formulated by Zuckerman as a twist on the imperative of authorial voice and is tethered to an examination of Zuckerman himself, longtime writer of interchangeably personal and quintessentially American themes. Should readers manage to resist offense, Zuckerman works to draw attention to the problematic centrality of race in the social, economic, and educational structures that shape the contemporary, 1990s world of *The Human Stain*; and this centrality, he suggests, transcends the novel's various historical contexts. Characters' involvement in (and inculcation by) racial ideology— or, racist structures and discourses—constitutes the various ways that *The Human Stain* engages the imaginative (and often problematic) dimensions of history- and community-making. Thus, the writer's story of Coleman's familial estrangement, racial passage, and late professional ruin offers the aging, institutionally unaffiliated Nathan Zuckerman occasion to reflect on his *own* life, values, and role as an author at the close of the twentieth century.

For instance, despite the fact that he and Coleman were unaware of one another while growing up in New Jersey (residing in different neighborhoods, having families of diverse backgrounds), readers of Roth's Zuckerman narratives may note that the two men nevertheless have more in common than geography: as a young man, Nathan Zuckerman also rejects his family (explored in *Ghost Writer*, c. 1979; *Zuckerman Unbound*, c. 1981; and *Counterlife*, c. 1986) in favor of his own "individualist" pursuits. Without family or community support (c. 1950s, six years Coleman's junior), Zuckerman cultivated his writerly métier in a literature program at Chicago (not unlike his depiction of

Coleman at New York University) where he developed an idealized image of himself, his vocation, and literary idols (which he retains into the twenty-first century): "American individualists," including Nathaniel Hawthorne, Herman Melville, Henry David Thoreau and, in particular, Emanuel Isadore Lonoff (a fictional Jewish writer).[15]

One social and narrative position that stands out in *The Human Stain* as a potential consequence of Zuckerman's particular métier is his imaginative rendering of Delphine Roux—Coleman's alleged, personal gadfly. Importantly, readers are not told *why* Delphine apparently seeks to ruin Coleman's reputation; therefore, readers cannot know why her mischief (particularly the anonymous letter) inspires in Coleman the kind of deranging perturbation which prompts Zuckerman to write on her rather extensively in *The Human Stain*.[16] While Zuckerman's rendition of Delphine's interior monologue reports that it is "the way [Coleman both] had sexually sized her up" and "had failed to sexually size her up" that leaves her seeking his recognition by any means, this characterization is also carefully (if contradictorily) curated to reveal how it is actually *a faulty image of herself* (and *not* her relationship with Coleman), which fuels Delphine's antagonism.[17] According to Zuckerman, Delphine perceives herself as entitled to recognition from Coleman (if not for her intellect and "École Normale sophistication," then) on the basis of her attractiveness, youth, or the exotic appeal of her French-ness.[18] In this depiction, Zuckerman takes care to draw Delphine as a woman academic who, due to *both* her intellect and apparently conventional good looks, has managed to make a name for herself by winning "over just about every wooable fool professor" (as Zuckerman puts it) with whom she works.[19]

Delphine is drawn so as to be read as proverbially *working* the traditionally white, male space of the academy to her advantage, directing aspects of her femininity toward her goals—for example, presumably ingratiating herself, flirting, and so on. These methods are of course relayed with disdain by Zuckerman (in narration, via Coleman, and through his depictions of Delphine), signaling the apparently distasteful nature of *this* character's subversion. Thus (and much like Coleman's misuse of his own privilege) Delphine is ultimately drawn by the writer as nevertheless blinded by her own sense of superiority to how she might aid Athena's marginalized students, or simply get along with her colleagues. Zuckerman presents Delphine in this arguably oversimplified manner for a twofold purpose: on the one hand, to clearly drive home a point about the academy (specifically, the humanities) being a male-dominated space in which women must politically jockey and/or work various complex angles in order to succeed (though rarely free of others' "sanctimony");[20] on the other hand, Delphine's depiction is also drawn to highlight the destructive, practical, and behavioral potentials inherent to these conditions—particularly in social (and official) displays of resentment or paranoia, like that in which Delphine presumably becomes entangled with Coleman.

In this dimension of Zuckerman's expression in *The Human Stain*, readers may perceive the operations of late-1990s racial ideology (specifically, President Clinton's 1997 Initiative on Race) through Zuckerman's cooptation of Delphine (a white woman) as an agent of disorder in Coleman's (a black man's) life. Within Zuckerman's immediate context, or narrative present (approximately 1998–2000), studies like President Clinton's are particularly notable for their faulty historicization of racism: such official language is often largely limited to discriminatory phenomenon and their impacts to the historical past, insisting that racial/cultural "*differences*" (not institutional, or more insidious forms of, racism) are the crux of the "American race problem."[21] Within this model, *dialogue* is proposed as the premier means by which Americans may reach the Clinton administration's goal of "One America"—or, "national unity with a multicultural gloss," to use the description of sociologist Claire Jean Kim.[22] Yet, dark-comically, within Zuckerman's narrative formulation of Delphine via Coleman, Coleman may only find peace if Delphine (in an out-of-character move) manages to see beyond herself and *have a dialogue* with Coleman outside of the "punishing immersion in meetings, hearings, interviews," which follow the spooks affair.[23] However, according to Zuckerman, Delphine's distorted perception of herself (*as well as* the conditions in which she works at Athena) forecloses this possibility as effectively as Coleman's angry resignation from the college. That is, her inability to honestly confront *herself* forecloses her ability to have a reasonable *dialogue* with Coleman, and vice versa.

Interestingly, however, the faultiness of a dialogic approach to combatting discrimination is not only expressed through sexist distortions like those affecting Delphine's characterization; the Clinton administration's prescribed brand of friendly dialogue is *also* unexpectedly foreclosed between Zuckerman and Coleman, as well. As with Delphine, the men's distorted perceptions of themselves, each other, *and* their contemporary conditions foreclose their potential to become closer friends. For instance, shortly after becoming acquainted, Coleman discontinues his nascent friendship with Zuckerman. This abrupt withdrawal occurs not long after he confides in the writer about an affair he is having with Faunia Farley, whom Coleman reportedly compares to his first love, Steena Paulsson, and describes as the perfect lover: "In bed [Faunia] is deep phenomenon."[24] Following Coleman's disclosure, the men see each other only two other times; in their last encounter, Zuckerman crosses paths with Coleman and Faunia at a concert in July 1998 and reports:

> When my calls were not returned, I assumed that Coleman wished to have nothing more to do with me. Something had gone wrong, and I assumed, as one does when a friendship ends abruptly—a new friendship particularly—that I was responsible, if not for some indiscreet word or deed that had deeply irritated or offended him, then by being who and what I am [i.e., a writer].[25]

Between the men, Zuckerman reasons that there is an unspoken and repelling force (or *difference*) that purports to elucidate their inaccessibility to, and incompatibility with, one another. Yet, while Zuckerman cannot account for Coleman's sudden retreat, he signals an important distortion of his self-perception (and perception of Coleman) in presuming this retreat has anything to do with Zuckerman's vocation as a writer; after all, Zuckerman misguidedly reasons, Coleman originally sought his acquaintanceship on the basis of his being a writer.[26] However, unbeknown to Zuckerman, the repelling and illusory force between the men merely indicates the writer's entrenchment in ideology's most troubling transformation at the end of the twentieth century: that is, into a political instrument and loose structuring agent for official American discourses on race and racism (e.g., as in Clinton's Initiative or earlier commissions politics).

Thus, whether despite or because of the sudden end to their familiarity, Zuckerman composes *The Human Stain*, dissembling behind layers of narrative a privileged intimacy with Coleman that he is not offered opportunity to establish. Through Zuckerman, *The Human Stain* demonstrates the problematic (if inevitable, as the writer suggests) response to Coleman's refusal: an imaginative one, from the writer's own position (rather than his protagonist's) within racial ideology. Simple as this narrative formulation may appear (drawing dark-comic effect in its application to Delphine), it is not without problematic implications in the case of Coleman's particular depiction. That is, the apparent impetus for Zuckerman's text clashes with official discourses defining racial discrimination (as well as the notion of *dialogue* as a foremost means to dispelling it), which hallmark the historical context of the novel's emergence (i.e., both in Zuckerman's fictional world *and* Roth's late-twentieth century actuality, as *The Human Stain* was published in both).

Importantly, however, as Eduardo Bonilla-Silva points out, racial ideology accommodates "contradictions, exceptions, and new information," which allows its often unwitting adherents (e.g., Zuckerman) to "maneuver within various contexts," and "produce various accounts and presentations of self" (and others) which enable them to discuss or argue certain issues while also appearing tolerant or ambivalent of race itself (and/or associated intersectional matters).[27] Within *The Human Stain*'s late-1990s context (which is interwoven with Coleman's youth in the early 1950s), readers meet Zuckerman embedded in a racial ideology that frames as *given* the interests of *his* (white, male) group (discursively, physically, and psychically) particularly in social and public contexts.[28] Zuckerman's disquieting fiction about the structures of race and gender in America at the end of the twentieth century thus amounts to much more than the writer's imaginative rendition of Coleman Silk's racial passage, as this chapter will explore.

Zuckerman's Late 1990s and Racial Discourse's Omissions

After the unexpected death of his father in 1969, a younger Nathan Zuckerman attempted to escape the writing life, disappearing into other endeavors and only publishing *The Ghost Writer* in the late 1970s. Zuckerman's non-authorial forays are humorously chronicled in Roth's first Zuckerman trilogy (published *c.* 1981–5), which may be read as inspired by issues within the young writer's family; following this, however, the style of Roth's ghost writer seems to expand away from the myopic, Salingeresque mode that characterizes his narrative style in *Ghost Writer* (1979).[29] Following the 1980s, Zuckerman returns to authorship—via *American Pastoral* (1997), *I Married a Communist* (1998), and *The Human Stain* (2000); in these books, the writer's new style is hallmarked by broad, non-fiction-inspired narrative.[30] This development in style and focus (from granular and personal to general and atmospheric) is also uncannily echoed in the style, focus, and narrative scope of the novels included in this study.

More pertinent to my reading of *The Human Stain*, however, is that the developmental changes which readers may track across Zuckerman's career are *also* paralleled by changes developing in commissions politics focused on race relations and racism (particularly following the Civil Rights Movement) in the United States. This is significant, as Zuckerman sets his rendition of Coleman's young adulthood and passing in New Jersey and New York of the early 1950s, a racially fraught historical moment (e.g., often noted for its "urban disorders") during which the writer also came of age. Zuckerman juxtaposes this historical past with *The Human Stain*'s contemporary narrative present, the late 1990s, when Coleman is accused of racism.

However, since the novel's publication, scholars and critics alike have conflated and collapsed *The Human Stain*'s apparently cynical outlook on contemporary political correctness with Philip Roth's purported own, personal sentiments.[31] None have considered the historical insight that Roth lends, however, particularly into late-twentieth-century American discourses on racism; and Roth makes these insights initially accessible via Zuckerman's specific depictions of his subject, Coleman. Zuckerman's juxtaposition of the early 1950s with the late 1990s holds deeper significance than pseudo-ironic historical contrast; this collocation illuminates distorted, rationalizing perceptions of racism and race relations inherent to Zuckerman's representations (regardless of the historical moment he depicts). This is not to suggest that Nathan Zuckerman is a racist writer; only that, as a writer who does not share Coleman's social or racial designations, Zuckerman's understanding (and therefore his narrative) of Coleman's race travel and social integration is limited to abstract identity politics: that is, presumed sets of differences between Coleman and himself that are constructed (*not* around the diversities in their experiences of *whiteness*, but) around his subject's sexual "audacity," Coleman's fervent "individuality," and ultimately ruinous personal investment in institutions.[32]

Zuckerman's formulation of Coleman is thus compelling for all it self-consciously *misses*, particularly, for instance, concerning Coleman's proclivity for using racial slurs. During their brief acquaintanceship, Zuckerman takes Coleman for a Jewish man like himself and participates in this (false) rendition of Coleman's life story; in fact, Zuckerman is apparently so invested in Coleman's false identity that he does not flinch when his acquaintance glibly compares his resignation from Athena College (i.e., "for being white") to a time he was "thrown out of a Norfolk whorehouse for being [he alludes, *mistakenly* profiled as] black."[33] Perhaps more troubling, Coleman also mocks Athena College and its students for blaming white Jews (such as himself—who is passing) for "black suffering" in a manner he claims is similar to the Germans' blaming "the same Old Testament monsters" for *their* suffering leading up to the Second World War.[34] Rather than question Coleman's harsh comments, Zuckerman (who is Jewish) participates in kind—and he does so, moreover, in a telling narrative aside to his readers, rather than directly to Coleman. In a provocative, if implicit, gesture of mutuality with Coleman's racializing discourse (and, presumably, also his readers'), Zuckerman admits that, to him (perhaps like to the doorman at Coleman's "Norfolk whorehouse"), his new friend's appearance *does indeed* recall "one of those crimp-haired Jews of a light yellowish skin pigmentation who possess something of the ambiguous aura of the pale blacks who are sometimes taken for white."[35]

Readers of Zuckerman's previous novels may not be surprised by the writer's casual application of controversial, racialized language. Yet it is through his subject's polarizing (i.e., politically incorrect) use of racial slurs that Zuckerman makes a larger point about the construction of not only Coleman's fabricated white identity, but also the operations of white identification in Zuckerman's depiction of America, overall. Because of Zuckerman's positioning at this early point in the novel, readers are meant to perceive Coleman's incendiary statements as reference to his frustration with being incorrectly profiled: first, as a passing youth during segregation (which was *not* incorrect) and more recently, as a racist, following his "spooks" incident at Athena. However, through Coleman's reportedly liberal use of racialized language in private with Zuckerman, the writer draws attention to an irony deeper than African American Coleman being racist: that is, the fact that it is "*through*, not despite, [his] participation in racism" that Coleman is able to successfully pass for so long and attain individualistic liberation.[36] Crucially, this suggests not only that racist discourses are constitutive of white identity in *The Human Stain*'s America, but that Coleman's participation is necessary to his success as a purportedly white individual in this racist society.

Racist structures and discourses abound in *The Human Stain*, but not exclusively in conversations between Coleman and Zuckerman during the late 1990s, these structures and discourses also pervade the writer's imaginative reconstructions of Coleman's youth in segregation-era New Jersey and Greenwich Village, New York. *The Human Stain* thus straddles the mid- to late-twentieth century and subtly compares these supposedly polar-opposite historical eras, in terms of race relations. For instance, early on in *The Human Stain*, Zuckerman informs readers that his narrative present coincides with the "summer [that] Bill Clinton's secret" affair with Monica Lewinsky "emerged" and "revived America's oldest communal passion, historically perhaps its most treacherous and subversive pleasure: the ecstasy of sanctimony."[37] The irony of Zuckerman's own participation in this ecstatic "sanctimony" (e.g., via Delphine Roux's characterization or Coleman's angry resignation) is implicitly and explicitly engaged in various facets of the writer's narrative present— particularly where Coleman's sexuality becomes Zuckerman's focus (which is rather often, particularly in the writer's reconstructed flashbacks to Coleman's young adulthood). Yet, Zuckerman's passive moralism does not approach Coleman's decision to abandon the Silk family of East Orange, New Jersey, and race travel; instead, this sanctimonious distaste reverberates in Zuckerman's representations of Coleman as an aging, Jewish academic living in western Massachusetts.

Less than a year prior to the publicity of Bill Clinton's sex scandal, the Clinton White House released the president's Initiative on Race in June of 1997; Zuckerman makes no mention of this text in *The Human Stain*.

However, contemporary formulations of race relations, like Clinton's, resonate with Zuckerman's depictions of Coleman, while they importantly diverge from Coleman's own (meager and fabricated) descriptions of his life as a Jewish boy in New Jersey to Zuckerman over drinks. This sketches a significant divide, transcending generations, in American conceptions of racial relations, which I explore in the next section of this chapter. Via rhetorical sleight, President Clinton's *One America in the 21st-Century* pseudo-historicizes de jure racism (institutional and individual) as "solved," implicitly claiming that "but for an occasional aberrational practice, future [i.e., non-racial] society is already here and functioning."[38] Racism, anti-Semitism, and historical aggressions between races are dissolved in Clinton's report to "racial/cultural differences," which may be solved through informed dialogue. However, Coleman confides that his (imaginary) Jewish identity is condescended to by his colleagues at Athena: "President Roberts," Coleman tells Zuckerman, "with his upper-class pedigree liked that he had this barroom brawler [referring to himself] parked just across the hall from him."[39] Although he is proud of his (albeit imaginary) kinship with "those stories about Jews and their remarkable rise from the slums," Coleman candidly sneers to Zuckerman, disdainful of colleagues like Roberts: "Gentiles actually hate those stories."[40]

Once again, readers find Coleman participating in racialized discourses, complaining about his colleagues' alleged anti-Semitism while simultaneously heaping limiting assumptions onto them, as well. By contrast, President Clinton's report trivializes instances of contemporary racism and anti-Semitism, such as those described (and perpetrated) by Coleman; the report even diminishes the total impact of *historical* racism by engaging nothing concerning the effects of white privilege on income and employment opportunities for people of color, with which Coleman's (actual) brother, Walter, is involved.

For instance, of Walter's efforts to integrate the schools in New Jersey, Ernestine relates:

> There were no colored teachers in the white Ashbury Park school system when Walter arrived there in 1947. You have to remember, he was the first. And subsequently their first Negro principal. And subsequently their first Negro superintendent of schools. That tells you something about Walt.[41]

What Ernestine seeks to articulate about Walter, in contrast with Coleman, is his investment in the actual, concrete outcomes, rather than "a fairy tale" (as she describes pre-Civil Rights-era fascinations with race travel).[42] Thus, Ernestine links Coleman's race travel to "fairy tale"-like ideals and dreams of unearned privileges, which implicitly undercut Walt's work in Ashbury park. Ernestine links Walt's work to the New Jersey governor's (c. 1947) amendments of the state's constitution, which "eliminated segregation in the public schools and in the National Guard."[43] In its moralistic stance, Ernestine's perspective indirectly coincides with 1950s legal doctrine on school integration, which was deeply influenced by the 1944 publication of Gunnar Myrdal's *An American Dilemma*.

For the first time (and in line with Ernestine and Walter Silks' values), Myrdal's text named the contradictions between America's racial practices and its founding values as a *moral dilemma* of national proportion. *American Dilemma* is further remembered for its influence on the Supreme Court's final decision in *Brown v. Board of Education* on May 17, 1954. The decision to desegregate public schools, and therefore enact the founding guarantee of "inalienable value and liberty" to all citizens in education, not only avowed Myrdal's moral discourse concerning the "American Creed," but garnered the kind of positive international attention that the American federal government craved by the early to mid-1950s.[44]

However, like the discourse of President Clinton's 1997 Initiative on Race, Myrdal's case against racism focuses on individual practices or instances of racism, thereby not only overlooking examples (historical and contemporary) of institutional and systemic racism, but by extension, also the economic, material, and opportunistic dimensions of these broad-based forms of discrimination. And importantly, this elision of systems and their material outcomes *also* looms in the bulk of Zuckerman's narrative, and particularly in his imaginative reconstructions of Coleman's past. After all, readers do not gain detail concerning Walter Silk's involvement in activism until Ernestine's conversation with Zuckerman late in the novel. In this way, Walt and the Silk family's disapproval of Coleman's passing is framed to indicate their (like many other African Americans') refusal to abandon the solidarity of their support networks for the sake of "fairy tale"-like, unearned privilege.

By speaking to Walter Silk's proactive work as an educator, activist, and community leader, Ernestine's narrative contribution thus subtly reminds Zuckerman (and readers) of the disproportionate material and economic burdens that often accompany racial identification in the United States. And as Freedman has pointed out, this late addition to the novel does inject it with an important (and heretofore, missing) historical quality. Her interjection in the novel offers an orderly "sense of history" to Zuckerman's tale, providing the "didactic payoff," presumably, for his audacious reconstruction of Coleman's life.[45] However, Freedman maintains that the sentimental didacticism imparted so late by Ernestine squares rather awkwardly with the rest of the novel. This is because, otherwise, Freedman points out, Roth "will have none [of the conventional passing narrative's] return to the racial under the sign of sentiment" throughout the rest of the novel.[46] I agree, insofar as Ernestine's addition to the narrative proffers a "sense of history" to Zuckerman's yarns; rather than unrealistically sentimental, I read Ernestine's perspective as imparting a different, *relational* sense of history to the novel. This stands in stark contrast to Zuckerman's conception of his subject's raw, historical individuality via secrecy.

Ernestine contrasts her (speculated) sense of Coleman's experience of his identity with their eldest brother, Walter, whose experiences as a teacher of color in New Jersey have long honed his focus on educational equity. Understood in relation to Walter, as Coleman is through Ernestine, Coleman is not permitted to be Coleman alone; rather, Coleman exists in relation to others: he is a cruel son to their mother, a polarizing rival to Walter, and he is the boy who (according to Ernestine) always seemed like "the breeziest, most optimistic child you ever wanted to see."[47] Even after Coleman's death, Ernestine's focus is not on (as Zuckerman sees it) Coleman's apparent personal destruction, but on her and Coleman's inconsolable (long-deceased) mother and a case of sibling rivalry gone awry. Ernestine tells Zuckerman about how their mother was heartbroken and confused by her son's choice to marry Iris Gittelman (a Jewish woman) and abandon the family, "what with all the success he had," both socially and academically, while growing up.[48] Ernestine distills the details of her brother's life very differently from Zuckerman's imaginative flashbacks, presenting a portrait that is nostalgic and tinged with tragedy; thus,

Coleman's individual tale of racial passing is subsumed by the Silk family's broader context and history, with which Coleman is inevitably entangled. In Ernestine's formulation, both readers and Zuckerman are therefore deprived of (even an imaginative sense of) Coleman's interiority, particularly his experiences as a "successful" co-ed at Howard University (which Zuckerman reports he despised) and then New York University.[49] Thus, while the writer grants that his post-funeral conversation with Ernestine offers "most of what I know about Coleman's growing up in East Orange," the writer is nevertheless aware that something is "missing from Ernestine's sense of Coleman's life."[50]

While Ernestine's relational history imparts Zuckerman's text with an abstract sense of the material and economic conditions from which Coleman emerged, its softly melodramatic and nostalgist framework elides several consequential factors in Coleman's life, which Zuckerman seeks to uncover (however imaginatively). For instance, like Myrdal's *American Dilemma*, Ernestine's image of young Coleman relies on its image of an optimistic Coleman to carry through the tragedy (or, dilemma) that Coleman's passing creates for her family:

> People grow up and go away and have nothing to do with their families ever again, and they don't have to be colored to act like that. [...] They hate everything so much they disappear. But Coleman as a kid was not a hater.[51]

By Ernestine's logic, unless Coleman hated his family *and* being black, he had no sensible reason to disown their family in the early 1950s. Myrdal's *American Dilemma* expresses a similar assurance of racial discrimination's future dissolution, providing that individual citizens are willing to socially cooperate. This appeal, however, was directed to the consciences of individual white Americans and their good sense (i.e., color-blindness), claiming they may finally realize America's ideals and set an example for the rest of the world.[52] However, this optimism, also reflected in Ernestine's comparative yarns about Walter, reads as disingenuous and incomplete to Zuckerman. While Ernestine cheerfully reasons that "Coleman couldn't wait to go through civil rights to get his human rights," Zuckerman's story of Coleman's life is *not* similarly invested in appealing to the consciences of his readers in his depictions or explanations of Coleman's passing.[53]

Importantly, Zuckerman's discursive avoidance of Ernestine's brand of assured, nostalgist optimism resonates with critiques received by Myrdal's moralistic text, particularly following the Civil Rights Movement (c. 1968); for example, *American Dilemma* was censured for explaining away and misframing discriminatory practices and conditions through its narrow narrative perspective. Although the military and many public schools had been desegregated from the mid- to late 1960s, critics of Myrdal, advocates of Black Power, and other race- and culture-conscious thinkers turned their attentions to racist *conditions*, such as severe poverty and ghettoized neighborhoods, that were still endured by many Americans. Further supporting critiques of Myrdal's work were numerous "urban disorders" that erupted across the country during the summer of 1967, inspiring many to wonder (including then-President Lyndon B. Johnson) whether the country's "dilemma" with race was in fact *not* an individual-level "Negro Problem" as historically claimed, but rather a broader "American problem."[54] This acknowledgment was followed by the 1967 creation of the National Advisory Commission on Civil Disorders and its "Kerner Report" (c. 1968, named for the group's research leader), to investigate the urban unrest as well as a 1970 report from President Richard Nixon's Commission on Campus Unrest, to examine college campus turbulences (e.g., Kent State University, Jackson State College) that, in terms of their racial catalysts, significantly recalled America's urban disorders. In line with the later-1960s' turn toward institutionally oriented concerns with culture and racism, both reports departed from Myrdal's conceptual and rhetorical optimism about the "American dilemma's" dissolution, as well as his moralistic, individual-level critique.

This is a line of cultural and economic logic with which Coleman is apparently familiar (if fabricated), as he discusses it in disclosures to Zuckerman about his (invented) Jewish upbringing in East Orange, New Jersey. And while this information *could* be used by Zuckerman to inform a rendering of Coleman's passing, interestingly, the material Coleman provides on his fabricated Jewishness is left unused in *The Human Stain*, presented (it seems) solely for its contrasts with Zuckerman's rendering. Coleman reportedly describes his hometown of East Orange as "the poor end of town," punctuating this statement with: "You're a Weequahic boy, you don't know East Orange."[55]

Much like Coleman's earlier, racialized expressions, Zuckerman neither responds to nor engages these class-conscious remarks (in either dialogue or narrative aside). However, readers of Roth's Zuckerman narratives such as *The Ghost Writer* (1979) may recall that in Weequahic, Zuckerman did not grow up wealthy or privileged in the ways he reports Coleman assuming. Nevertheless, Zuckerman does not correct Coleman, allowing his acquaintance (as well as his uninitiated readers) to assume he is more privileged than Coleman.

Following Zuckerman's collaborative silence, Coleman thus describes his imaginary Jewish father as:

> One of those Jewish saloon keepers, they were all over Jersey and, of course, they all had ties to the Reinfields and the Mob—they had to have, to survive the Mob. My father wasn't a roughneck but he was rough enough, and he wanted better for me.[56]

Like Coleman's remarks concerning his non-Jewish colleagues' distaste for "those stories [with which he identifies] about the Jews and their remarkable rise from the slums," his reference to his father as "one of those Jewish saloon keepers" constitutes another application by Coleman of racialized, stereotyping discourse. Although Coleman attempts to deflect the image of a "brawling" and bar-owning "roughneck" from his depiction of his (fabricated) Jewish father, seasoned readers of Zuckerman's narratives may note the descriptive echoes of the writer's own contentious cousin, Sidney, in this depiction.

Sidney is introduced in *The Ghost Writer* and is cast as an offensive character in one of young Nathan Zuckerman's early, successful stories of Jewish family life. Indeed, if Coleman's father *had actually* owned a saloon, Zuckerman's cousin Sidney may well have frequented it.[57] In Zuckerman's early-career short story, "Higher Education," the college-aged writer depicts his cousin Sidney, along with other members of his family, in a narrative of Jewish domestic life. At this early point in his career, Zuckerman's predominating conflicts crystallize around the bittersweet success he attains with this story. Although Roth does not include the text of "Higher Education" in *The Ghost Writer* (nor is it mentioned in *The Human Stain*), readers are informed that (akin, perhaps, to Buddy Glass) Zuckerman is anything but flattering and affirmative in his story's characterizations.

Set in the mid-1950s, *The Ghost Writer* thus depicts young Zuckerman's struggles to live his idealistic notion of being an "individualist" American writer (i.e., to whom nothing is sacred but his own authorial voice) in the face of his disapproving family and Weequahic neighborhood community. This is a major issue that Zuckerman's father (a soft-spoken, locally popular chiropodist), Victor Zuckerman, takes with "Higher Education." Victor reproaches his son for the narrative's offensive depictions, claiming that the story doesn't "leave anything disgusting out"—and arguably encourages anti-Semitism in readers.[58] Zuckerman's father continues:

> From a lifetime of experience I happen to know what ordinary people will think when they read something like this story. And you don't. You can't. You have been sheltered from it all your life. You were raised here in this neighborhood where you went to school with Jewish children.[59]

Victor warns that "Higher Education," and other stories like it, will not be interpreted by a majority of Zuckerman's readers as being about "immigrants like [Zuckerman's great aunt, Meema] Chaya who worked and saved and sacrificed to get a decent footing in America"; rather, "as far as Gentiles are concerned," his story will be interpreted as being about "kikes and their love of money."[60] To his father's entreaties, however, a 23-year-old Zuckerman only replies, "I didn't go into Meema Chaya's life" because "that isn't *this* story."[61] Although the young Zuckerman does not articulate it as such, his frustration with and rejection of his father's pleas reveal their contradictory (i.e., at once culture-conscious *and* universalist) structure—a frustration similar to that which he registers with Ernestine's perspective on Coleman near the end of *The Human Stain*.[62]

Victor's comments on his son's early fiction are striking, on the one hand, for his awareness of institutional discrimination and, on the other, for Victor's consciousness of individual-level prejudices as *not* social aberrations (as Myrdal *and* Clinton would claim), but as "ordinary" occurrences.[63] Victor alludes to the presumed benefit of Zuckerman attending an all-Jewish school, while concurrently admitting to its problematically sheltering effects on his son; thus, Victor's perceived solutions to these American dilemmas are (perhaps unsurprisingly) where he and Zuckerman diverge. In a similar manner (if much later in life), Ernestine reminds Zuckerman (and readers) that, like Victor's disapproval of "Higher Education," Walter's banishment of Coleman speaks to a similar, morally based disapproval of forgetting (or choosing to dispose of) one's origins. Similarly, as a professional fiction writer, Zuckerman is expected by Victor to offer only affirmative depictions of Jewish people in his stories—not "disgusting" ones. Read as counterpoints to Myrdal's moral entreaty to white Americans against racist social practices, Victor's and Walter's stances in favor of cultural and racial solidarity illuminate the faultiness of this didactic theory. For instance, in *The Ghost Writer*, Zuckerman reports being raised on stories of "the slums" by Victor; these stories praised the Weequahic community's most admired member, Judge Wapter, who was "born of Galician Jews in the slums adjacent to the city's sweatshops and mills some ten years before our family arrived" in 1900.[64] By 1956, Judge Wapter had ascended to "a position of prestige and authority rather like that accorded in [the Zuckerman] household to President [...] Roosevelt."[65] Although Zuckerman does not state as much in *The Human Stain*'s narration or dialogue, the authority associated with those, like Wapter, who achieved this "rise" is a concept that has been lost on him since his youth. This places Zuckerman in an interestingly parallel relation with the "gentiles," who, Coleman distastefully concludes, "hate those stories" about Jewish immigrants' ascensions from the slums.[66]

According to Victor, and other disapproving voices like Wapter's, anti-Semitism is perpetuated by the dissemination, particularly for entertainment purposes, of negative stereotypes. However, unlike his father, the young Zuckerman of *The Ghost Writer* is less concerned with optimistically rendering the personalities and facts of his Jewish characters' lives, and more invested in deploying his fictions to carefully strip away the layers (e.g., sundry social expectations, practices) that constitute his childhood community's conception and perception of Jewish identities. Moreover, readers may observe, the older Nathan Zuckerman of *The Human Stain* takes a similar position on Coleman's identity, evidenced by his dissatisfaction with Ernestine's familial account. However, despite the supposedly "post-racial," politically correct context in which readers of *The Human Stain* meet Zuckerman, the writer's dissatisfaction with formulaic conceptions of cultural identity does not prevent him from uncritically incorporating them into his profile of Coleman. This begins with his subject's propensity to use racial slurs when angry and is carried through Coleman's descriptions of his (imaginary, Jewish) upbringing. In fact, Coleman's imaginary family portrait is more resonant with the narratives of Jewish resilience that are propounded by Zuckerman's father.

Thus, while Coleman's invented story and use of derogatory racial language are not meant to express his conscious dissemination of racist ideology, Zuckerman's uncritical incorporation of these elements into *The Human Stain* nevertheless reveals the inarguable presence of racism (at individual and institutional levels) in his text's narrative present, and not merely its historical past—despite what official discourses on racism in the late 1990s would claim. In this way, Zuckerman (not unlike his own father) is astute to note his subject's individual use of racist language as part and parcel of his identification as white, as well as this (racist) discourse's role in his own professional (i.e., institutionally linked) downfall. However, as Zuckerman's narrative notes these elements for readers, their disengagement from the writer's rendition of Coleman's life speaks to Zuckerman's inability to square these trickily negative aspects of Coleman's identity with the optimistic (if dissatisfying) image of Coleman that he is offered by Ernestine. Zuckerman's inability to grasp the concurrence of these polarizing images in a single subject (Coleman) reveals the writer's inability to grasp a primary difference between his own story of familial estrangement and Coleman's: that is, the legal and social stakes (and, in many cases, ramifications) of identifying as black in the United States.

In *Who Is Black? One Nation's Definition* (1992), F. James Davis notes that, for Americans of any black lineage, full integration into political, economic, social spheres and institutions has been historically blocked and directly discouraged via miscegenation.[67] And importantly, the United States' rules for determining who may be considered socially and legally black (e.g., the one-drop rule) subsisted well beyond the release of Myrdal's 1944 text and the subsequent Civil Rights Movement; this led many *post*-Civil Rights critics of Myrdal to question his assurance in the American Creed's color-blind ideals.[68] Meanwhile, as discussed in Chapter 2, during the Cold War, America's internationally recognized racist social and institutional practices brought the country under significant political fire concerning its abilities to fight communism abroad. According to Davis: Even "before World War I, it was clear that in questionable cases the one-drop rule would generally prevail in social practice *and* in the courts, and in the North as well as the South."[69]

Reflecting the United States' unique definition of black Americanness, combined with the social and institutional barriers historically associated with this identity, the social phenomenon of "passing for white" thus emerged in the United States even before Jim Crow instituted de jure segregation of neighborhoods, schools, and public facilities (e.g., concert venues, voting booths, restrooms, athletic facilities).[70] Therefore, it likely comes as little surprise that Davis dates the "peak years for passing as white" in America as "probably from 1880 to 1925"; "by 1925," he claims, particularly in light of the Black Renaissance of the 1920s, black communities in America "had fully accepted the one-drop rule, as even the lightest mulattoes [who might have passed, instead] allied themselves more and more firmly with [black Americans]."[71] Importantly, however, in Zuckerman's rendition of Coleman's racial passing, his protagonist flouts the one-drop rule and refuses alliance with his small, dispersed black community in East Orange, New Jersey; thus audaciously out of step with segregationist social norms of 1952 (according to Zuckerman's timeline), Coleman disowns his birth family decades *after* the practice might have been considered even remotely acceptable.

With the initiatives of the Civil Rights Movement at hand, the concept of race travel toward acquiring social and material privileges reads as deeply disrespectful, implying bad faith in (not only governments' willingness to meet citizens' demands for equality, but) black communities' and activists' abilities to effectively and sustainably convince governments to fulfill their demands. Critics of Myrdal pointed out that racial inequality (particularly at material levels) is relatively easy to maintain via discriminatory institutions and the maintenance of the vastly different economic privileges and opportunities they produce and sustain; therefore, race travel may be read, in this context, as a means for sustaining discriminatory institutions and the practices that exclude people of color from their ranks.[72]

Coleman's late racial passing thus forms an important (if narratively unarticulated) facet of the character that Zuckerman draws of his acquaintance. Coleman's choice to race travel as late as the 1950s marks him as a distinctly *unmoral* figure (i.e., one who is objectively uninfluenced by morality and moral argument) within an otherwise morally directed context. This is necessary to Zuckerman's rendering because *without* this historical detail (despite the fact that Zuckerman neglects to delve into its contextual significance), Coleman's passing might otherwise be read as the character's sole, pragmatic choice within a racist context. Indeed, Ernestine suggests as much, when she tells Zuckerman: "Of course, if you look at it narrowly, from the point of view of social advantage, of course it was advantageous in the well-spoken Negro middle class to do it Coleman's way."[73] However, though Zuckerman does not directly make this connection to either Ernestine or his readers, "narrowly" is precisely *how* he depicts (as the writer imagines it) Coleman's motivations and final decision to race travel.

This, I argue, is precisely why the bulk of Coleman's marriage to Iris Gittelman (e.g., the "million difficulties of the Silks' marriage," the births of their four children) is blotted from Zuckerman's rendition of Coleman's life, as are the details of his ascension and tenure at Athena College. These intimate and personal details delve a little *too* deeply for Zuckerman to manage in his craft. That is, beyond any clear issues that Zuckerman had with (and/or was influenced by) his birth family in his early fiction, *The Human Stain* features a brief subplot (pp. 35–7, 44) in which Zuckerman discusses his own conditions of incontinence, impotence, and his "reclusive existence" following a prostate cancer procedure in the earlier-1990s.[74] Prior to the procedure, readers of Roth might note, Zuckerman never married, had children, nor joined the ranks of a university or college as either a writer-in-residence (as had his hero, E. I. Lonoff) or creative writing instructor (like Buddy Glass). Thus, the writer possesses no basis from which to depict Coleman's experiences of this sort. Because of this, in concert with the writer's renewed awareness of his solitude and impotence in the face of Coleman's affair with Faunia Farley, Zuckerman's reconstruction is shaped by his focus on Coleman's sexuality and relationships (romantic or otherwise) with women as well as the unknown cause of Coleman's death, which Zuckerman convinces himself is linked to the misdirected, anti-Semitic hatred of Faunia's estranged husband, Lester Farley.[75]

However, by simultaneously goading readers with the historical taboo of miscegenation *and* softly aligning Coleman with problematic myths of black sexuality, Zuckerman exposes both himself and his context as woefully ill-equipped to narratively tackle the experiences of those living outside of white, male experiences and paradigms. Importantly, as Antonio Bonilla-Silva points out, this default (narrative) position not only is central to the color-blind racial ideology that distinguishes much late-twentieth-century official doctrines on race, but it also delegitimizes expressions of racially specific experiences (material, emotional, or otherwise).[76] It is not coincidental, then (in either Zuckerman's oeuvre or his historical context), that both Coleman's professional downfall and eventual death are brought about by his involvement with white women. The liaisons that Zuckerman chronicles coerce readers to imagine a life which seeks neither to bolster cultural institutions nor to allay concerns of community ostracism; however, by the time Coleman decides to race travel, these are precisely the injunctions to which he ultimately submits in marrying Iris Gittelman. In this way, women become outlets for Coleman's "transgressive audacity": first, as means for Zuckerman's narrative elision of the moral costs of mid-century racial passing and, second, as diversions from the writer's failure to clearly articulate Coleman's motivations for race travel (which neither Zuckerman nor Ernestine apparently comprehends).[77]

In the final analysis, where Zuckerman might be (and, via Roth, has been) credited with rethinking and reshaping the passing genre in *The Human Stain*, I claim that his fixation on Coleman's mysterious and untimely death reduces his rendering to another conventionally tragic figure within the passing genre. This ultimately presents readers with the question of whether or not anything has, in fact, changed in American race relations (particularly since before the Civil Rights Movement) amid the twentieth century's tides of ideological and discursive change.

Coleman Silk and Women (According to Zuckerman)

In Zuckerman's recreation of Coleman's young adulthood, he meets "the churned-up, untamed," and decidedly "non-Jewish Jewish Iris" Gittelman in about 1951. About two years later, they become engaged and Coleman decides to pass, despite the fact that:

It wouldn't have fazed [Iris] for five minutes to learn that he had been born and raised in a colored family and identified himself as a Negro nearly all his life, nor would she have been burdened in the slightest by keeping that secret for him if it was what he'd asked her to do. [...] Iris's open-mindedness wasn't even a moral quality of the sort liberals and libertarians pride themselves on; it was more on the order of a mania, the cracked antithesis of bigotry.[78]

Apart from Coleman's fervent desire "to be neither this nor that but something in between," the writer does not delve very deeply into his subject's decision to flout "officialdom" on race relations and liberal morality.[79] Rather, Zuckerman transfers Coleman's historically contradictory behavior onto the "clever, furtively rebellious" Iris and her (as she reportedly portrays them) "anarchist" parents: "two uneducated immigrant atheists who spat on the ground when a rabbi walked by."[80] With this narrative sleight of hand, transposing contrary cultural practices onto the woman whom Coleman chooses to marry (and her "non-Jewish Jewish" family), Zuckerman adapts passing as a narrative strategy to avoid explaining the motivational contours of Coleman's decision. Further, and more importantly, this narrative elision also allows Zuckerman to merge practical and economic factors that may have also been linked to Coleman's ultimate decision to racially pass, and to which *The Human Stain* also passively alludes.

Compellingly, even the text's faint allusions to the practical or economic dimensions of Coleman's decision are *also* conjoined to women in his life. For instance, five months before meeting Iris Gittelman and deciding to disown his birth family, Coleman becomes involved with Ellie Magee, "a petite, shapely colored girl, tawny-skinned" who goes out with both "white NYU guys" and "colored NYU guys," as both "are drawn to her."[81] Like Coleman, she is an African American who allows others to presume that she is white as circumstances suit her.[82] According to Zuckerman's account, Ellie's "naturalness" and "ease" provide Coleman with a non-threatening relation in which he can also be "natural" himself.[83] Zuckerman claims that Ellie is the first woman with whom Coleman feels he can be himself; and so much so, in fact, "that one night the truth [about his being African American] just comes bubbling out" and the "utterly unnarrow-minded" girl is not only unfazed, she is unsurprised.[84] Within the four narrative pages that Zuckerman allots to Coleman's presumed affair with Ellie, readers (like Zuckerman's imaginary, young Coleman) may believe that "she's a contender, this one."[85] Her "ease and lively innocence" remind Coleman of his first love, Steena Paulsson; only Ellie is not white, and therefore, Zuckerman relates, Coleman does not feel the need to bring her home to meet his family (as he had with Steena) "and they don't go visiting hers," either.[86]

This point is troubling for its allusion to the casualness with which Zuckerman depicts Coleman proceeding—without compunction—in his affair with Ellie, as opposed to the stricter conduct to which he holds himself in Steena's company earlier on. Furthermore, Zuckerman also does not mention Coleman being in love with Ellie, nor does the writer present Coleman as considering a future with her, as he had with Steena (and soon will with Iris Gittelman). While Ellie provides occasion for Coleman to consider life lived between the borders that separate black and white in America, the context in which Coleman receives this lesson (i.e., among the bars and shops of Greenwich Village, "the four freest square miles in America") only serves to render the enterprise shallow and grotesque, according to Zuckerman.[87] Thus, when Coleman meets Iris, he quickly decides to move on from Ellie because, as Zuckerman puts it: "Iris gives more. She raises everything to another pitch. Iris gives him his life on the scale he wants to live it," the narrator reports.[88]

Although the nature of the "pitch" and "scale" that Iris provides is not described by Zuckerman, her merits are related in terms of the different conditions (compared to Ellie) that a long-term relationship with her would provide:

> Some dimension is missing [with Ellie]. The whole thing lacks ambition—it fails to feed that conception of himself that's been driving him all his life. Along comes Iris and he's back in the ring. [...] [He has] the gift to be secretive again [...] It was fun [with Ellie]. But insufficiently everything else.[89]

Zuckerman's narration leads readers to presume that Ellie affords Coleman opportunity to "play" his racial identity any way he likes, becoming the audacious man par excellence, for 1951, unabashedly romancing a racially ambiguous woman. However, as Zuckerman tells it, with Ellie, Coleman is merely "racially cross-dressing," to use Freedman's verbiage, rather than manifesting his radical (if nebulous) conception of "anarchist" "self-freedom."[90] That is, partnered with Ellie, Coleman appears as a white man inhabiting a role in order to gain privileged access to the libidinal freedom with which his 1950s white, male contemporaries apparently associated blackness: "The guys he knows from school all think he's taking out a colored girl," Zuckerman reports, whom Coleman proudly tells them is "hot."[91]

The "dimension" and "ambition" that Coleman's brief affair with Ellie purportedly lacks, however, are left unexplained by Zuckerman; during their brief acquaintanceship, Zuckerman does not report the men discussing a young woman named Ellie Magee whom Coleman dated before marrying Iris, and she is not mentioned in the novel's late conversation with Ernestine. For all intents and purposes, Coleman's four-page, "five-month interlude" named Ellie is an invention of Nathan Zuckerman's imagination, potentially applied for a strategic, narrative purpose; key to this consideration is not whether Ellie truly existed in Coleman's youth, but what her invention within Zuckerman's representation of Coleman's life might imply. Zuckerman's rendering of Coleman's Ellie affair is defined, on the one hand, by the pleasure it provides in "playing the ambiguity" of their appearances in public and, on the other, by her unceremonious disposal with the introduction of Iris (despite Ellie once being a "contender"). Through this reversal, the writer represents Coleman's conception of his identity as unmoral and divergent from official theories like Myrdal's on race and racism in the early 1950s.[92] Furthermore, this sequence (particularly as it is likely fabricated) also suggests that Zuckerman himself does not conceive identity as linked to individual morality. Further, as he is Coleman's author and contemporary (approximately six years Coleman's junior, p. 10), Zuckerman's deviation from Myrdal's official mood on race and racism in this period is particularly significant; it suggests that (whatever the race of the individual in question) a good sense of attentiveness to issues of race and racism in social contexts is (or *was*, c. Coleman's early 1950s) *neither* an individual nor a *moral* process for many Americans, as Gunnar Myrdal suggests in *American Dilemma*.

According to the morally directed individual focus suggested in Myrdal's analysis, remaining with Ellie Magee and eventually introducing her to his family *would* have been the appropriate choice for Coleman to make. However, speculating about Coleman's choices otherwise (i.e., as a counterpoint to Ernestine's perspective) constructs for Zuckerman an intimate (and, indeed, privileged) proximity through which readers may become immersed in a reconstruction of Coleman's psychic space. In so doing, Zuckerman suggests that this space is home to the cause of Coleman's desire: an agile state of "raw I," divorced from any "coercive, inclusive, historically inescapable moral we" for which he restlessly strives.[93] Thus, Coleman's various love affairs become Zuckerman's means for entering into this psychic space, so he may narratively hypothesize how this desire experientially manifests in his subject's life.

For instance, Zuckerman's rendition of Coleman's affair with Steena Paulsson appears in the novel long after Coleman's own brief mention of her to Zuckerman over a game of cards early on in the novel. Importantly, in the early scene in which Coleman discusses Steena, the conclusion of their three-year romance is not brought up; however, in Zuckerman's reconstruction, this end is presented as abrupt and potentially traumatic. Injected into Zuckerman's rendition of Coleman's life with renewed significance, the end of this relationship denotes Coleman's acceptance, signifying the historical moment's problematically concrete and necessarily oppositional relation between black and white. After meeting Coleman's mother and Ernestine and spending what seems like a pleasant Sunday afternoon in East Orange, Steena does "not phone him or try ever to see him again."[94] Without explanation, she "raced alone from the train as though from an attacker"; and an inexpressive Coleman is left alone on the emptying commuter rail, holding Steena's forgotten hat.[95]

The year of the breakup is 1950, and the matter-of-fact tone with which Zuckerman relates Coleman's reaction to the relationship's end transmits it as *given* in the context of its occurrence: "I can't do it [Steena said]. There was a kind of wisdom in that, an awful lot of wisdom for a young girl, not the kind one ordinarily has at only twenty."[96] According to Zuckerman, Steena is only able to maintain closeness with Coleman insofar as she is able to misrecognize him as white, like herself; once that "fairy tale" is shattered by the concrete reality of his parentage, there can be no turning back. Steena's leaving Coleman brings to readers' attention the apriority of whiteness as a concrete position—although, once again, Zuckerman demurs from delving any further into this idea.

Steena's sudden reaction to Coleman's identity denotes an abstract dimension at work in Zuckerman's conception of whiteness, as well. The issue of race, thus, enters Coleman and Steena's relationship as a generic disruption, an element unassimilable to Steena's conception of social normativity. That is, according to Zuckerman, Coleman's racial identity confronts Steena with the reality of her own desire, which is rooted in an image of powerful, *a priori* whiteness. Steena may not be aware of her own creative desire, which generates an image of a white Coleman; however, despite being born of her imagination, or a "fairy tale," this desire is nevertheless real in Zuckerman's rendering and therefore all the more upsetting to Steena.

Through Coleman's idealized relationship with Steena, Zuckerman carefully probes the simultaneously concrete and ideological bases of racial identity, as her unconscious desire and its power are not merely ramified by her skin tone, but in the ways she inhabits her body at specific, intimate moments with Coleman. Freedman speaks to the emergence of desire and "the power of her whiteness" in such moments, discussing a scene in which Steena sings and dances for Coleman to "a black man's version of a Jewish man's version of a black-inspired musical idiom": Artie Shaw's rendition of "The Man I Love," featuring Roy Eldridge on the trumpet.[97] "Prompted by a colored trumpet player playing it like a black torch song," Steena's impromptu, "slithery" dance and evocative crooning make immediately visible for Coleman "[t]hat big, white thing."[98] Her performance, Freedman notes, is another example of "racial cross-dressing": addressing, at once, "the Jewish accession to whiteness via blackface minstrelsy" and a white person's enactment of "a black role in order to access for her or himself the libidinal freedom stereotypically associated with 'blackness'" (not unlike Coleman in his brief affair with Ellie Magee).[99] Following the performance, Steena hides her face, "half meaning, half pretending to cover her shame" for this explicit, and apparently transgressive, display of her body.[100] The power of Steena's whiteness thus lies in her ability to inhabit this other idiom, enacting a momentary freedom from the image of power which drives her attachment to Coleman. And while the power of her whiteness becomes clear to Coleman, as does her desire, through this performance he adores her all the more: she is powerful, she desires him, and Coleman seems to want nothing more than to inhabit the parallel, powerful image of himself in which Steena is invested.

However, it is this very imaginative desire, attended by an unsettlingly concrete reality, that ultimately drives Steena away, teaching Coleman (as Zuckerman tells it) a hard lesson about the "accidental" nature of "fate" when one is black "or, how accidental it all may seem when it is inescapable."[101] Coleman's fate is presented as accidental here because, as a black American in the 1950s, he represents a stereotypical idiom of transgression: Steena's reaction shows Coleman that *he* is that which inspires Steena to cover her face after "The Man I Love" ends. Zuckerman's reconstruction alludes to the fact that this is likely so unsettling for Steena because all the while, she had presumed Coleman's particular display (though this is not explicitly narrated) to be, like her own, an intimate performance. And more importantly, the account that readers find—of Steena's dance, of the Sunday with Coleman's family, and her swift departure—is Zuckerman's fabrication (as Ernestine barely speaks on this subject, either). By constructing Steena's chapter in Coleman's life in this way, the writer implicitly (and rather perceptively) aligns himself with Steena, insofar as both are duped by Coleman's secret. But more presciently, Zuckerman uses the Steena's affair to highlight its effects on Coleman's competence; in Zuckerman's reconstruction, this relationship's contingency and instability (while reportedly unsurprising) inspire Coleman to search for a new sense of individuality that stipulates breaking with his family and community—elements of his identity that are linked to the loss of Steena.

Thus, despite the fact that Ellie reportedly made Coleman feel that his "fate" was no longer "inescapable" (as it had felt with Steena), Zuckerman's narrative necessitates his leaving her following the loss of Steena, so as to fulfill the (uncannily ideological and non-material) motivational schema (i.e., unmoral, individualist) that the writer has defined for Coleman. According to Zuckerman, Coleman is open about his racial identity with Ellie; and in doing so, he finds "all his relief" and suddenly feels "like a boy again."[102] While being with Ellie helps Coleman to find reassurance in his ability to successfully inhabit whiteness *and* regain "his innocence," Zuckerman reports, Coleman nevertheless quickly decides: "What use is innocence?"[103] While the Ellie interlude is reaffirming, it cannot affect Coleman's attachment to conventional (read: white) conceptions of autonomous individuality. In the end, Ellie inspires in Coleman a revelation somewhat like Steena's, when she learns that Coleman is black: that is, the attention that Ellie and Coleman receive when they are out, and the interested lines of questioning from his colleagues at New York University, demonstrates for Coleman that he has come to fully inhabit an image of whiteness.

His relationship with Ellie thus plays a very similar role in Zuckerman's narrative as Steena's dance to "The Man I Love." This construction is troubling as it presumes that Ellie constitutes little more than play-acting, or performance for Coleman: entertaining, but not sustainable in a permanent way. Like Steena's dance (and Faunia's much later), Zuckerman's vision of Coleman's affair with Ellie Magee thus problematically represents a self-indulgent performance of power by his protagonist. While Zuckerman's narration does not level judgment against Coleman for any of his relationships, it is important to note that Coleman's affair with Ellie is constructed, presented, and disposed of in a manner similar to that which Delphine Roux presumes of his relationship with Faunia in her (alleged) antagonistic, anonymous letter. In this way, Zuckerman compellingly aligns his vision of Coleman with the callous, chauvinistic depiction for which he originally credits Delphine Roux's anonymous letter.

After Coleman resigns from Athena, he ostracizes himself from the community and begins a secretive affair with Faunia, who works at the College as part of the custodial staff. With the additional exception of his brief acquaintanceship with Zuckerman, Coleman supposedly associates with no one else in their Massachusetts town. By taking these rather drastic steps to separate himself from society, Zuckerman presumes that Coleman is trying forge a sense of autonomy configured around a fantasy of social and material disregard—not unlike he claims of himself. It is thus due to his protagonist's apparently reasoned, social self-exile that Zuckerman presumes that, besides the symbolic Ellie Magee, Faunia Farley is the woman to whom Coleman reveals his racial identity. However, of this, readers cannot be certain, as Zuckerman makes this deduction when he runs into Coleman and Faunia one summer evening at a rehearsal for the Boston Symphony Orchestra. At this mid-point in the novel, readers learn that Coleman has inexplicably stopped returning Zuckerman's calls and has disconnected his answering machine. Zuckerman reasons that, since his trip to the dairy farm where Faunia works for free room and board (to which Coleman invited him to watch her milk the cows), "the last thing [Coleman] now wanted" was "permitting this [...] writer to nose around in his private life"—"dropping me in the middle of that summer made sense for every possible reason, even if [at the time] I had no way of imagining why."[104]

Encountering Coleman and Faunia at the concert, and pondering their serenity—"I found them looking nothing like so unusual or humanly isolated as I'd been coming to envision"—Zuckerman is reportedly struck by a pivotal moment that forces him to reevaluate Coleman:

> I sat on the grass, astonished, unable to account for what I was thinking: he has a secret. [...] Why a secret? Because it is there when he's with her. And when he is not with her it is there too [...]. There is a blank. [...] a blotting out, an excision, though of what I can't begin to guess [...]. Faunia alone knew how Coleman Silk had come about being himself. How do I know she knew? I don't. I couldn't know that either. I can't know. [...] For better or worse, I can only do what everyone does who thinks that they know. I imagine. I am forced to imagine.[105]

At the concert, Coleman and Zuckerman have a brief exchange, from which Coleman and Faunia are rather quick to depart; in the resulting moment, Zuckerman finds himself encased in an intense present. With the line, "I can only do what everyone does who thinks they know," Zuckerman recalls Delphine's anonymous letter, which begins with the foreboding phrase: "Everyone knows ...."[106] Furthermore, in sensing that Coleman harbors a secret which only Faunia knows, Zuckerman also implicitly calls attention to his earlier reconstructions of the relationships with Steena and (the likely imaginary) Ellie. In this converging moment of interwoven perspectives (i.e., narrating-Zuckerman colliding with experiencing-Zuckerman), Roth's ghost writer deftly entices readers along the path of existential assumptions that essentially underlie narrative creation.

Zuckerman thus calls readers' attention not to merely his own unreliability as Coleman's biographer, but to the necessarily impossible set of conditions that comprise the narrative act. Zuckerman's initial image of Coleman (as possessing a particularly conscientious, hard-nosed dean-of-faculty charm) is despoiled as soon as Coleman speaks to the notion of himself as a lover. To the very end of the novel, following his brief exchange at the symphony rehearsal, the image of Coleman the lover (and the privileges this relation affords the women he loves) is replayed again at Coleman's grave site after a conversation with Ernestine:

> I began by wondering what it had been like when Coleman had told Faunia the truth about that beginning—assuming that he ever had [...] Assuming that what he could not outright say to me on the day he burst in all but shouting, "Write my story, damn you!" [...] he could not in the end resist confessing to her [...] the first and last person since Ellie Magee for whom he could strip down and turn around so as to expose [...] the mechanical key by which he had wound himself up to set off on this great escapade.[107]

Folding the narrative back some two hundred pages to recall Coleman's brief "interlude" with Ellie, Zuckerman calls attention to the discord among Coleman's various identities: the (passing for) Jewish Coleman known to the Athena College community, the sentimental and optimistic Coleman known to Ernestine, and Zuckerman's own mistaken image of Coleman as "one of those crimp-haired Jews." Once again unable to square the contradictions inherent to his protagonist, Zuckerman ultimately decides that Coleman, in the role of a lover (beyond his secret), is the most authentic image of his subject that he is able to render.

Importantly, however, this is an image of Coleman Silk to which neither Ernestine or Delphine Roux is privy; like Zuckerman, neither has access to the intimacy which *The Human Stain* dissembles via numerous flashbacks to Coleman's early life. Ironically, however, these are also the only women from Coleman's life to whom Zuckerman has any reasonable access, particularly following Coleman's (and Faunia's) death. Because of the inconvenience of Zuckerman's context, for his construction of Coleman's passing narrative to *work*, the writer must strike a contrast between himself and these women; thus, he emphasizes Ernestine's and Delphine's perspectival distances from Coleman by chasms of time and space, while creatively amplifying (through the imaginative, narrative inclusions of Steena, Ellie, and Faunia) a sense, throughout the narrative, of Zuckerman's own closeness with his subject. By incorporating data from and on Delphine and Ernestine in *The Human Stain*, but nevertheless keeping their impressions of Coleman at a narrative distance from his own vision, Zuckerman attempts to reveal, through Coleman's intimacies, how shifting relations between imaginative constructions (psychic, discursive) and blunt materialities shapes the bases of human life—beyond the racial identities that concern Delphine or Ernestine. According to Zuckerman's formulation, then, beyond identifications (whether familial, communal, etc.) is the subject's interior psychic space; and as this is home to the subject's most intimate desires, only the most intimate *Other* (an oxymoron in itself) may begin to perceive the subject as a *Self*, whole in its un-cohesiveness. Zuckerman assigns this pinnacle position of intimacy to the unlikely Faunia Farley, Coleman's final lover.

However, particularly within the conventions of the passing genre, Zuckerman's calculation of Coleman's character via his intimacies with white women—and particularly, at last, Faunia—is not without its deep historical implications. Coleman and Faunia perish in a car accident together under mysterious circumstances only months after their affair initiates; with this event, Zuckerman imagines Coleman's death to be (not absurd or accidental, as in Silko's *Almanac* or other of Zuckerman's texts, but) as an anti-Semitic hate crime by Faunia's husband, a severely PTSD-inflicted war veteran.[108] Faunia's husband, Lester Farley, is a stranger to Zuckerman and readers directly meet him only once, in the novel's closing scene; yet, well in advance of this meeting, Zuckerman reasons that Lester commits the double murder out of rage over his wife leaving him for "a two-bit kike professor."[109] This hunch compels Zuckerman, who then seeks affirmation of his suspicion in conversations with those he sees or meets at Faunia and Coleman's funerals.

For instance, just before his chance meeting with Ernestine, Zuckerman discloses that Coleman's adult sons, Jeffrey and Michael Silk, are not amused by Zuckerman's apparently sudden, postmortem interest in their father:

> They let me know that I was to knock it off: to forget about […] the circumstances of the accident and about urging any further investigation by the police. They could not have made clearer that their disapproval would be

boundless if their father's affair with Faunia Farley were to become the focal point of a courtroom trial instigated by my importuning.[110]

Interestingly, the caretaker of Faunia's father (whom Zuckerman accosts outside of a local diner) has a similarly repellent reaction to the writer's inquiries; and once again, as he assumes of Coleman's rejection of his friendship, Zuckerman attributes the behavior of Coleman's eldest son and the hostility of Faunia's father's caretaker to his being a writer. Although implicit to the novel's narrative action, Zuckerman's late series of difficulties in cobbling together his narrative speculations constitute an important signal to readers: since about the nineteenth century, the "tragic mulatto trope" has been a popular one among white American novelists, including Harriet Beecher Stowe, Mark Twain, and George W. Cable.[111] However, like the act of passing itself, its unacceptability is echoed in post-1925 (and post-Harlem Renaissance) African American-authored narratives of passing, via these characters' inevitably tragic ends.[112]

Zuckerman's choice for Coleman's end, however, may be read as a bit more obscure—or, at the very least, more divided—than such conventional formulations of the passing genre's protagonist. For instance, one potential, with-the-grain reading of Coleman's death is precisely as Zuckerman speculates: that is, his subject was mistakenly "killed as a Jew."[113] This reading, interestingly, recalls fictional passers of *pre*-Harlem Renaissance literature, who were, as M. Guilia Fabi notes in *Passing and the Rise of the African American Novel* (2004), "rarely tragic figures"; moreover, she adds (much like Zuckerman proposes of Coleman) "when tragedy [would] befall them, it is most clearly indicated to be the result of virulent prejudice and discrimination."[114] The detachment of the passing character from association with tragedy neatly delinks their choice to race travel from moral issues around racial identity via solidarity; in Coleman's case, however, this unmoral storyline would be difficult for Zuckerman to carry to its conclusion, as his subject's experiences in passing transcend the moral imperatives with which many American anti-racist discourses were inflected in the first half of the twentieth century.

Because Coleman's passing continues into the 1990s and collides with President Clinton's deflective formulation of racism as a problem of America's past, Zuckerman must *also* leave this line of depiction (e.g., framing Coleman as a victim of anti-Semitism) open to readers' own speculations and interpretations.[115] Thus, the resistance that Zuckerman faces as he attempts to uncover details about Lester's nefarious involvement in Coleman and Faunia' deaths signals Zuckerman's flawed calculations about (not only the couple's affair, but) Coleman and Faunia as victims of discrimination during the late 1990s. Because Coleman dies during a historical moment in which racism is framed as so many "racial differences" that may be dialogically resolved, the Silk family's consideration of Coleman's death as foul-play becomes a moot, and likely also painful, point (from Jeff and Michael's point of view) because neither Coleman or Lester is present to confer, and such a conclusion would reduce the memory of the already-deceased Iris (their mother) in relation to her husband, Coleman.

This construction of racism, while appropriate to *The Human Stain*'s narrative present, is also fascinating, on the one hand, for its elision of the *a priori* position of whiteness in its presumption that racism has been "solved."[116] On the other hand, this construction also compels, due to its *inability* to incorporate a notion of systemic, extant racisms that cannot reliably be tracked via citizens' explicit behaviors or practices. Moreover, the anti-Semitic and classist circumstances with which Zuckerman associates Faunia and Coleman's deaths reflect the writer's *own* fears around mortality—in particular, Zuckerman's long-standing fears concerning the potentially violent capabilities of others.[117] Indeed, Zuckerman's readers discover in *Exit Ghost* (2007) that this is the writer's reason for relocating to the Berkshire Mountains from Manhattan in 1993, two years before the cancer diagnosis that readers discover in *The Human Stain*.[118]

In this way, Coleman's death *reminds* Zuckerman of his own, fear-based (i.e., irrational) rationale for relocating to the woods of New England; and although Zuckerman's narration is unclear about whether Coleman discusses Lester Farley with the writer, the writer's decision to perceive Lester as Coleman's killer and delink Coleman's depiction from moral trespass speaks to his impulse to create meaning from a life's otherwise untold (and perhaps unspeakable) elements, as Zuckerman applies only vague impressions and the writer's (not Coleman's) perspectives on them. However, because of the generally (if passively) racialized nature of Zuckerman's vision of the late 1990s (particularly as depicted through Athena's reaction to Coleman's "locution"), it becomes difficult for readers to stably link the novel's vision of late-century conceptions of race and racism to *either* morality or amorality. The moral indecision with which Zuckerman thus leaves readers at the end of *The Human Stain* signals (not only all actors' participation in racist structures and discourses, but) the troublingly instrumental role of generalized racism in the formation of characters *besides* Coleman.

Thus, via Coleman's relationships with women, Roth directs Zuckerman to expose both the virtues and the dangers of identification, however conceived: while its intent may be euphemistic or optimistic, identification is nevertheless formed around perceived threats to an ideal (or, to use Ernestine's terminology, a "fairy tale") of both society and the self, that it works to uphold. In this way, Roth asks readers to consider the kind of creative life (whether collective or individual) that may be, if a *meaningful* existence were not bound to a necessarily polemical narrative.

Conclusion: Toward Renewing Readers' Experiences of American Novels

The Cold War novels that I read (*Franny and Zooey* and *The Flagellants*) articulate a renewed understanding of ideology's demise as its qualitative transformation through numerous vectors of American culture. This altered understanding of ideology's end, these novels show, may aid readers (of American histories and literatures) in perceiving precisely *how* the lives and potentials of certain Americans can be subtly and gradually limited by means one might not initially realize to be ideological: that is, via advertising copy, social and cultural criticism, commissions documents, etc.—*and* in the virtual absence of these Americans' awareness or consent. Rather than focusing on the political conditions or outcomes of their characters' worlds, Salinger's and Polite's Cold War narratives hone in on the effects of ideology's transformations on characters' families, social relationships, and career prospects.

In this way, the novels read in Chapters 1 and 2 themselves function in manners that are similar to the hermeneutics of *critique*: subtly aligning their contentious main characters with various histories of *resistance* (e.g., second-wave feminisms, nationalist discourses). As such, these novels interrogate their worlds' given values, expose their flawed beliefs, and reveal their corrupt systems. Yet, the types of ideological critique that occur in Salinger's and Polite's Cold War-era texts (while compellingly descriptive and reminiscent of today's modes of literary critique) nevertheless fail to articulate any alternative(s) to the values-based (i.e., ideological) issues they purport to expose. Indeed, however, articulations of alternative values may not necessarily be the *point* or objective of the novels' expressions (much as articulating alternative ideologies is not the *point* of ideological literary critique). Nevertheless, this narrative *and* critical blindness to alternatives are significant, particularly in the context of the Cold War.[1]

When readers meet Franny, Ideal, and others, the Cold War is a silent, non-event that accumulates in the backgrounds of their lives: it constitutes a variety of creeping forces generating normalized atmospheres of intolerance (i.e., inequality, exploitation, and injustice) and despair. After all, both *Franny and Zooey* and *The Flagellants* end with characters stagnating in their unsatisfactory circumstances; and by extension, readers are left to speculate (or moralize about) under *what* conditions (*how* or *when*) the characters' lives could possibly improve. In the absence of posited alternatives to the private and public conditions faced by Salinger's and Polite's characters, both Cold War novels close with Franny, Zooey, Ideal, and Jimson indefinitely embedded in the rounds of their variously uncomfortable lives. In this way, *no actual change*, it seems, may be expected by or from the endings of *either* novel. And this is largely because in both *Franny and Zooey* and *The Flagellants*, characters are depicted as, at once, paradoxically responsible for their "substandard" lives *and* inadvertently entangled with autonomous, ramifying forces that adversely affect them (e.g., social and legal responses to their gender, income level, age, race, marital status). As a result, both novels' atmospheres and settings impart demoralized senses of well-being on the main characters, making space for *unfocused desire* (specifically configured as *problematic lack*) to take root in them, and to register with readers.

Yet, neither Salinger's stories nor Polite's novel offers readers any advice for avoiding the dread stalemates of unfocused desire. This construction of character uncannily embodies the double-edged nature of America's Cold War discourses on *freedom* (i.e., *from* and *to*). No alternatives exist for characters like Franny, Ideal, or Jimson toward understanding their worlds or their places therein (and by extension, readers are *also* not offered alternative ways to imagine the characters' lives). This chillingly apropos, sweeping representational irony, inheres to *both* Cold War narratives that I read in this study, echoing the era's no-alternative, either-or political logic.

However, to settle on such a resigned interpretation would itself constitute a telling, ideological move—merely describing, and then enacting, the ensnarement depicted as the narratives' ends. Instead, I read in Salinger's and

Polite's precarious endings, representational *traps* (or, distortions), that the writers have set for their readers. These traps delineate—not only the novels' contexts amid the Cold War, but also—precisely how the novels will interact with (and find interpretation via) critical hermeneutics that out-last the Cold War. Apropos of the Cold War's defensive stance toward ideological consensus, the novels' internal engagements with histories of resistance do *not* aid their contentious main characters in breaking free from their unsatisfactory conditions. Rather, these traps are cobbled from the images, arguments, and advice that populate the main characters' lives; in effect, the novels' endings read as culminations of readers' distorted experiences of narrative reality (or, realism), which mirrors the ensnarement (via bewildering distortion) of the novels' main characters. This is a dread fate that savvy American readers may (somehow) avoid, although the novels do not disclose how. Thus, interpreting Salinger's and Polite's narratives as hinged on their contentious characters' *inabilities* to hone in on (and then successfully pursue) specific ambitions is also problematic.[2] That is, positing Salinger's Franny, and Polite's Ideal (and/or Jimson) as troublesomely immature, difficult, or unambitious amounts to limiting incomplete assessments that ironically recall postwar disciplines of defining reality according to symbolic, polarizing standards (e.g., Red or dead, good versus evil).

Consider, for instance, the depiction of communism imparted to *Life Magazine*'s (perhaps unlikely) readership by John Foster Dulles in 1946. In his two-part article, "Soviet Foreign Policy and What to Do about It," Dulles outlines the basic doctrines of the Soviet Communist Party (i.e., the concept of "one world" and or *Pax Sovietica*) as constituted by an ideological consensus that re-imagines (or, distorts) important policy principles such as democracy, the definitions of fascism, and "friendly" foreign governments.[3] Dulles's focused interpretation of this common enemy as conniving and totalitarian presumes an understanding of how that enemy might be vanquished: that is, via its own methods, sustained ideological consensus (however forced or coerced). Taken to its end, this understanding of necessary, defensive American ideological consensus would read circumstances like those faced by Franny, Ideal, or Jimson as of their own making; that is, evidence of their individual failures to assimilate the correct ideological cause or perspective (an arguably broad and dispassionate stance to take on the characters' diverse personal struggles). Likewise, Dulles's article charged *Life*'s readership with correctly recognizing the postwar moment as an imminent ideological threat. The struggle between godless totalitarianism and the United States' righteous, god-fearing democracy is thus re-imagined (or, distorted) by Dulles to read as a necessary, moral struggle between good and evil; this duality would be recovered near the end of the Cold War, during the 1980s, by President Ronald Reagan.

However, Dulles' proposed moral and ideological (i.e., *freedom from*) crusade sharply contrasts with the *material* image of freedom (i.e., *freedom to*) that was customarily showcased across the pages of *Life Magazine*, and many other popular and ephemeral media of the time. Of this point, Andrew Bacevich notes:

> Bracketing Dulles's call to arms were ads for facial soap, shampoo, hair oil, mouthwash, cosmetics, deodorant, cologne, and other personal products. [...] Other ads touted the latest in nylon stockings, women's undergarments, swimwear, and men's shirts that were "handkerchief soft" while "richly-masculine."[4]

The brand of proto-self-entrepreneurship (i.e., where one may purchase the trappings of an abundant American life) featured in *Life*'s advertising copy harkens to the slightly later, self-help-oriented discourses of 1950s and 1960s women's service magazines. In both instances, popular and mass-oriented visions of American lives are based in difficult-to-define qualities of *choice* (i.e., a brand of *freedom to*). Thus, while various official (e.g., academic and federal) and often anti-populist channels championed American exceptionalism, Christian morality, and the power of focused hard work, much of the messaging found in mass advertising copy organized and broke these values down into, what appears to be, their material building blocks (i.e., into various products). However, as many like Ideal and Jimson well knew, the material elements of plentiful, postwar American life (however purportedly virtuous) were not accessible to all, and particularly *not* during the forty-plus years that constituted the Cold War.

As *Life Magazine* advertised Omega watches and Franny Glass attended college, non-professional wages in America stagnated; Richard Nixon disgraced the American presidency; key figures in civil freedom struggles were assassinated or imprisoned; and "urban disorders," including police brutality, continued relatively unabated. And while critical and scholarly heterogeneity abounded in the now-various areas of American humanities, the Cold War's many anxieties (often described, as in Dulles's piece, as the totalitarian threat, nuclear destruction, etc.) weighed heavily on most Americans residing beyond the insular and privileged academy. Thus, for many in America, the end of the Cold War perhaps could or *should* have marked an important occasion for remorse and/or restitution (even if only in the realm of ideas). Instead, however (as discussed in Chapter 3), the Cold War's end was *greeted with fanfare*: democratic capitalism, globalization, and global leadership had prevailed. In the years immediately after the Cold War, between the Reagan and first Bush administrations (1989–91), it almost seemed as if the promise of postwar American abundance might *finally* become the legacy of *every American citizen*.

However, the individualism and ambition associated with the post–Cold War generated a blindness to a tension that is built into democratic capitalism. Here, there is an innate tension between *individual freedom* (e.g., the material abundance implied by late capitalism's risk society) and the *common good*—or, various objective apparatuses (such as infrastructure) that regulate, transport, and/or otherwise support the general well-being of a country's populations. The individualism and ambition associated with triumphant, post–Cold War late-capitalist society are sharply at odds with the logic of *common good*. Such mechanisms and apparatuses are constituted by shared services and/or spaces; they are *not* constructed with the goal of generating a return (or prestige) for investors and stakeholders. Leslie Marmon Silko's *Almanac of the Dead* (1991) deftly recreates the difficulties of this tension-blindness, via her novel's sweeping cast of variously disaffected, self-interested characters. Similarly, Philip Roth's *The Human Stain* echoes this obliviousness to these contradictions via Zuckerman's oddly color-blind (i.e., a purported universal, *common good*), but identity politics-infused (i.e., or race-conscious and individualist) rendition of Coleman Silk's passing narrative.[5]

Moreover, unlike the texts I engage in Chapters 1 and 2, the post–Cold War narratives featured in Chapters 3 and 4 do not *earnestly* align their primary characterizations with histories of resistance. Rather, a brand of *cynical*, narrative lip-service is paid to revolutionary ideas, such as postcolonial Marxian or Civil Rights thought. This occurs through empty narrative events and gestures that ultimately amount to nothing, such as: Angelita's execution of Bartolomeo in *Almanac of the Dead*; or, *The Human Stain*'s oddly late introduction of Ernestine Silk (and by extension, activist, Walter Silk) into Zuckerman's portrait of Coleman. Purportedly radical or groundbreaking acts are woven into the narratives, such as Coleman's untimely passing or Clinton's involvement in the Homeless Army, but only for their preparations to fall flat, availing nothing (much like Angelita's and Lecha/Zeta's proposed revolutions). Thus, not only do the post–Cold War novels of Chapters 3 and 4 refuse non-cynical alignment with critical hermeneutics that might expose (and/or offer correctives to) the ideological inconsistencies in their respective worlds, these novels *also* refuse any pretense of sustainable alternatives to their worlds' de jure systems and practices. In this way, the Cold War fantasy of actual, concrete, and permanent change is *not* innocently entertained in the post–Cold War. Instead, processes of making change to the circumstances of one's life are understood as individual, high-risk, and indefinite performances that are not necessarily guaranteed to yield any real, sustainable satisfaction.

Nevertheless, in the worlds of *Almanac of the Dead* and *The Human Stain*, characters' abilities to alter the circumstances of their lives (however riskily or temporarily) figure as forms of *freedom* (specifically, *freedom to*). Yet, one important outcome of this individualistic, personalized understanding of freedom is the necessity of its perceived, yielded changes as being non-revolutionary. By design, these changes are tailored and personal (within specific parameters) and thus *not* constitutive of actual change, in the grand scheme. In effect, this understanding of freedom may read as a revenant of *unfocused desire*, and a testament to indictments like those made by Daniel Bell and Lionel Trilling in the 1950s and 1960s, which claim the need for an American cultural elite to guide the ignorant masses.

As Bell notes in "The Mood of Three Generations," the youth of the postwar United States were predisposed to pointless and arguably *unfocused* acts of rebellion and dissent; and importantly, this is *not* a point that Fukuyama would refute in the late 1980s and early 1990s. Thus, despite Fukuyama's claims that the ideological stimuli of historical progress had been exhausted by the end of the Cold War, his triumphant conception of a late-capitalist democratic brand of *freedom* nevertheless reads as softly cynical. In the cases of *Almanac* and *The Human Stain*, this cynicism stems from characters' persevering belief in *themselves* as heroes of their own stories; and it manifests as their preternatural willingness to opportunistically and ruthlessly navigate the scenes of their lives, with little true regard for others. The effect of this cynicism is comic-ironic (if often violent) in *Almanac of the Dead*, with its stable of seventy-plus self-important characters; and in *The Human Stain*, this cynicism reads as tragic, as Coleman's ultimate passing cannot clearly be interpreted as either heroic or righteous (no matter how or when Zuckerman depicts America).

Troublingly, according to these novels, this individualistic and cynical post–Cold War vision of freedom does *not* fully recognize itself as the costly illusion that it is; it is a cynicism that is blind to its own machinations. In *Almanac of the Dead*, for instance, readers encounter a striking variety of de jure cynicism in characters' general *freedoms* to choose among various *styles* of capitalism (i.e., neutralized revolutionary ideas, Marxist critiques, etc.), through which they may change and more deeply identify with their lives and work. However, in this formulation, the necessary domination of people's lives by capital reveals the illusory nature of this choice within the democratic society depicted (e.g., *Almanac*'s narrative present). As capital is so general and dominant, it functions beyond the reach of democratic processes, more often figuring as their impetus. As a result, the chaotic and ethically uncentered world of *Almanac* may be attributable to its long-standing domination by capital over people's motivations and movements. This variety of presumed, post–Cold War freedom thus operates to conceal various, concrete *unfreedoms* that encroach on characters' everyday lives; in *Almanac of the Dead*, characters' general vulnerability to *sorcery* signifies just one variety of seemingly inexplicable *unfreedom* that menaces them.

The concealment of *unfreedoms* with seemingly pervasive and permissive *freedoms to* constitutes a tricky, post–Cold War logic that also plays out (and perhaps a bit more clearly) in Philip Roth's *The Human Stain*. Within the novel's capitalist mid-century (i.e., Cold War) America, Coleman *chooses* to pass for white. This choice, as his sister Ernestine tells it, can be read on the one hand as a risky bid for *further freedoms*; on the other hand, however (in line with Coleman's brother, Walter Silk), Coleman's choice can *also* be historically situated as more insidious than Ernestine would believe. Whichever way Coleman's choice is read, the very existence of the concept of racial passage (in the world of *The Human Stain*) as a prospective *choice* Coleman could make immediately belies any *freedom* it would feign to bestow to those who select it. Although *freedom* is configured in Coleman's case as the *freedom to* live however he chooses, because his *choice* involves an ideological move that cements the very discriminatory and exploitative systems that he aims to subvert, Coleman's *choice* can, at best, be read as reactive (but certainly not as heroic): a reaction, perhaps, against various, unfulfilled postwar promises of American abundance. In this construction, the concept of *freedom* once again becomes a cynical one; the *freedom to* live and do as Coleman chooses is generally touted as positive. But sadly, the costs of (and collateral damages caused by) this *freedom* are only allotted the sparsest of narrative reflection by Zuckerman.

In a similar way, but on a smaller scale, Coleman is given the *freedom* to choose between Iris and Ellie for a future life-partner. However, because Coleman's *choice* is based on cynical (albeit imaginary, originating with Zuckerman) assumptions concerning Coleman's personal incentives, desires, and presumed grudges—his perceived *choice* between Ellie and Iris quickly dissolves into no choice at all. Indeed, readers may not be surprised that Coleman ultimately selects Iris for a partner. Yet, because the young Ellie Magee is so easily and brusquely eliminated from Zuckerman's reconstruction, an important but dangerous coldness inherent to (not only cynicism itself, but) de jure cynicism's blindness to itself becomes alarmingly clear. Indeed, Zuckerman's narrative decision to cut Ellie from *The Human Stain* may be read as functioning similarly to the merciless elimination of certain characters in the world of *Almanac of the Dead*: not only removing specific figures (Menardo, Bartolomeo, and others) from the narrative, but *freeing* those who answer to these figures (e.g., Tacho, Angelita, and their various forms of capital) for cooptation and use by still others. In the case of Ellie, Zuckerman crafts a compelling reversal: her removal from the storyline of *The Human Stain* frees up a second woman, who has been waiting in the wings—Iris Gittelman—to finally be absorbed by Coleman.

According to the Cold War texts explored here, during the Cold War, creative expressions of lives in America found much of their narrative bases (for better and worse) in characters' relationships within their small communities and/or family units (whether in a narrative's present, character's memory, etc.). And importantly, as discussed in the cases of *Franny and Zooey* and *The Flagellants*, running parallel to this narrative foundation is an underlying concern with the nature and quality of the education (or, upbringing) characters garner in the imperfect microcosms of family and town (particularly concerning the world beyond). While it may initially read as ironic that so few (if any) of the family's or town's snippets of counsel turn out to be sustainable for these characters, this perceived irony (a harbinger for cynicism) is precisely the expressive point intended: Ideal (like Franny *and* Jimson) is aware that the lessons of her past hobble her in the present. However, because these lessons originate with early preservers of her survival (however imperfect, for example, her great-grandmother), Ideal becomes unwittingly willing to deceive herself until, before readers know what has happened, she is "bowing" under the weight of her life on a daily basis. This configuration is costly and harsh for Ideal; further, it is miserably constructed in a manner quite similar to Franny Glass' association with her luxe, frivolity-signifying raccoon coat. For all intents and purposes, Ideal and Franny have made their *choices* in life—but these choices were mere illusions placed before them, not choices, at all.

Unlike the permissive (if easily predictable), self-interested *choices* made by characters in *Almanac* or *The Human Stain*, in *Franny and Zooey* and *Flagellants*, characters are not even granted the fantasy (or, to adopt Ernestine's verbiage, the "fairy tale") of believing they have created the lives they wish. They are only allowed the fantasy of what might *someday* come to be (if not for themselves, then for others). By contrast, in the post–Cold War texts I engage, readers may perceive a certain strain of radicality in characters' (albeit often resigned) ruthless honesty with themselves about the self-interested (i.e., distinctly non-communal and non-familial) nature of life in America. However, as readers may particularly see in the case of Coleman Silk, this perceived ruthless honesty becomes a lie, as it conveniently paves over the various *unfreedoms* it necessarily stipulates.

The work of literary interpretation need not take on the often contentious, socio-political task of outlining alternative beliefs, values, and so on, to those that may be found in Cold War and post–Cold War American novels (i.e., doing so could recast the Cold War fantasy of building an American cultural elite). Social constructivism is neither a practical nor wise companion to literary scholarship. Yet, rather than simply describing the novels' problematic value claims and purported beliefs, throughout *The American Novel After Ideology*, I have mined these novels' investments for information about the social, political, and broader cultural contexts in which they were written and initially received. Rather than stepping outside of history, reading each novel as an artifactual compendium of metaphorically resonant symbols, I work to hold the novels up to their specific historical contexts (as one holds a prism up to a window) toward reverse-engineering *how* the novels may have been shaped *by* those contexts. This begins to generate a historicization of each literary context (a kind of intellectual map) that surveys specific sets of social, political, and cultural conditions from which both critical *and* creative literary expressions emerge. Accordingly, rather than offering with my study some diagnostic of my fellow scholars' alleged disavowals or a symptomatic reading of some professional unconscious, *The American Novel After Ideology* simply asks readers of American novels to consider anew (beyond conventional *critique*) the effects of long-form fictional literatures within and upon the United States and its citizens.

Notes

Introduction

1. Fredric Jameson, *The Ideologies of Theory* (London: Verso, 2008): 5.
2. Ibid., 7.
3. See J. D. Salinger, *Franny and Zooey* (New York: Back Bay Books, 2001); as well as, Carlene Hatcher Polite, *The Flagellants* (New York: Farrar, Strauss & Giroux, 1967).
4. Rita Felski, *The Limits of Critique* (Chicago: Chicago University Press, 2015): 124. While I consider my concept of *interpretation* a close relative to Felski's *critique* (i.e., I read *interpretation* as a posited *product*, or outcome, of *critique*), my plan here is neither to *apply* nor to *critique* (pun intended) Felski's points on the fault-lines and pit-falls of *critique*. By and large, I agree with her assessments. Rather, in *American Novel after Ideology*, I develop a Felskian *postcritical* approach to interpreting American novels which engages not only the texts in question, but their contemporaneous receptions and intersections with various other cultural, social, and political forces.
5. Susan Sontag, "Against Interpretation," in *Against Interpretation and Other Essays* (New York: Picador, 1966): 3–14.
6. See Jameson, *Ideologies of Theory*, 7 & 9; and Sontag, "Against Interpretation," 3–5.
7. See Gerard A. Brandmeyer and R. Serge Denisoff, "Status Politics: An Appraisal of the Application of a Concept," in *Pacific Sociological Review* (Spring, 1969): 5–11.
8. Lionel Trilling, "Our Country and Culture," *Partisan Review* (19.3, 1952): 318–26.
9. See Mary McCarthy, "Characters in Fiction," in *On the Contrary* (New York: Noonday Press, 1962): 271–92.
10. McLuhan's thought anticipates the cultural consequences of technological innovation; importantly, the question of media as cliché (as explored in *Mechanical Bride*, c. 1951) expands in *Understanding Media* (1964) and *From*

Cliché to Archetype (1970), beyond the logical and linguistic to the pervasive and decentralized. Uncannily, Salinger was obliquely credited, by John Updike in a 1961 review of *Franny and Zooey*, for "seek[ing] the words for things transmuted into human subjectivity" (rprnt. in Grunwald, ed., 54). In "an age of nuance, of ambiguous gestures and psychological jockeying on a national and private scale," Updike writes, "Salinger's intense attention to gesture and intonation help make him, among the contemporaries, a uniquely pertinent literary artist" (54).

11 Janet Malcolm, "Justice for J. D. Salinger," *New York Review of Books* (48.10: June 21, 2001).

12 However, in contrast with Malcolm, I do not believe that either Salinger or *Franny and Zooey* has been permanently "relegated" to the margins of literary study by influencers like Kazin, Didion, and others. I do not believe critics— these or others, necessarily—would have wanted this fate for Salinger. This is a point I try to support in this essay, exploring aspects of *Franny and Zooey* that went unexamined by critics in its time (e.g., Franny's breakdown; her diverse narrative framings; and the important historical, cultural implications of the sections' individual narrative voices).

13 Noteworthy, critical articles on *Franny and Zooey* by contemporaries of Salinger include (to name only a few): Joan Didion, "Finally (Fashionably) Spurious"; Leslie Fielder, "Up from Adolescence"; Alfred Kazin, "Everybody's Favorite"; and John Updike, "Anxious Days for the Glass Family." All reprinted in: *Salinger: The Classical, Critical, and Personal Portrait*, ed. Henry Anatole Grunwald (New York: Harper, 2009).

14 Gordon Hutner, *What America Read: Taste, Class, and the Novel* (Chapel Hill: University of NC Press, 2009). According to Hutner, many literary critics at the time of *Franny and Zooey*'s release saw the integrity of literary achievement as threatened by "the middlebrow" (270). During the 1950s, "the middlebrow" emerged as a common term used to categorize mass American culture.

15 See Leslie Fielder, *Love and Death in the American Novel* (McLean, IL: Dalkey Archive Press, 1960): 289–90, 333.

16 Daniel Patrick Moynihan, *The Negro Family: The Case for National Action* (Washington: US Department of Labor, Office of Policy Planning and Research, 1965).

17 Interestingly, there are only two surviving, contemporary treatments of *The Flagellants* from BAM-era intellectuals. One is a mostly positive, if brief, review

by Nikki Giovanni (1968) (*Negro Digest* 17, January: 97–8). The second is a very brief mention of Polite in the book *From Apology to Protest*, by Noel Schraufnagel (1973), in which *The Flagellants* is referred to as a "disaster of accommodationism" (*From Apology to Protest: The Black American Novel* [DeLand: Everett/Edwards]: 121 and 129–30). Apart from this, *The Flagellants* seems to have only garnered passing, infrequent mention in BAM-era publications. Perhaps even more compelling, if problematic: the only American reviews made widely available for research scholars came from mainstream sources featuring reviews of the novel. These include a (mostly negative) review in *The American Scholar* by Roger Ebert, titled, "First Novels by Young Negroes," (Autumn 1967): 682–6; another (also negative) review in *Publishers Weekly* by Herbert Lottman, "Authors and Editors," (June 12, 1967): 20–1. In 1967, there was also a (scathing) piece published by Frederic Raphael in *The New York Times Book Review* ("Jimson and Ideal," June 11: 40); and a (mixed) review from Nora Sayre, which appeared in *The Nation* ("Punishing," October 9, 1967): 344.

As for scholarly engagements with the novel, only a handful were published after the novel's second printing, and all rely on a biographical reading to account for the novel's content and style. Of the five total articles published in peer-reviewed journals, three appeared together in the same journal issue (Newson 1992, "The Poet's Distance Achieved through a Parisian Sojourn; Carlene Hatcher Polite's The Flagellants," 22–6; Reid 1992, "Carlene Hatcher Polite and the French Connection," 32–7; and Worthington-Smith 1992, "Salvation of the African American Male; Carlene Hatcher Polite's Efforts in The Flagellants," 27–31—all included in MAWA Review 7.1). Of these, Reid and Worthington-Smith revised and/or expanded their original MAWA Review pieces for publication a second time (thus, the articles on The Flagellants totals 5). Worthington-Smith's revised article appeared in MAWA Review in 1993; and Reid's, in The Connecticut Review, 1996 (Spring 18.1, pp. 39–50).

18 Roger Ebert, "First Novels by Young Negroes," *The American Scholar* (Autumn, 1967): 682–6.
19 Nina Sayre, "Punishing," *The Nation* (October 9, 1967): 344.
20 See Ebert, "First Novels by Young Negroes," 684.
21 Madhu Dubey, *Black Women Novelists and the Nationalist Aesthetic* (Bloomington: Indiana University Press, 1994); Aldon Nielsen, *Black Chant: Languages of African American Post-Modernism* (New York: Cambridge University Press, 1997); James Edward Smethurst, *The Black Arts Movement:*

Literary Nationalism in the 1960s and 1970 (Chapel Hill: University of North Carolina Press, 2005); and Cynthia Young, *Soul Power: Culture, Radicalism, and the Making of a U.S. 3rd World Left* (Durham: Duke University Press, 2006).

22 The term "misogynoir" was coined around 2008 by Moya Bailey and Trudy, and can be found (particularly today) rather widely explored, defined, and discussed in internet articles, forums, blogs. An excellent, concise, and recent engagement with the term by Bailey and Trudy ("On Misogynoir: Citation, Erasure and Plagiarism") may be found in *Feminist Media Studies,* 18.4 (2018): 762–8. The term's first appearance, however, seems to have been in a 2010 article by Bailey for crunkfeministcollective.com, entitled "They Aren't Talking about Me … " Available at: http://www.crunkfeministcollective.com/2010/03/14/they-arent-talking-about-me/

23 See Jeanine Basinger, *A Woman's View: How Hollywood Spoke to Women 1930–1960* (Hanover: Wesleyan University Press, 1993): 55. Also see *Franny and Zooey*: 5.

24 Luc Boltanski and Eve Chiapello, *The New Spirit of Capitalism*, trans. Gregory Elliot (London: Verso, 2018): xxi–xxiii.

25 See Sidney Hook in *Partisan Review* (19.5, 1952): 569.

26 See Boltanski & Chiapello, *The New Spirit of Capitalism,* xxii.

27 See, Polite, *The Flagellants*, 16.

28 See Guyatri Spivak, *Death of a Discipline* (New York: Columbia University Press, 2003); as well as, François Cusset's *French Theory: How Foucault, Derrida, Deleuze & Co. Transformed the Intellectual Life of the United States* (Minneapolis: University of Minnesota Press, 2008).

29 Here I refer to the term "under-class" as coined by sociologist Gunnar Myrdal in the 1960s. See Herbert J. Gans, *Sociology and Social Policy: Essays on Community, Economy, and Society* (Columbia University Press); Chapter 5 "Studying the Bottom of American Society": 57–70.

30 For more on this allusion, see Boltanski and Chiapello, *The New Spirit of Capitalism,* xxiii–xxv.

31 This elision in Fukuyama's reasoning has already been aptly explored in a literary study of the 1990s, namely, in the Introduction to Samuel Cohen's *After the End of History: American Fiction in the 1990s* (Iowa City: University of Iowa Press, 2009): 3–29. Here, Cohen discusses the importance of the 1960s to the public life of the 1990s, particularly in relation to the Rodney King beating in 1991; Clarence Thomas' nomination to the Supreme Court and Anita Hill's testimony against him; and the controversies surrounding Bill Clinton's campaign and presidency (11–12).

32 Claire Jean Kim, "Clinton's Race Initiative: Recasting the American Dilemma." *Polity* (33.2, Winter 2000): 175–97. See, in particular: 186, 191.
33 See Leslie Marmon Silko, *Almanac of the Dead* (New York: Penguin, 1992).
34 Francis Fukuyama, *The End of History and the Last Man* (New York: Free Press, 2006): xii.
35 "Sorcery" is also referred to in the novel as the work of "witches"; and synonymously denoted as "witchcraft" or "magic," depending on the narrative context and historical moment in which "sorcery," as such, appears. Importantly, however, the function and operations of "sorcery" in *Almanac of the Dead* amount to much more than mythical magic or witchcraft; while mythical and speculative historical tales inform the novel's understanding of this concept, its operations are framed and highlighted by various "real-world" events that call readers' attention to its effects and importance, well beyond the mythical, or mystical, realms (Silko: 32, 156, 469, 472, 477–8, 522, 570, 589, 721, 759; linked terms: 8, 10, 20, 190, 121, 206–9, 232, 279, 316, 336, 339, 411, 416, 438, 469, 471, 475, 476, 477–8, 479, 481, 494, 503, 520, 522, 529, 570, 601–3, 604, 607, 625, 701, 720, 722, 759, 760).
36 Indeed, in Marx's manuscripts (particularly his early work), labor's place in human life is largely seen as a productive activity through which humanity might creatively fulfill itself. However, what Marx does not consistently acknowledge is whether his image of work as fulfilling and creative is an ideal image, a specter—and therefore, continually unattainable in the material realm.
37 Skow, J. "People of the Monkey Wrench." *Time* (138.23, December 9, 1991): 86.
38 See Antonio Barrenechea, *America Unbound: Encyclopedic Literature and Hemispheric Studies* (Albuquerque: University of New Mexico Press, 2016): 105.
39 For Alan Ryan's review, "An Inept *Almanac of the Dead*," see *USA Today* (January 21, 1992): D6. Citing Susan Lundquist's *Native American Literatures: An Introduction* (Continuum, 2004), Antonio Barrenechea points out that during the 1990s, the operations of the Native American Literary Renaissance (a term coined in 1983 by Kenneth Lincoln in a book by that name) were generally expected as aesthetic criteria. The three levels of the Renaissance's operations include: "confidence on the part of contemporary Native authors in reclaiming their heritage in their own literary expressions; concern with finding and reevaluating early literary works by Native authors; and renewed interest in anthologies of translations of traditional artistic expressions" (Lundquist 38). Although Barrenechea does not explore this point in detail, I claim that *Almanac*

does operate on all three levels expected of Renaissance authors (not that such criteria should be required by artists on the basis of their familial origins), albeit through heretofore unseen (in 1991) discursive and aesthetic processes.

40. Some recent scholars (mostly writing for more than nine to ten years following *Almanac*'s original publication) who make reference to and critical use of *Almanac*'s divided, often vituperative, early reviews include: Carmen Irr, "The Timelines of *Almanac of the Dead*, or a Postmodern Rewriting of Radical Fiction," in *Leslie Marmon Silko, A Collection of Critical Essays*, ed. Louise K. Barnett and James L. Thorston (University of New Mexico Press, 1999), 223–44; Roderick Nash, *Wilderness and the American Mind* (Yale University Press, 2001): 1–3; Rebecca Tillet, *Howling for Justice* (University of Arizona Press, 2014), 5–7; Barrenechea, *America Unbound*, 105. In Tillet's case, *Almanac*'s rancorous critical reception is framed as the ground upon which her edited collection's included pieces are built, while other scholars, such as Womack, Irr, Barrenechea, and Nash note the novel's many negative reviews as indicative of its significance as a work of American literature. Furthermore, this is not an exhaustive list of scholars who've made reference to, and critical use of, *Almanac*'s reception, as there are many others; here I list some of the more recent and compellingly (if uncannily) related in their approach.

41. Rebecca Tillett, "Introduction: *Almanac* Contextualized," in *Howling for Justice: New Perspectives on Leslie Marmon Silko's* Almanac of the Dead, ed. Rebecca Tillett (Tucson: University of Arizona Press, 2014): 5–13. See 6, in particular.

42. See Philip Roth, *The Human Stain* (Boston: Houghton Mifflin, 2000).

43. Consider, for example: Gunnar Myrdal, *An American Dilemma: The Negro Problem & Modern Democracy* (New York: Harper Brothers, 1944). Also see Clinton White House, *One America in the 21st-Century: Forging a New Future: The President's Initiative on Race & The Advisory Board's Report to the President*, United States Federal Government. Available at: https://clintonwhitehouse2.archives.gov/Initiatives/OneAmerica/PIR.pdf

44. See Roth, *The Human Stain*, 16.

45. Ibid., 169.

46. Mark Maslan, "The Faking of the Americans: Passing, Trauma, and National Identity in Philip Roth's *Human Stain*," *Modern Language Quarterly: A Journal of Literary History* (66.3, September 2005): 365–89.

47. Dean J. Franco, "Being Black, Being Jewish, and Knowing the Difference: *The Human Stain*; or, It Depends on What the Meaning of 'Clinton' Is," *Studies in Jewish American Literature* (23, 2004): 88–103.

48 Ibid., 89–90.
49 Ibid., 94.
50 Derek Parker Royal, "Fictional Realms of Possibility: Reimagining the Ethnic Subject in Philip Roth's *American Pastoral*," *Studies in Jewish American Literature* (20, 2001): 1–16.
51 See Kim, "Clinton's Race Initiative: Recasting the American Dilemma," 190–1.
52 Ibid., 191.

Chapter 1

1 For instance, "good sportsmanship," which I discuss later in this chapter.
2 Daniel Bell, *The End of Ideology: On the Exhaustion of Political Ideas in the 50s* (Cambridge: Harvard University Press, 2001): 39–46.
3 Ibid., 300–1.
4 Ibid., 301.
5 Importantly, however, clichés always appear connected to and interwoven with other, sometimes unrelated, cultural clichés (McLuhan 1951, 98–101; McLuhan 1970, 42–50). They do not generally appear/iterate in isolation.
6 See Marshall McLuhan, *The Mechanical Bride* (Berkeley: Ginkgo Press, 1951): 3. As McLuhan's fame reached its apex and the 1960s came to a close, his reputation waned and his work fell into obscurity (not unlike Salinger). McLuhan is often credited as one of the first media theorists; given his literary background, he perhaps may also be considered one of the original thinkers of interdisciplinary literary studies.
7 For instance, he notes that media (including mass media) never uses itself as content: "The content of writing is speech, just as the written word is the content of print, and print is the content of the telegraph" (McLuhan 1995, 151). McLuhan's work anticipates the cultural consequences of technological innovation; the question of media as cliché (in *Mechanical Bride*, 1951) expands in *Understanding Media* (1964) and *From Cliché to Archetype* (1970), beyond the logical and linguistic to the pervasive and decentralized.
8 Stories comprising *Franny and Zooey*: "Franny," *New Yorker* (January 29, 1955): 24; and "Zooey," *New Yorker* (May 4, 1957): 32. Critiques of *Franny and Zooey* by named contemporaries include (to name a few): Joan Didion, "Finally (Fashionably) Spurious"; Leslie Fielder, "Up from Adolescence"; Alfred Kazin, "Everybody's Favorite"; and John Updike, "Anxious Days for the Glass

Family." All reprnt. in: *Salinger: The Classical, Critical, and Personal Portrait*, ed. Grunwald (2009, Harper). According to Gordon Hutner in *What America Read: Taste, Class, and the Novel* (2009), many critics at the time of *Franny and Zooey*'s release saw the integrity of literary achievement as threatened by "the middlebrow"—a term also used by Fielder in reference to Salinger's writing in *Love and Death in the American Novel* (1960): 289–90, 333. During the 1950s, "the middlebrow" emerged as a common term used to categorize mass American culture; see Christina Klein, *Cold War Orientalism: Asia in the Middlebrow Imagination, 1945–1961* (Berkeley: University of California Press, 2003), 64.

9 Franny's depictions in *Franny and Zooey* echo a variety of women's film leading ladies; her pluckiness in "Franny" recalls Susan Vance (Katherine Hepburn) in *Bringing Up Baby* (1938), among other of Hepburn's roles, while her affect in "Zooey" resonates with Greta Garbo's Grusinskaya in *Grand Hotel* (1932). And although Franny is described as beautiful (perhaps recalling a young Elizabeth Taylor), in "Zooey," Franny's undermining by favored brothers, Zooey and Buddy, recalls Charlotte Vale (Bette Davis) early on in *Now, Voyager* (1942).

10 See, Jeanine Basinger, *A Woman's View: How Hollywood Spoke to Women 1930–1960* (Hanover: Wesleyan University Press, 1993): 15.

11 See, Alfred C. Kinsey et al., *Sexual Behavior in the Human Female: By the Staff of the Institute for Sex Research*, Indiana University (Bloomington: Indiana University Press, 1981): 715.

12 There was a particular interest on the origins and development of neuroses within the American nuclear family, particularly among Freudians and some behavioralists, appearing in women's magazines at the time. Buddy also alludes to this point in "Zooey's" narration (54–5). By the mid-1950s, Coontz points out, it was difficult to find a women's magazine that *didn't* contain some article or knowing reference to one of the many alleged neurotic disorders that might manifest as a result of a woman's inability to properly perform her roles within family and society.

13 See Stephanie Coontz, *A Strange Stirring: The Feminine Mystique and America Women at the Dawn of the 1960s* (New York: Basic Books, 2011): 66.

14 For example, in an early essay titled, "J. D. Salinger: 'Everybody's Favorite,'" Alfred Kazin credits Salinger for possessing an "exciting professional mastery of a peculiarly charged and dramatic medium, the American short story" (111). Kazin refers to Salinger as "the expert performer and director" who

understands "gesture," and associated observational details as the "essence" of short fiction; his stories are thus "particularly exciting" due to Salinger's "almost compulsive need" to populate his stories with intensive detail (111–13). Similarly, in *On the Contrary* (1962), McCarthy alludes that Salinger's characters are "impersonations" by the author; "like some prankster on the telephone," she maintains, impersonators like Salinger use "an assumed voice" to shape narrative and characterization (282–3). However, Salinger's method serves neither reader nor story: "One wonders whether the care expended on the mechanics of the imitation [...] does not constitute a kind of advertisement for the author, eliciting such responses as 'Think of the work that went into it!'" (283).

15 See, Leslie Fielder, "Up from Adolescence," in *Salinger: The Classical, Critical, and Personal Portrait*, ed. Henry Anatole Grunwald (New York: Harper, 2009): 58.
16 See, Bell 301. This is also echoed in Zooey's evaluation of Franny's use of the "Jesus Prayer," which I will not analyze here. I read Zooey's evaluation as a narrative red herring by Salinger/Buddy: that is, a prankish and ironic narrative attempt to capitalize on readers' tendency to value religious references as symbolically significant to characterization and narrative resolution. Buddy informs readers early on: "Zooey" is neither a religious nor mystical story, but a "multiple" love story, "pure and complicated."
17 Buddy may not have written "Franny," but he knows the plot (likely from Bessie's, tri-monthly, 500-word letters).
18 See, Salinger, *Franny and Zooey*, 7, original emphasis.
19 After falling out of fashion with the Great Depression, by 1955, the raccoon coat became vogue again—this is when "Franny" was first published in *The New Yorker* and the year in which *Franny and Zooey* is set. For an account of the vintage raccoon coat's rise among fashionable women in the 1950s, and the coat's symbolic associations with New York City socialites and high society, see Jennifer Le Zotte's, *From Goodwill to Grunge* (Chapel Hill: University of North Carolina Press, 2017): 122–9.
20 See, Le Zotte, *From Goodwill to Grunge*, 126; 128–9.
21 Ibid., 127.
22 Ibid., 131.
23 Ibid., 128. Also see Salinger, *Franny and Zooey*, 7.
24 See Basinger, *A Woman's View*, 15.
25 See McLuhan, *Mechanical Bride*: xi.

26 See Basinger, *A Woman's View*, 17, 60. By presenting Franny through involved, yet emotionally distant, narrative framing, readers are encouraged to adopt Franny's point of view; however, as in women's film, this construction is not equivalent to empathetic relation.
27 McLuhan, *Mechanical Bride*, xi.
28 See Sainger, *Franny and Zooey*, 11.
29 Ibid.
30 Salinger, *Franny and Zooey*, 11.
31 See, Mary McCarthy, "Up the Ladder from *Charm* to *Vogue*," in *Women's Magazines, 1940-1960: Gender Roles and the Popular Press*, ed. Nancy A. Walker (Boston: Bedford St. Martin's, 1988): 247–57.
32 See Basinger, *A Woman's View*, 55–82.
33 See, Betty Friedan, *The Feminine Mystique* (New York: W. W. Norton, 2013): 69–70.
34 See, McLuhan, *Mechanical Bride*, vi–vii; as well as Friedan, *Feminine Mystique*: 508. Through mass media, McLuhan observes, women's bodies become cliché through their complicity with products: specific parts of women's bodies are presented as detached parts that may be seamlessly switched out of one context and into another—legs sell stockings, mid-sections sell blouses, etc. (McLuhan, *Mechanical Bride*, 99–100).
35 See, Basinger, *A Woman's View*, 57.
36 Salinger, *Franny and Zooey*, 5–6.
37 Ibid., 14.
38 Ibid., 15.
39 Ibid., 20.
40 Ibid.
41 See Melissa A. Ames, "Memoirs of a Bathroom Stall," *The Keep*, Faculty Research and Creative Activity. Eastern Illinois University, Paper 13 (2006): 70. Available at: http://thekeep.eiu.edu/eng_fac/13
42 Salinger, *Franny and Zooey*, 21.
43 Ibid., 21–2.
44 Ibid., 23.
45 Ibid., 22–3.
46 Ibid., 20, 23.
47 See, Alva Myrdal and Viola Klein, *Women's Two Roles: Home and Work* (London: Routledge, 1956): 146–7.

48   Ibid.
49   See, Joan Didion, "Marriage a la Mode," in *Women's Magazines, 1940–1960: Gender Roles and the Popular Press*, ed. Nancy A. Walker (Boston: Bedford St. Martin's, 1988): 258.
50   Ibid., 259–60.
51   Ibid., 259.
52   See, Friedan, *Feminine Mystique*, 107–9. Also see, Coontz, *A Strange Stirring*, 67–8.
53   See, Salinger, *Franny and Zooey*, 47.
54   These retroactive authorial credits may be read as impersonations by Salinger, distancing himself from criticism received during the stories' *New Yorker* days. Like Franny's letter, which rhetorically releases Lane and herself from connection to her complaints, Salinger releases himself from authorial connection to these stories (and their criticism) by directing Buddy to claim authorship.
55   See, Salinger, *Franny and Zooey*, 47–8.
56   Ibid., 70–7, 80, 82–4.
57   Ibid., 47.
58   See, David Seed, "Keeping It in the Family: The Novellas of J. D. Salinger," in *J. D. Salinger*, ed. Harold Bloom (New York: Infobase, 2008): 69–87.
59   See, Salinger, *Franny and Zooey*, 49.
60   See, Salinger, *Franny and Zooey*, 148. For two Glass family stories that chronicle the various, early adventures of the Glasses (particularly during Franny's childhood and Les's days in Hollywood), see Salinger's two composite texts, *Raise High the Roof Beam, Carpenters and Seymour: An Introduction* (Little, Brown & Co., 1963).
61   See, Salinger, *Franny and Zooey*, 98.
62   Basinger, *A Woman's View*, 57.
63   See, Friedan, *Feminine Mystique*, 71.
64   See, *Feminine Mystique*, 70. In *A Strange Stirring*, Coontz supports this point, noting that "the only women regularly featured in the news were movie stars and presidents' wives" at this time in American history (17).
65   See, Salinger, *Franny and Zooey*, 76. Franny has an elder sister, Beatrice (or, Boo Boo), a.k.a., Mrs. Tennenbaum in "Down in the Dinghy" of *Nine Stories*. Boo Boo does not appear in *Franny and Zooey*, but is mentioned several times, receiving no introduction by Buddy. In "Down in the Dinghy," she is a housewife living in Connecticut. She is first mentioned in "Zooey" by Bessie, who bemoans her absence during Franny's crisis; then, by Franny, who asks Zooey if Boo Boo

had a "religious philosophy" (153); and finally, Zooey in response to Franny, insults Boo Boo claiming that her "religious philosophy" amounts to an oblique reference to a claim made in a book (Rev. Francis Kilvert's *Diaries*, *c.* 1920), which Zooey suggests Boo Boo takes very seriously. Because of her housewife role and superficial interest in religious ideas (not unlike Franny's), Boo Boo becomes another insufficient private image for Franny.

66 For more on the Glass parents and vaudeville, see *Seymour: An Introduction*, 139, 168-71. In J. D. Salinger, *Raise High the Roof Beam, Carpenters and Seymour: An Introduction* (Back Bay Books, 2001).
67 See, Salinger, *Franny and Zooey*, 77, 98.
68 See, ibid., 99; 84-6.
69 See, Salinger, *On the Contrary*, 271, 274.
70 Ibid., 271.
71 Ibid., 275.
72 To make her point, McCarthy cites two directions in which these "narrative experiments" went: British writers' interest in recording "sensibility" (a "feminine' discourse or genre) and American counterparts" "masculine" experiments representing "sensation" (McCarthy 274-6).
73 See, Salinger, *On the Contrary*, 273-4.
74 See, Salinger, *Franny and Zooey*, 98. Also see *On the Contrary*: 273. Franny is also a different "social type" (in McCarthy's words) from sister, Boo Boo, who enlisted in the military when she was Franny's age. See *Raise High the Roof Beam*.
75 See, Salinger, *Franny and Zooey*, 125-6, original italics.
76 See, Basinger, *A Woman's View*, 57.
77 See, Salinger, *Franny and Zooey*, 123.
78 See, ibid., 125-6.
79 Ibid., 126.
80 See, ibid., 52; 146-71.
81 Ibid., 143; 147-50.
82 See, Lucinda Rosenfeld, "The Trouble with Franny," in *With Love and Squalor: 14 Writers Respond to the Work of J. D. Salinger*, ed. Kip Kotzen and Thomas Beller (New York: Broadway Books, 2001): 78-87.
83 See, Salinger, *On the Contrary*, 283.
84 See, Bell, *The End of Ideology,* 301, 359-60.
85 Ibid., 301.

86 See, Salinger, *Franny and Zooey*, 165–7.
87 Ibid., 162–4.
88 See, Friedan, *The Feminine Mystique*, 140–51.
89 Salinger, *Franny and Zooey*, 148.
90 Ibid., 171.
91 See, Joan Didion, "On Self-Respect: Its Source, Its Power" in *Vogue* (August 1, 1961): 62–3.
92 Bell, *The End of Ideology*, 299.
93 Friedan, *The Feminine Mystique*, 150.
94 Ibid., 151, 141–2.
95 Bell, *The End of Ideology*, 301.
96 See, Bell, *The End of Ideology*, 301 and 303. Bell reasons that this shift in aesthetic and discursive attitude (episteme) may account for "irony, paradox, ambiguity, and complexity" dominating literary critical discourse, c. 1960.
97 Ibid., 308–11.
98 Salinger, *Franny and Zooey*, 161 and 165.
99 Ibid., 194.
100 Ibid., 197.
101 In *Postmodern Belief* (2010), Hungerford examines "faith in faith" in the 1950s–early 1960s, American postwar years; specifically, in political and literary critical discourses. She also considers how this civic and national episteme may have inflected critics' reception of *Franny and Zooey*. Deviating from Hungerford, my work inspects how "faith in faith" finds reification and reiteration in this scene of *Franny and Zooey*, beyond the doctrinal (syncretic or specific) divisions of religion or 1950s literary criticism. That is, along with Zooey's discussions on society, art, religion, and his mass culture-reminiscent characterization as "leading man," I read Zooey as adopting epistemic "faith in faith" as a discursive mode to try to reach Franny, appealing to her by framing her crisis (professionally and morally) in a manner inconsistent with her presumed immaturity. Thus, Zooey's final attempt at "spiritual counsel" generates no new insights or effects in Franny.
102 Salinger, *Franny and Zooey*, 148.
103 Ibid., 197. Also see, Basinger, *A Woman's View*, 13.
104 See, Mary McCarthy, "Salinger's Closed Circuit," in *If You Really Want to Hear about It: Writers on J. D. Salinger on His Work*, ed. Catherine Crawford (New York: Thunder's Mouth Press, 2006): 27–33, 29.

105 See, Salinger, *Franny and Zooey*, 198. Zooey's comment concerning "'unskilled laughter'" suggests his reference to an earlier remark by Franny, on her frustration with audiences. This rhetorical move is meant to lend support to Zooey's counsel; however, nowhere in *Franny and Zooey* does Franny make such a comment.
106 Ibid.
107 Ibid., 27–9.
108 Franny shows interest in Zooey's work in television, expressing excitement about scripts he (boredly) receives and expresses interest in his upcoming trip to France for a film shoot (129–37). Given this, it is difficult to imagine Franny finding spiritual satisfaction along the professional track Zooey suggests (particularly as a woman actor).
109 See, Jackson Lears, "A Matter of Taste: Corporate Cultural Hegemony in a Mass-Consumption Society," in *Recasting America: Culture and Politics in the Age of the Cold War*, ed. Lary May (Chicago: University of Chicago Press, 1989): 38–57. In the postwar, post-ideological (and mass-oriented) cultural climate of the 1950s, perspectives like Bell's found new relevance, while Buddy's distant, inarticulate style would have smacked of the generation's earlier, lost purposes (particularly to some of Salinger's contemporaries). This may account for critics' often evaluating "Zooey" as offering more compelling fodder for analyses than "Franny," due to its philosophically uncertain, explicit, and implicit entanglements with various competing discourses (especially religious, professional, and creative).
110 See, Coontz, *A Strange Stirring*, 106.

Chapter 2

1 See Carlene Hatcher Polite, *The Flagellants* (New York: Farrar, Straus & Giroux, 1967): 17.
2 Ibid., 16.
3 Ibid., 13.
4 Ibid., 17.
5 Ibid., 20.
6 Ibid., 16.
7 See, Jean Carey Bond and Patricia Peery, "Is the Black Man Castrated?" in *The Black Woman: An Anthology*, ed. Toni Cade Bambara (New York: Washington Square Books, 2005): 141–8, 145.

8 See, Roger Ebert, "First Novels by Young Negroes," *American Scholar* (Autumn 1967): 584. Encouraged by the 1954 Supreme Court desegregation decision, many writers foresaw the end to the separateness and inequality that characterized their lives and informed their art; as a result, many believed that, as they began enjoying the privileges heretofore reserved for whites, their work would also, eventually, come to be associated with the privilege and success of white American art. As the 1950s became the 1960s, however, black Americans' experiences became arguably worse and few black writers found themselves treated fairly or equally by publishers or bookstores. In response, the BAM defined a full-scale rejection of earlier integrationist strategies. These artists worked alongside the Black Power activists, relying upon the black American masses (rather than the middle class) to provide their arts' raw material *and* audience. Directing their art exclusively to the black community, writers of the Black Aesthetic were disinterested in collaborating, or assimilating, with white society.

9 See Malcolm X's (1964) Speech at the founding rally of the Organization of Afro-American Unity. Available at: https://www.blackpast.org/african-american-history/speeches-african-american-history/1964-malcolm-x-s-speech-founding-rally-organization-afro-american-unity/

10 See Larry Neal, "The Black Arts Movement," in *The Portable Sixties Reader*, ed. Ann Charters (New York: Penguin, 2003): 446–54.

11 See Schraufnagel's, *From Apology to Protest: the Black American Novel* (DeLand: Everett/Edwards, 1979): 129.

12 Ibid. 129–30. Schraufnagel's critical survey of contemporary African American literature stands as the only scholarly writing on *The Flagellants* predating the 1990s. In his very brief treatment of the novel (approximately two pages), Schraufnagel pejoratively names *The Flagellants* an example of "accommodationist" black American literature. He defines acccommodationism: "[Literature which] concentrates basically on the adjustment an individual makes to function in accordance with the standards of white society" (121).

13 See Alphonso Pinkney, *Red, Black, and Green: Black Nationalism in the United States* (Cambridge: Cambridge University Press, 1976): 14.

14 See James Edward Smethurst, *The Black Arts Movement: Literary Nationalism in the 1960s and 1970s* (Chapel Hill: North Carolina University Press, 2005): 15.

15 For more on this subject, see Neal, "The Black Arts Movement," in *The Portable Sixties Reader*, 446–54.

16 Of course, the Harlem Renaissance was invested in dismantling Jim Crow racism of the earlier twentieth century. However, in terms of its artistic aims

and aesthetic theories and practices, as a movement, the Renaissance's priorities varied from the more politically oriented BAM.

17 See, James Zeigler, *Red Scare Racism and Cold War Black Radicalism* (Jackson: University of Mississippi, 2015): 9–11. Abolitionism, and later the Second World War, engendered a necessary break with structures of institutionalized racism—but only theoretically. This break nevertheless spurred on subtler forms of systemic racism that, in turn, expanded black Americans' real conditions of oppression. Some examples include the Black Codes, vagrancy laws, bureaucratic voting restrictions, and other decrees that (while not rhetorically coded to be exclusively for African Americans) were only ever enforced against African Americans, thereby seriously restricting and criminalizing black life. The intent of such insidious, underhandedly institutional racism was, practically speaking, bent on making it impossible for African Americans (and especially African American men) to participate in public American life in any significant or broadly meaningful way.

18 See, Smethurst, *The Black Arts Movement*, 33.

19 See, ibid. Also see Ziegler, *Red Scare Racism and Cold War Black Radicalism*, 9 and 11–13. By the time of his term as president, Truman had been long astute to the needs and concerns of African American voters. Raised in a racist Southern culture and with political experience working as a senator for Missouri, Truman had become perceptive about the color question long before most other American politicians; his career had long been reliant upon being responsive to African American voters. For more on the political career of Harry S. Truman and his "Double V" campaign following the Second World War, see Rawn James Jr., *The Double V* (London: Bloomsbury, 2014).

20 See, Madhu Dubey, *Signs and Cities: Black Literary Postmodernism* (Chicago: Chicago University Press, 2003): 19.

21 Ibid., 17.

22 For an excellent examination of the ways black women's roles and images have been limited and stigmatized in both black and white cultural discourses, see Angela Davis, *Reflections on the Black Woman's Role in the Community of Slaves* (Malden: Blackwellm, 1998): 111–28.

23 See, Bambara, *The Black Woman*, 4.

24 The work of literary recovery may be ideological, but sometimes, it is also personal and/or institutional. Because of this, an examination of precisely why Carlene Hatcher Polite was ultimately omitted from 1980s and 1990s

reclamation projects (especially when writers like Gayl Jones were not) is a study that warrants a separate article. Indeed, a piece akin to Madhu Dubey's study of Gayl Jones's omission from 1980s reclamation projects, which she published in 1995, is more than overdue for Polite in 2021 (see Dubey 1995, "Gayl Jones and the Matrilineal Metaphor of Tradition" in *Signs*, 20.2). Although a second printing of *The Flagellants* was authorized in 1987 through Beacon Press, the novel never took hold in the academy as relevant or particularly valuable to the history of black women's literature in the United States. Polite wrote in a similar critical context as Gayl Jones; and like Jones, she was critiqued for her ideological ambivalence and questionable depictions of black lives. As Dubey has pointed out, like Jones, Polite's work posed "serious and disquieting questions" about tradition-building and ideology's invisible work in everyday life; and like Jones, Polite's use of communal framing devices and nontraditional oral narrative modes does not signify a positively unified cultural voice. Unlike Jones, however, the research on Polite's omission does not yet exist.

25 Although there are many others, Toni Morrison's early novels, *The Bluest Eye* (1970) and *Sula* (1973), along with Gayl Jones' first novel, *Corregidora* (1975), have been credited as excellent examples of texts from this period that illustrate the discursive constructedness of African American women's ideological absence from or silence within black nationalist discourses (see Dubey 1994). It is worth noting, however, that these much more well-known texts were published several years following the US release of Polite's *The Flagellants*, which has yet to be credited with such creative achievements.

26 See, Hazel V. Carby, "The Politics of Fiction, Anthropology and the Folk: Zora Neal Hurston," in *New Essays on Their Eyes Were Watching God*, ed. Michael Awkward (Cambridge: Cambridge University Press, 1991): 71–93.

27 See, Polite, *The Flagellants*, 13.

28 See, Polite, *The Flagellants*, 4. Ideal's childhood in Black Bottom may have contributed to 1990s readings of the novel, which attributed its obscurity to its presumed autobiographical nature. Black Bottom was a Detroit neighborhood, and Polite was from Detroit. Many African Americans migrated here from the South during the Great Migration, bringing with them Southern culture. The Bottom was demolished in the early 1960s for "urban renewal." However, 1990s readers have not engaged with how black cultural nationalism reproduced black femininity through countless cultural patterns, including narrative

strategies that exclude or absorb black female consciousness and experiences; nor did they consider how *The Flagellants* performs these strategies. However unintentional, these readings confer Polite with little creative dexterity, recalling that biographical analysis does not permit understanding Polite's expression of ideological inscriptions.

29　Ibid.
30　Ibid., 16.
31　Ibid., 5, emphasis added.
32　Ibid.
33　See, Alice Walker, "In Search of Our Mothers' Gardens," in *In Search of Our Mothers' Gardens: Womanist Prose* (San Diego: Harcourt Brace, 1983): 231–43.
34　See, Dubey, *Signs and Cities*, 144–58.
35　Polite, *The Flagellants*, 20.
36　Ibid., 20–1.
37　See, Bambara, *The Black Woman*, 141–5.
38　See, Melissa V. Harris-Perry, *Sister Citizen: Shame, Stereotypes, and Black Women in America* (New Haven: Yale, 2011): 52.
39　Polite, *The Flagellants,* 27.
40　Ibid., 28.
41　Ibid., 38–40.
42　Ibid. 51.
43　Ibid., 55.
44　Ibid., 56, 57.
45　Ibid., 58.
46　Ibid., 59–60.
47　Ibid., 60.
48　Ibid.
49　Ibid.
50　Ibid., 111–12, emphasis added.
51　Ibid., 112.
52　Ibid., 113–14.
53　See, Harris-Perry, *Sister Citizen*, 93.
54　Ibid.
55　See, bell hooks, *Ain't I a Woman? Black Women and Feminism* (London: Pluto Books, 1986): 79.
56　Polite, *The Flagellants,* 112.

57 Ibid., 129.
58 Ibid., 130.
59 Ibid.
60 Ibid.
61 Ibid., 185–6.
62 Ibid., 192–3.

Chapter 3

1. See, Francis Fukuyama, *The End of History and the Last Man* (New York: Free Press, 1992): 287. Also see Alexandre Kojeve, *Introduction to the Reading of Hegel Lectures on the Phenomenology of Spirit*, ed. Allan Bloom, trans. James H. Nichols (Ithaca: Cornell University Press, 1969): 158–62, n. 6.
2. See, Fukuyama Francis, "The End of History?" *The National Interest* (No. 16, Summer 1989): 3; 3–18.
3. Ibid., 4.
4. See, Fukuyama, *The End of History*, 288–90. Also see Kojeve, *Introduction to the Reading* (1969): 159.
5. The concept of humanity as various forms of historical agency (i.e., struggles for material status and ideological recognition) theoretically "died," according to Hegel, with the widespread assertion of democratic principles (e.g., equality, liberty, fraternity) during the early-nineteenth century. As the nineteenth century progressed, Marx would assert history's "end" at mid-century.
6. Fukuyama, *The End of History*, 300.
7. What Marx did not acknowledge (or rather, inconsistently acknowledges in his conception of human history and labor's role therein) was that his image of work as fulfilling a free and creative role in humanity's experience is an ideal image, a specter—or, an unstable image and therefore an unstable role that cannot be stably achieved within the material realm.
8. See, Leslie Marmon Silko, *Almanac of the Dead* (New York: Penguin, 1992): 14.
9. While Franny resigns herself, at the end of *Franny and Zooey*, to sleeping away the rest of her day, and Ideal, long nursed on discourses of her own wickedness, closes *The Flagellants* by facilitating Jimson's abandonment (once again), a strange assurance resides in Salinger's and Polite's depictions of Franny's and Ideal's interminable trials and failures toward attaining agency.

10 Silko, *Almanac of the Dead,* 709.
11 Ibid., 311.
12 Ibid., 291, 314 and 525–7.
13 Ibid., 310 and 515–16.
14 Ibid., 536.
15 Ibid., 590.
16 Ibid., 189–91.
17 Ibid., 519–20.
18 Ibid., 519.
19 See, John Gerring, "Ideology: A Definitional Analysis," *Political Research Quarterly* (50.4 December 1997): 957–94.
20 See Andre Gunder Frank, "No End to History! History to No End?" *Social Justice* (17.4 Winter 1990): 7–29.
21 Ibid., 7–8.
22 Indeed, in Marx's manuscripts (particularly his early work), labor's place in human life is largely seen as a productive activity through which humanity might creatively fulfill itself. However, what Marx does not consistently acknowledge is whether his image of work as fulfilling and creative is an ideal image, a specter—and therefore, continually unattainable in the material realm.
23 "Sorcery" is also referred to in the novel as the work of "witches"; and synonymously denoted as "witchcraft" or "magic," depending on the narrative context and historical moment in which "sorcery," as such, appears. Importantly, however, the function and operations of "sorcery" in *Almanac of the Dead* amount to much more than mythical magic or witchcraft; while mythical and speculative historical tales inform the novel's understanding of this concept, its operations are framed and highlighted by various "real-world" events that call readers' attention to its effects and importance, well beyond the mythical, or mystical, realms (Silko: 32, 156, 469, 472, 477–8, 522, 570, 589, 721, 759; linked terms: 8, 10, 20, 190, 121, 206–9, 232, 279, 316, 336, 339, 411, 416, 438, 469, 471, 475, 476, 477–8, 479, 481, 494, 503, 520, 522, 529, 570, 601–3, 604, 607, 625, 701, 720, 722, 759, 760).
24 See, Fukuyama, *The End of History*, xii.
25 Here, I am citing Andre Gunder Frank's (1990) argument against Francis Fukuyama's much-referenced, 1989 pieces "The End of History?" and "End of History: So Misunderstood by So Many" published in *The National Interest* and excerpted by the author in the *Washington Post* and *International Herald Tribune*.

Frank notes that Fukuyama's answer to critics like himself was similarly widely publicized, including an excerpt in the *International Herald Tribune* (December 15, 1989) as well as Madrid's *El Pais*, which devoted a Sunday supplement to four pages' worth of reply and about six of the countless comments from around the world (Frank 29). Where Fukuyama's work asserts that a specific ideal of history has died (*c.* 1989), Frank rebuts Fukuyama's claim as too reliant upon a specific, idealistic definition of history (via ideology) which by design overlooks the real, material conditions (such as economic dependence), which actually move history along—beyond any historical work that an ideological position may hold claim to making.

26 See, J. B. Harley, *The New Nature of Maps: Essays in the History of Cartography*, ed. Paul Laxton (Baltimore: Johns Hopkins University Press, 2001): 137.
27 See Silko, *Almanac of the Dead*, 14–15, for Silko's "Five Hundred Year Map"
28 See, Mishuana Goeman, *Mark My Words: Native Women Mapping Our Nations* (Minneapolis: Minnesota University Press, 2013): 167.
29 See, Harley, *The New Nature of Maps*, 63.
30 *Ibid.* Also see, Goeman, *Mark My Words*, 167.
31 See Harley, *The New Nature of Maps,* 112–13, 117 and 137.
32 Ibid., 15.
33 Ibid., 62.
34 In Harley, *The New Nature of Maps*, Harley widely discusses the use of illustration, particularly during the age of North America's colonization by Western European powers, toward noting class stratification and relations (particularly racial) of superiority and inferiority (see especially, ch. 4, pp. 110–47). This illustrative practice is, perhaps unsurprisingly, absent in the maps featured in print news media from the time of *Almanac*'s publication. However, I suggest here that her Five Hundred Year Map's inventories of character names simultaneously serve to supplant and recall historical maps' highly racialized illustrations—thus keeping with, while exposing certain agendas within, the aesthetics of maps used during her own historical moment.
35 See, Silko, *Almanac of the Dead*, 418.
36 Ibid.
37 Ibid., 416, 420 and 742.
38 Ibid., 424.
39 Ibid., 423–4.
40 Ibid., 396 and 400–10.

41 Ibid., 15.
42 See, Harley, *The New Nature of Maps*, 136–8.
43 Ibid., 135.
44 See, Harley, *The New Nature of Maps*, 67–8.
45 See, Silko, *Almanac of the Dead*, 416.
46 Ibid., 277.
47 Ibid., 301.
48 Ibid., 258.
49 Ibid., 301.
50 Ironically, "Menardo's had been the first insurance company to employ a private security force to protect clients from political unrest" (p. 261).
51 See, Silko, *Almanac of the Dead*, 261, 258 and 590–1.
52 As possibly the most fearful character toward snakes in *Almanac*, for instance, Menardo must first search his new property for "poisonous snake[s] and drunken Indians" before he can bring himself to move into his newly constructed, jungle-adjacent mansion (283).
53 See, Silko, *Almanac of the Dead*, 321, 323 & 340.
54 Ibid., 322–6 and 508–9.
55 Ibid., 722.
56 Ibid., 88.
57 Ibid., 91–8.
58 Ibid., 34.
59 Ibid., 91–8 and 762.
60 Ibid., 87, 90–1, 93.
61 Ibid., 96.
62 Ibid., 25, 31–5.
63 Ibid., 96.
64 Ibid., 90–8.
65 Ibid., 91 and 97.
66 Ibid., 25. For the sake of precision, just before Sterling decides to leave Tucson, Lecha and Zeta's ranch, and his associated employment there, the narrator mediates: "These people from Tucson were too strange for him. He'd try to find his cousin in Phoenix. High wages weren't everything" (588). While Sterling may have a family member available to him in Phoenix, readers nevertheless do not learn this information until the final third of the novel.
67 Ibid., 15, emphasis added.
68 Ibid.

69   Ibid., 26, 39 and 80–1.
70   Ibid., 374.
71   Ibid.
72   Ibid., 133.
73   Ibid., 15 and 374.
74   Ibid., 374.
75   Ibid., see 374, original emphasis; 362–3, 374, 598 and 660.
76   Ibid., 133.
77   Ibid.
78   Ibid., 14–15.
79   Ibid., 14 and 73–81.
80   Ibid., 316.
81   Ibid.
82   Ibid., 15.
83   Ibid., 80.
84   Ibid., 14.
85   Ibid., 134.
86   Ibid., 14 and 573.
87   Ibid., 478.
88   Ibid., 478, emphasis added.
89   Ibid., 313.
90   Ibid., 224.
91   Ibid., 189, emphasis added.
92   Ibid., 703.
93   Ibid., 709.
94   See Fukuyama, *The End of History,* 330.
95   Ibid., 328–31.
96   Ibid., 329.
97   See Silko, *Almanac of the Dead,* 326.
98   Ibid., 578.
99   Ibid., 135.
100 Ibid., 14.
101 See, Claire Jean Kim, "Clinton's Race Initiative: Recasting the American Dilemma," *Polity* (33.2 Winter 2000): 185. Also see, Robert C. Lieberman, "The Storm Didn't Discriminate: Katrina and the Politics of Color Blindness," *Du Bois Review* (3.1 2006): 11.

Chapter 4

1. For instance, *American Pastoral* (1997) chronicles the unlikely and tragic personal downfall of kindly Seymour "Swede" Levov, a Nordic-looking athletics star-turned-family-man who attended high school with Zuckerman in New Jersey. The trilogy's second installment, *I Married a Communist* (1998), follows the destruction of Ira Ringold, younger brother to Zuckerman's high school English teacher, Murray (who is one of his earliest heroes); Ira strikes it big as a radio star, but his success is ruined by an expose alleging his Russian and Communist sympathies—written by his wife. In these sketches, national themes and topics such as terrorism, McCarthyism, racism, and the concept of national fictions are highlighted.
2. See, Philip Roth, *The Human Stain* (Boston: Houghton Mifflin, 2000): 109. *Human Stain*, on the other hand, focuses on the life of a man whom Zuckerman does not know and to whom he has no ties; and although they grew up nearby to one another, their admitted unawareness of each other in adulthood (despite Coleman's fabricated passing story) may signal important, narratively insurmountable differences that Zuckerman ultimately (if unwittingly) reveals for analysis.
3. Ibid., 316–17. Herb Kebel is one of very few African American faculty members at Athena College, and according to Zuckerman he was hired by Coleman during his stint as dean (pp. 16, 308, 315–16).
4. See, *Klezmer America: Jewishness, Ethnicity, Modernity* (New York: Columbia University Press, 2008: 172.
5. Readers of Roth's fiction may note that a younger Nathan Zuckerman's own conception of social mobility and success (for himself, as a Jewish writer from New Jersey) is also framed as ideological (as in *Ghost Writer*, c. 1979), which I discuss later in this chapter.
6. In terms of the "survival" of passing fiction beyond this historical moment in African American fiction, Juda Bennett notes Roth's *The Human Stain* (among other "anomalous" examples of contemporary passing narratives), but predominantly focuses on the oeuvre of Toni Morrison in "Toni Morrison and the Burden of the Passing Narrative" (*African American Review* 35.2, 2001: 205–17). Fascinatingly, Morrison is the sole contemporary author whom Bennett credits with adapting passing as a narrative strategy in her representations of race travel, suggesting that following passing fiction's popularity (i.e., roughly, from

the 1930s onward) the topic and genre became taboo territory (to many, if not all writers) in African American literary circles. The fact that Zuckerman adopts in *The Human Stain* many of the very same indirect, circuitous narrative strategies observed in Morrison calls attention to the fact that, as social praxis and literary genre, passing also became forbidden discursive terrain for American authors beyond African American literary traditions. To account for this, I will explore, Zuckerman attempts to offer the most realistic (while also respectable and inoffensive) narrative of race travel possible for a white author who, for all intents and purposes, seems to also perceive himself as having abandoned his own birth family for reasons very similar (in his point of view) to Coleman's.

7 See, Roth, *The Human Stain*, 135.
8 Ibid., 324.
9 Ibid., 327.
10 See, Freedman, *Klezmer America*, 171.
11 See, Roth, *The Human Stain*, 5 and 98.
12 Ibid., 6.
13 Ibid.
14 Ibid., 39. I cannot help but wonder (though there is little data in the novel to support this hunch) if, in a gamble to learn personal information about Coleman via his reaction, Zuckerman did not *himself* pen the anonymous, harassing letter that Coleman found in his mailbox.
15 Ibid., 2, 5, 44, and 310.
16 Elaine Safer has cited Delphine's antagonistic conquest and "eagerness to punish Coleman for racism and exploitation of women" as a means for her to compensate "for her frustrated desire to be the object of his affection" (222). This reading coincides with Zuckerman's free indirect discourse of Delphine's inner monologue, which suggests that she perceives her job at Athena as "déclassé," not providing her with "the kind of recognition she was trained to get" (Roth 189, 190). She is further described by the writer as being like a "precocious child" with "a considerable talent for being wounded" when she is not positioned as an object of either envy or desire, as she is accustomed (Roth 185, 187). However, Safer's reading, like Zuckerman's rendering of Delphine, requires a further analytical step in order to perceive how the narrator's own position (especially as Zuckerman is also a character in *The Human Stain*) informs his characterizations.
17 See, Roth, *The Human Stain*, 185.

18 Ibid., 190.
19 Ibid.
20 Ibid., 2.
21 See, Claire Jean Kim, "Clinton's Race Initiative: Recasting the American Dilemma," *Polity* 33.2 (Winter 2000): 190–1.
22 Ibid., 191.
23 See, Roth, *The Human Stain*, 12.
24 Ibid., 31.
25 Ibid., 204.
26 Shortly after resigning from the professorate, Coleman accosts the writer at home and demands that he compose a memoir (working title: Spooks), exposing Athena College's institutional "absurdity" (p. 11). Zuckerman is startled by the spectacle of "a man I did not know, but clearly someone accomplished and of consequence now completely unhinged," careening about his work room and alternately speaking and yelling (p. 11).
27 See, Eduardo Bonilla-Silva, *Racism without Racists: Color-blind Racism and the Persistence of Racial Inequality in America* (New York: Rowman Littlefield, 2014): 10.
28 Ibid.
29 Roth's first Zuckerman trilogy includes the novels, *Zuckerman, Unbound* (1981); *Anatomy Lesson* (1983); and *The Prague Orgy* (1985).
30 See, Philip Roth, *The Facts: A Novelist's Autobiography* (New York: Vintage, 1988): 7.
31 Concerning *The Human Stain*'s late-1990s narrative present: in the aftermath of his utterance, the behavior of Coleman's Athena colleagues has been read as cruel and ridiculous; according to Jay Halio, their ostracizing of Coleman illustrates Roth's own "powerful indictment of political correctness" (p. 173). Elaine Safer similarly describes Roth's depiction of Athena College as a "microcosm for the political correctness fever," which, she reminds readers, Roth himself refers to as a "calculated frenzy" (p. 212). Historically, readers of *The Human Stain* have collapsed the novel's cynicism toward political correctness with Philip Roth's alleged, personal sentiments; however, I claim there is a historical deeper point that Roth seeks to illustrate for readers, particularly by attributing this depiction of the 1990s to Nathan Zuckerman.
32 See, Roth, *The Human Stain*, 37; 322–3; 334–5.
33 Ibid., 16.

34 Ibid.
35 Ibid., 15–16.
36 See, Michele Elam, "Passing in the Post-Race Era: Danzy Senna, Philip Roth, and Colson Whitehead," *African American Review* (41.4 2007): 758, emphasis added. There is a significant amount of this toxic passivity on the topic of racism between the men. For instance, Roth's ghost writer also does not challenge Coleman when he reportedly raves "about black anti-Semitism" and proceeds to compare "white Jews" being blamed for "black suffering," as akin to the Germans' holding "the same evil Old Testament monsters responsible for [their] suffering" during the Second World War (Roth, *The Human Stain*, 16).
37 See, Roth, *The Human Stain*, 2.
38 See, Freeman, Alan David. "Legitimizing Racial Discrimination through Antidiscrimination Law: A Critical Review of Supreme Court Doctrine," in *Critical Race Theory: The Key Writings That Formed the Movement*, ed. Kimberle Crenshaw et al. (New York: The New Press, 1996): 41.
39 See, Roth, *The Human Stain*, 23.
40 Ibid.
41 Ibid., 322.
42 Ibid., 323.
43 Ibid.
44 See, Mary L. Dudziak, *Cold War Civil Rights: Race and the Image of American Democracy* (Princeton: Princeton University Press, 2000): 102 and 107. Also see, James Zeigler, *Red Scare Racism and Cold War Black Radicalism* (Jackson: University of Mississippi, 2015): 37.
45 See, Freedman, *Klezmer America*, 171.
46 Ibid., 169.
47 See, Roth, *The Human Stain*, 325.
48 Ibid., 324.
49 Ibid., 341–2.
50 Ibid., 317 and 322.
51 Ibid., 325.
52 See, Kim, "Clinton's Race Initiative," 180. Also see Gunnar Myrdal, *An American Dilemma: The Negro Problem & Modern Democracy* (New York: Harper Brothers, 1944): 1020–1.
53 Roth, *The Human Stain*, 327.
54 See, Dudziak, *Cold War Civil Rights*, 232.

55 Roth, *The Human Stain*, 22.
56 Ibid.
57 See, Philip Roth, *The Ghost Writer* (New York: Vintage, 1995): 81. Interestingly, however, despite having admired Sidney as a young man and featured a fictionalized version of him in an early story titled "Higher Education" during the 1950s, Zuckerman withholds this parallel from both readers and Coleman in *The Human Stain*.
58 Ibid., 86.
59 Ibid., 91–2.
60 Ibid., 94.
61 Ibid., 88, emphasis added.
62 See, Roth, *The Human Stain*, 332–3.
63 See, Roth, *The Ghost Writer*, 91.
64 Ibid., 96.
65 Ibid., 97.
66 See, Roth, *The Human Stain*, 23.
67 See, James F. Davis, *Who Is Black? On Nation's Definition* (University Park: PA State University Press, 2008): 54.
68 Since about the turn of the twentieth century and bolstered by Jim Crow segregation of the 1930s and 1940s (especially in the South), black Americans have been defined as "anyone person with any known African black ancestry," regardless of appearance or other factors; by 1915, white Americans accepted the one drop rule, while not being assigned social or legal determination of their identity (Myrdal, *An American Dilemma*, 113–18, qtd. in Davis 5).
69 See, Davis, *Who Is Black?*, 77 emphasis added.
70 Ibid., 14 and 77. Importantly, however, both the one-drop rule and white Americans' anxieties over instances of racial passing originated much earlier in the United States, alongside the institution of slavery. These rules, however, were made official due to the powerful reinforcement they received under the Jim Crow system.
71 Ibid., 77–8. In *Who Is Black?*, Davis notes that between 1880 and 1925 approximately 12,000 people crossed the color line each year, although, he admits, "such estimates are most likely inflated. By 1940 the annual number passing as white did not exceed between 2,500 and 2,750 a year (Burma, 1946: 18–22), and possibly no more than 2000 to 2500 (Eckard, 1947: 498)" (*Who Is Black?*, 56).

72 See, Bonilla-Silva, *Racism without Racists,* 2–3. Also see, Kim, "Clinton's Race Initiative," 182.
73 Roth, *The Human Stain,* 326.
74 Brief subplot on Zuckerman, ibid., 35–7, 44.
75 Ibid., 71 and 308.
76 See, Bonilla-Silva, *Racism without Racists,* 1 and 32–3.
77 Roth, *The Human Stain,* 31 and 326.
78 Ibid., 130.
79 Ibid., 127.
80 Ibid.
81 Ibid., 132.
82 Ibid.
83 Ibid., 135.
84 Ibid., 133–4.
85 Ibid. 134.
86 Ibid., 133.
87 Ibid., 135.
88 Ibid., 136.
89 Ibid., 135.
90 See, Freedman, *Klezmer America,* 183. Also see, Roth, *The Human Stain,* 130.
91 Ibid., 131 and 133.
92 Ibid., 133.
93 Ibid., 108, original emphasis.
94 Ibid., 125.
95 Ibid.
96 Ibid., 126.
97 Ibid., 116. Also see Freedman, *Klezmer America,* 183.
98 Roth, *The Human Stain,* 115.
99 See, Freedman, *Klezmer America,* 183.
100 Roth, *The Human Stain,* 116.
101 Ibid., 127.
102 Ibid., 135 and 134.
103 Ibid., 136.
104 Ibid., 204–5.
105 Ibid., 212–13.
106 Ibid., 213 and 38.

107 Ibid., 337.
108 Ibid., 294–5 and 300–1.
109 Ibid., 70, 344 and 350.
110 Ibid., 308.
111 See, Giulia Fabi, *Passing and the Rise of the African American Novel* (Urbana: University of Illinois Press, 2001): 2–3.
112 Ibid., 3–5.
113 See, Roth, *The Human Stain*, 325.
114 See, Fabi, *Passing and the Rise of the African American Novel*, 3.
115 Interestingly, the 1960s through the 1980s (i.e., likely as they are defined by his marriage to Iris) are left uncovered in Zuckerman's account. This is an unfortunate, though sadly telling, historical omission that the writer makes, I argue, for the sake of preserving his intricate reconstruction of Coleman's race travel.
116 See, Freeman, "Legitimizing Racial Discrimination through Antidiscrimination Law," 34–5.
117 Readers of Roth's Zuckerman novels may recall the writer's earlier experiences, particularly following the publication of *Carnovsky*, receiving death threats, dodging obsessive fans, and fearing for his safety, while both living in Manhattan as a young writer and traveling abroad in Jerusalem and London. In fact, in Roth's final Zuckerman novel, *Exit Ghost* (2007)—set four years after the publication of *The Human Stain*—Zuckerman admits in narration that his receiving regular, anti-Semitic death threats during his time in Manhattan during the early 1990s (coupled with the FBI's inability to guarantee his safety) led to his leaving off urban life for a pastoral existence reminiscent of those by Henry David Thoreau, Ralph Waldo Emerson, and E. I. Lonoff, Zuckerman's idol.
118 See, Philip Roth, *Exit Ghost* (New York: Vintage, 2007): 53–8.

Conclusion

1 Today, conventional ideological *critiques* of either *The Flagellants* or *Franny and Zooey* might yield readings that focus on issues such as misogyny, domestic dysfunction, or abuse in the texts. Furthermore, themes like American exceptionalism's blindness to intersectional experiences of violence,

discrimination, and/or their effects may also find exploration. By contrast, my readings work to illuminate the *novels'* (not my own) commentaries on the reductionisms of both *critique* and dominating discourses in the contexts the novels' specific, embodied historical moments.

2   To reiterate an important point made in this study's Introduction: None of these characters are presented with unique models or bases from which to imagine or formulate life circumstances that are any different from those lived by their direct peers or family members. Furthermore, other American media (i.e., contemporaneous with the texts' publications) barely offered readers any such bases, either.

3   See, John Foster Dulles, "Thoughts on Soviet Foreign Policy and What to Do about It," (two-part article) in *Life*, Issues for June 3 and June 10 (1946): 112–18, 120, 123–6; and 118–20, 122, 124, 127–8, 130 (respectively).

   For instance, according to Dulles's account, "in Russian," a "friendly" government is one that "profess[es] their belief in Soviet ideals and who prove[s] their sincerity by working to promote them" (June 3, 1946: p. 113). He also discusses specifically "Russian" definitions of "fascism" (i.e., anything "non-Soviet"), "democracy" (i.e., a proletariat dictatorship, which Dulles leaves unexplicated), and so on. The primary point of this expository interpretation, Dulles explains, is to clarify for American readers specifically how Soviet leaders employ the same terminology as American leaders, but with catastrophically *different* meanings attached (113–14).

4   See, Andrew Bacevich, *The Age of Illusions: How America Squandered Its Cold War Victory* (New York: Metropolitan Books, 2020): 13.

5   For Roth, in particular, this stylistic move is a distinct departure from his earlier, more myopic work, such as 1979's *The Ghost Writer*.

Bibliography

Alexander-Floyd, Nikol G. 2007. *Gender, Race, and Nationalism in Contemporary Black Politics*. New York: Palgrave.

Althusser, Louis 1971. *Lenin and Philosophy and Other Essays*. New York: Monthly Review Press.

Ames, Melissa A. 2006. "Memoirs of a Bathroom Stall," *The Keep, Faculty Research & Creative Activity*. Eastern Illinois University, Paper 13. Available at: http://thekeep.eiu.edu/eng_fac/13

Bacevich, Andrew 2020. *The Age of Illusions: How America Squandered Its Cold War Victory*. New York: Metropolitan Books.

Barrenechea, Antonio 2016. *America Unbound: Encyclopedic Literature and Hemispheric Studies*. Albuquerque: University of New Mexico Press.

Basinger, Jeanine 1993. *A Woman's View: How Hollywood Spoke to Women, 1930–1960*. Hanover: Wesleyan University Press.

Bell, Daniel 1960. *The End of Ideology: On the Exhaustion of Political Ideas in the Fifties*. Cambridge: Harvard University Press.

Bennett, Juda 2001. "Toni Morrison and the Burden of the Passing Narrative." *African American Review*, 35.2 (Summer): 205–17.

Boltanski, Luc and Eve Chiapello 2018. *The New Spirit of Capitalism*, trans. Gregory Elliot. London: Verso.

Bonilla-Silva, Eduardo 2014. *Racism without Racists: Color-blind Racism and the Persistence of Racial Inequality in America*. New York: Rowman Littlefield.

Bonilla-Silva, Eduardo 2015. "More Than Prejudice: Restatement, Reflections, and New Directions in Critical Race Theory." *Sociology of Race and Ethnicity*, 1.1: 73–87.

Brandmeyer, Gerard A. & R. Serge Denisoff 1969. "Satus Politics: An Appraisal of the Application of a Concept." *Pacific Sociological Review*, 12.1 (Spring): 5–11.

Burnham, James 1941. *The Managerial Revolution: What Is Happening in the World Now*. London: Putnam & Co, Ltd.

Cade Bambara, Toni, ed. 2005. *The Black Woman: An Anthology*. New York: Washington Square Press.

Cade Bambara, Toni 2005a. "Preface." *The Black Woman: An Anthology*. New York: Washington Square Press: 1–7.

Cade Bambara, Toni 2005b. "On the Issue of Roles." *The Black Woman: An Anthology*. New York: Washington Square Press: 123–35.

Carby, Hazel V. 1990. "The Politics of Fiction, Anthropology and the Folk: Zora Neal Hurston." *New Essays on Their Eyes Were Watching God*, ed. Michael Awkward. Cambridge: Cambridge University Press: 71–93.

Carey Bond, Jean and Patricia Peery 2005. "Is the Black Man Castrated?" *Black Woman: An Anthology*, ed. Toni Cade Bambara. New York: Washington Square Press: 141–8.

Centrie, Craig 2015. "When Black Girls Became Pretty: Teacher Biography as Source of Student Information." *Female Students and Cultures of Violence in Cities*, ed. Julia Hall. New York: Routledge: 150–69.

Clayborn, Carson 1995. *In Struggle: SNCC and the Black Awakening of the 1960s*. Cambridge: Harvard University Press.

Clinton White House. 1998. *One America in the 21st-Century: Forging a New Future: The President's Initiative on Race & The Advisory Board's Report to the President*. United States Federal Government. Available at: https://clintonwhitehouse2.archives.gov/Initiatives/OneAmerica/PIR.pdf

Cohen, Samuel 2009. *After the End of History: American Fiction in the 1990s*. Iowa City: University of Iowa Press.

Coontz, Stephanie 2001. *A Strange Stirring: The Feminine Mystique and American Women at the Dawn of the 1960s*. New York: Basic Books.

Crawford, Catherine, ed. 2006. *If You Really Want to Hear about It: Writers on J. D. Salinger and His Work*. New York: Thunder's Mouth Press.

Davis, Angela 1998. "Reflections on the Black Woman's Role in the Community of Slaves." *The Angela Y. Davis Reader*, ed. Joy James. Malden: Blackwell: 111–28.

Davis, F. James 2008. *Who Is Black? On Nation's Definition*. 1991. University Park: Pennsylvania State University Press.

Delgado, Richard and Jean Stefancic 2012. *Critical Race Theory: An Introduction*. New York: New York University Press.

Denning, Michael 1998. *The Cultural Front: The Laboring of American Culture in the Twentieth Century*. New York: Verso.

Didion, Joan 1961. "On Self-Respect: Its Source, Its Power." *Vogue*, 138, August 1: 62–3.

Dubey, Madhu 1994. *Black Women Novelists and the Nationalist Aesthetic*. Bloomington: Indiana University Press.

Dubey, Madhu 1995. "Gayl Jones and the Matrilineal Metaphor of Tradition." *Signs* 20.2: 245–67.

Dubey, Madhu 2003. *Signs and Cities: Black Literary Postmodernism*. Chicago: Chicago University Press.

Dudziak, Mary L. 2000. *Cold War Civil Rights: Race and the Image of American Democracy*. Princeton: Princeton University Press.

Dulles, John Foster 1946. "Thoughts on Soviet Foreign Policy and What to Do about It: Part I." *Life*, 20.22 (June 3): 112–18, 120, 123–6.

Dulles, John Foster 1946. "Thoughts on Soviet Foreign Policy and What to Do about It: Part II." *Life*, 20.23 (June 10): 118–20, 122, 124, 127–8, 130.

Ebert, Roger 1967. "First Novels by Young Negroes." *American Scholar*, 36.4 (Autumn): 682–6.

Elam, Michele 2007. "Passing in the Post-Race Era: Danzy Senna, Philip Roth, and Colson Whitehead." *African American Review*, 41.4: 749–68.

Fabi, Giulia 2001. *Passing and the Rose of the African American Novel*. Urbana: University of Illinois Press.

Fielder, Leslie *Love and Death in the American Novel*. McLean: Dalkey Archive Press, 1997.

Frank, Andre Gunder 1990. "No End to History! History to No End?" *Social Justice*, 17.4 (Winter): 7–29.

Freedman, Jonathan 2008. *Klezmer America: Jewishness, Ethnicity, Modernity*. New York: Columbia University Press.

Freeman, Alan David 1996. "Legitimizing Racial Discrimination through Antidiscrimination Law: A Critical Review of Supreme Court Doctrine." *Critical Race Theory: The Key Writings That Formed the Movement*, ed. Kimberle Crenshaw et al. 1995. New York: The New Press: 29–46.

Fukuyama, Francis 1989. "The End of History?" *The National Interest*, 16 (Summer): 3–18.

Fukuyama, Francis 1992. *The End of History and the Last Man*. New York: Free Press.

Gates, Henry Louis Jr. 1983. "The 'Blackness of Blackness': A Critique of the Sign and the Signifying Monkey." *Critical Inquiry*, 9.4 (June): 685–723.

Gerring, John 1997. "Ideology: A Definitional Analysis." *Political Research Quarterly*, 50.4 (December): 957–94.

Giovanni, Nikki 1968. "Review of *The Flagellants*." *Negro Digest*, 17 (January): 97–8.

Goeman, Mishuana 2013. *Mark My Words: Native Women Mapping Our Nations*. Minneapolis: Minnesota University Press.

Grunwald, Henry Anatole, ed. 2009. *Salinger: The Classic, Critical and Personal Portrait*. New York: HarperCollins.

Halio, Jay 2001. "The Human Stain." *Shofar*, 20.1: 173.

Hardison, Ayesha K. 2014. *Writing through Jane Crow: Race and Gender Politics in African American Literature*. Charlottesville: Virginia University Press.

Harley, J. B. 2001. *The New Nature of Maps: Essays in the History of Cartography*, ed. Paul Laxton. Baltimore: Johns Hopkins University Press.

Harris-Perry, Melissa 2011. *Sister Citizen: Shame, Stereotypes, and Black Women in America*. New Haven: Yale University Press.

Hegel, Georg Wilhem Friedrich 2018. *Phenomenology of Spirit (The Phenomenology of Mind)*, trans. J. B. Baillie. San Bernadino, CA: Pantianos Classics.

Hodgson, Godfrey 1996. *The World Turned Right Side Up: A History of Conservative Ascendancy in America*. Boston: Houghton Mifflin.

hooks, bell. *Ain't I a Woman? Black Women and Feminism*. London: Pluto Books, 1986.

Hungerford, Amy 2010. *Postmodern Belief: American Literature and Religion since 1960*. Princeton: Princeton University Press.

Hutner, Gordon 2009. *What America Read: Taste, Class and the Novel, 1920–1960*. Chapel Hill: North Carolina University Press.

James, Rawn Jr. 2014. *The Double V: How Wars, Protest, and Harry Truman Desegregated the American Military*. London: Bloomsbury.

Jones, Le Roi (Amiri Baraka) 1994. "The Myth of a 'Negro Literature.'" Reprinted in *Within the Circle: An Anthology of African American Literary Criticism from the Harlem Renaissance to the Present*, ed. Angelyn Mitchell. Durham: Duke University Press: 165–71.

Kim, Claire Jean 2000. "Clinton's Race Initiative: Recasting the American Dilemma." *Polity*, 33.2 (Winter): 175–97.

Kinsey, Alfred C. et al. 1981. *Sexual Behavior in the Human Female: By the Staff of the Institute for Sex Research, Indiana University*. Bloomington: Indiana University Press.

Klein, Christina 2003. *Cold War Orientalism: Asia in the Middlebrow Imagination, 1945–1961*. Berkeley: California University Press.

Kojeve, Alexander 1969. *Introduction to the Reading of Hegel: Lectures on the Phenomenology of Spirit*, ed. Allan Bloom, trans. James H. Nichols, Jr. Ithaca: Cornell University Press.

Lakoff, George 2006. *Whose Freedom? The Battle over America's Most Important Idea*. New York: Farrar, Strauss & Giroux.

Lears, Jackson 1989. "A Matter of Taste: Corporate Cultural Hegemony in Mass-Consumption Society." *Recasting America: Culture and Politics in the Age of Cold War*, ed. Lary May. Chicago: Chicago University Press: 38–57.

Le Zotte, Jennifer 2017. *From Goodwill to Grunge*. Chapel Hill: University of North Carolina Press.

Lieberman, Robert C. 2006. "The Storm Didn't Discriminate: Katrina and the Politics of Color Blindness." *Du Bois Review*, 3.1: 7–22.

Malcolm, Janet 2001. "Justice for J. D. Salinger." *New York Review of Books*, 48.10 (June 21).

Marx, Karl 1973. *Grundrisse: Foundations of the Critique of Political Economy (Rough Draft)*. Penguin Books in association with New Left Review. Available at: https://www.marxists.org/archive/marx/works/1857/grundrisse/

McCarthy, Mary 1962. *On the Contrary*. New York: Noonday Press.

McCarthy, Mary 2006. "J. D. Salinger's Closed Circuit." *If You Really Want to Hear about It: Writers on J. D. Salinger and His Work*, ed. Catherine Crawford. New York: Thunder's Mouth Press: 127–33.

McDowell, Deborah 1989. "Boundaries: Or Distant Relations and Close Kin." *Afro-American Literary Study in the 1990s*, ed. Houston Baker, Jr. and Patricia Redmond. Chicago: University of Chicago Press: 51–70.

McLuhan, Eric and Frank Zingrone, eds. 1995. *Essential McLuhan*. New York: Basic Books.

McLuhan, Marshall 1951. *The Mechanical Bride*. Berkeley: Ginkgo Press.

McLuhan, Marshall 1964. *Understanding Media, the Extensions of Man*. New York: McGraw Hill.

McLuhan, Marshall and Wilfred Watson 2001. *From Cliché to Archetype*, ed. Terrence Gordon. Berkeley: Ginkgo Press.

Moynihan, Daniel Patrick 1965. *The Negro Family: The Case for National Action*. Washington: United States Department of Labor, Office of Policy Planning and Research. Web. May 29, 2014.

Myrdal, Alva and Viola Klein 1956. *Women's Two Roles: Home and Work*. London: Routledge.

Myrdal, Gunnar 1944. *An American Dilemma: The Negro Problem & Modern Democracy*. New York: Harper Brothers. Available at: https://archive.org/stream/AmericanDilemmaTheNegroProblemAndModernDemocracy/AmericanDelemmaVersion2_djvu.txt

Neal, Larry 2003. "The Black Arts Movement." *The Drama Review*, 12 (Summer 1968). Reprinted in *The Portable Sixties Reader*. New York: Penguin: 446–454.

Newson, Adele 1992. "The Poet's Distance Achieved through a Parisian Sojourn; Carlene Hatcher Polite's The Flagellants." *MAWA Review*, 7.1: 22–6.

Nielsen, Aldon 1997. *Black Chant: Languages of African American Post-Modernism*. New York: Cambridge UP.

Pinkney, Alphonso 1976. *Red, Black, and Green: Black Nationalism in the United States*. Cambridge: Cambridge University Press.

Polite, Carlene Hatcher 1967. *The Flagellants*. New York: Farrar, Strauss & Giroux.

Ransby, Barbara 2005. *Ella Baker and the Black Freedom Movement: A Radical Democratic Vision*. Chapel Hill: North Carolina University Press.

Reid, Margaret 1992. "Carlene Hatcher Polite and the French Connection." *MAWA Review*, 7.1: 32–7.

Reid, Margaret 1996. "The Diversity of Influences on Carlene Hatcher Polite's *The Flagellants* and *Sister X and the Victims of Foul Play*." *Connecticut Review*, 18.1 (Spring): 39–50.

Roth, Philip 1979. *The Ghost Writer*. New York: Vintage, 1995.

Roth, Philip 1981. *Zuckerman Unbound*. *Zuckerman Bound: A Trilogy and Epilogue 1979–1985*. New York: Library of America, 2007. 117–262.

Roth, Philip 1983. *The Anatomy Lesson*. *Zuckerman Bound: A Trilogy and Epilogue 1979–1985*. New York: Library of America, 2007. 263–450.

Roth, Philip 1985. *The Prague Orgy*. *Zuckerman Bound: A Trilogy and Epilogue 1979–1985*. New York: Library of America, 2007. 451–506.

Roth, Philip 1986. *The Counterlife*. New York: Vintage, 1996.

Roth, Philip 1988. *The Facts: A Novelist's Autobiography*. New York: Vintage, 1997.

Roth, Philip 1997. *American Pastoral*. New York: Vintage, 1998.

Roth, Philip 1988. *I Married a Communist*. New York: Vintage, 1999.

Roth, Philip 2000. *The Human Stain*. Boston: Houghton Mifflin, 2001.

Roth, Philip. 2007. *Exit Ghost*. New York: Vintage.

Rosenfeld, Lucinda 2001. "The Trouble with Franny." *With Love and Squalor: 14 Writers Respond to the Work of J. D. Salinger*, ed. Kip Kozen and Thomas Beller. New York: Broadway Books: 78–87.

Safer, Elaine 2002. "Tragedy and Farce in Roth's The Human Stain." *Critique: Studies in Contemporary Fiction*, 43.3 (Spring): 211–27.

Salinger, Jerome David 1989. *Franny and Zooey*. New York: Little, Brown & Co.

Schraufnagel, Noel 1974. *From Apology to Protest: The Black American Novel*. DeLand: Everett/Edwards.

Seed, David 2008. "Keeping It in the Family: The Novellas of J. D. Salinger." *J. D. Salinger*, ed. Harold Bloom. New York: Infobase: 69–87.

Silko, Leslie Marmon 1991. *Almanac of the Dead*. New York: Penguin.

Silko, Leslie Marmon 1996. *Yellow Woman and a Beauty of the Spirit: Essays on Native American Life Today*. New York: Simon & Schuster.

Smethurst, James Edward 2005. *The Black Arts Movement: Literary Nationalism in the 1960s and 1970s*. Chapel Hill: North Carolina University Press.

Smith, David Lionel 1995. "Chicago Poets, OBHC and the Black Arts Movement." *The Black Columbiad: Defining Movements in African American Literary Culture*, ed. Werner Sollors and Maria Deitrich. Cambridge: Harvard University Press: 253–64.

Tate, Claudia 1987. "Introduction." *The Flagellants* (second printing). Boston: Beacon Press.

Tillet, Rebecca 2014. "*Almanac*, Contextualized." in *Howling for Justice: New Perspectives on Leslie Marmon Silko's* Almanac of the Dead, ed. Rebecca Tillet. Tucson: University of Arizona Press: 5–13.

Trilling, Lionel 1952. "Our Country and Culture." *Partisan Review*, 19.3: 318–26.

Walker, Alice 1983. "In Search of Our Mothers' Gardens." *Ms. Magazine*, 1974. Reprinted in Alice Walker, *In Search of Our Mothers' Gardens: Womanist Prose*. San Diego: Harcourt Brace: 231–43.

Walker, Nancy A., ed. 1988. *Women's Magazines, 1940–1960: Gender Roles and the Popular Press*. Boston: Bedford St. Martin's.

Wallace, Michele 1990. *Black Macho and the Myth of the Superwoman*. New York: Dial Press.

Washington, Cynthia 1979. "We Started from Different Ends of the Spectrum." Reprinted in Sara Evans' *Personal Politics: The Roots of Women's Liberation in the Civil Rights Movement and the New Left*. New York: Vintage: 238–40.

Whyte, William H. 2002. *The Organization Man*. Philadelphia: University of Pennsylvania Press.

Young, Cynthia 2006. *Soul Power: Culture, Radicalism, and the Making of a U.S. 3rd World Left*. Durham: Duke University Press.

Zeigler, James 2015. *Red Scare Racism and Cold War Black Radicalism*. Jackson: University of Mississippi.

Index

African American literature 11–12, 24, 26, 54, 58
Almanac of the Dead. See also Silko, Leslie Marmon
   Angelita 87–92, 99–101, 104–5, 112–13, 115–16, 119–21
   Bartolomeo 87–91, 115, 123
   Blue, Leah 112–13, 119
   characterization 85–9, 91–5, 97–9, 101, 103, 105–6, 111, 113–14, 116, 119–24, 126
   Clinton 100–1, 103–6
   Cuban imperial interest 87–91, 95, 97, 115
   dark comic twist 108, 123
   Five Hundred Year Map 94–9, 101–4, 106–7, 110–11, 113–14, 116–20, 122–5, 197 n.27, 197 n.34
   Fukuyama's "end of history", reconceptualization 84–6, 88–96, 101, 109–10, 113, 119, 122–4, 126
   "*Giant stone snake*" 101–3
   humanity, depiction in 83–6, 88–90, 92–5, 110, 113–14, 122, 125
   ideological response 19–23
   Lecha 114, 116–19, 121, 198 n.66
   Menardo 103–6, 108–10, 112–13, 115–21, 123, 198 n.52
   narrator 103, 107–8, 112–13, 116, 118–19, 123
   "*Prophecy*" panel 114–15, 117–18
   racial discourse 88, 93, 98, 125–7
   reality, conception in 88, 92, 95, 113, 122
   sorcery influence 83, 92–6, 99–101, 103, 105–6, 108–9, 112–15, 117–20, 123, 196 n.23
   Sterling 105–14, 116–17, 121, 198 n.66
   Yoeme 99–100, 114, 117–18, 121–2, 124–5
   Zeta 112–19, 121, 125, 198 n.66

American culture 4, 12–13, 30, 52
   clichés to 30, 33
   conceptions of women 11, 35, 43, 53–4
   early-1960s 54
   late-twentieth-century 26
   power relations 7
American novels. *See also specific novels*
   after ideology 7–11
   Cold War and post–Cold War conditions 2–5, 7, 176
   power relations 7, 10–11, 16, 18, 102
   transformed iterations 6–7
   women, conceptions 6, 8–11, 13–14, 17–18
American society 5, 16, 18, 29–30, 40, 48, 59, 62, 125
Ames, Melissa A. "Memoirs of a Bathroom Stall" 186 n.41
audiences 6, 13, 34–5, 50–1, 80, 124, 190–1

Bacevich, Andrew 170
   Age of Illusions: How America Squandered Its Cold War Victory 207 n.4
Bailey, Moya, "On Misogynoir: Citation, Erasure and Plagiarism" 180 n.22
Bambara, Toni Cade 190 n.7
   "On the Issue of Roles" 74
BAM (Black Arts Movement) 5, 11–12, 54, 57–64, 68, 71, 81
   developmental influence 61
   imperfect models 16
   women writers 13
Barrenechea, Antonio 181 n.39
   America Unbound: Encyclopedic Literature and Hemispheric Studies 181 nn.38–40
Basinger, Jeanine 31, 52
   A Woman's View: How Hollywood Spoke to Women 1930–1960 180 n.23, 184 n.10

behavior 36, 39, 42, 46, 50–1, 53, 109, 153, 163
beliefs 20, 59–60, 66, 79, 85, 92–4, 108–9, 113, 120, 167
Bell, Daniel 5, 9–11, 15, 18–19, 28–9, 32, 47–9, 172, 185 n.16
  The End of Ideology: On the Exhaustion of Political Ideas in the 50s 4, 29, 183 n.2, 189 n.96
  The Mood of Three Generations" 29, 172
Beller, Thomas 188 n.82
Bennett, Juda 200 n.6
Black Power movement 17, 58–9, 61, 64, 81, 86, 145, 150
black women 11, 61–2, 71, 73–4, 192–3 n.24. See also BAM (Black Arts Movement)
  1970s and 1980s artists 64
Boltanski, Luc, *The New Spirit of Capitalism* 180 n.24
Bond, Jean Cary 69
  "Is the Black Man Castrated?" 190 n.7
Bonilla-Silva, Antonio 152
Bonilla-Silva, Eduardo 137, 152
  Racism without Racists: Color-blind Racism and the Persistence of Racial Inequality in 202 n.27
Brandmeyer, Gerard A. "Status Politics: An Appraisal of the Application of a Concept" 177 n.7
Burnham, John 6–7, 15
  Managerial Revolution: What Is Happening in the World Now 6

Cade Bambara, Toni 190 n.7
  "On the Issue of Roles" 74
capitalism 14–15, 17, 48, 84, 86, 91, 94, 120, 123, 126
capitalist democracy 17, 19, 84
Carby, Hazel V. "The Politics of Fiction, Anthropology, and the Folk: Zora Neal Hurston" 64, 193 n.26
Carey Bond, Jean, "Is the Black Man Castrated?" 190 n.7

cartography 21, 96–8, 102–3, 110–11, 117, 120
Chiapello, Eve, *The New Spirit of Capitalism* 180 n.24
Civil Rights Movement 1, 25, 131, 138, 145, 149–50, 152
Clinton, Bill 140–1, 163, 180 n.31
  "Initiative on Race", *One America in the 21st Century* 19, 135–6, 141–2
Cohen, Samuel, *After the End of History: American Fiction in the 1990s* 180 n.31
Cold War 1, 17–18, 24–5, 60, 83–5, 91, 149, 167–73, 175–6, 190
Coontz, Stephanie 184 n.12
  A Strange Stirring: The Feminine Mystique and America Women at the Dawn of the 1960s 184 n.13, 187 n.64
cosmologies 95, 101, 113, 115
Crawford, Catherine 189 n.104
criminals 109–12, 114, 116, 118, 120–1
cultural clichés 8, 30, 33, 35, 49, 51–2, 54, 183
cultures 2, 5, 18–19, 30, 44, 94–5, 101, 114, 120
Cusset, François, *French Theory: How Foucault, Derrida, Deleuze & Co. Transformed the Intellectual Life of the United States* 180 n.28

Davis, Angela
  Reflections on the Black Woman's Role in the Community of Slaves 192 n.22
Davis, F. James 150
  Who Is Black? One Nation's Definition 149, 204 n.71
Deleuze, Gilles 18
democracy 19
Denisoff, R. Serge
  "Status Politics: An Appraisal of the Application of a Concept" 177 n.7
Derrida, Jacques 18, 180
Didion, Joan 9, 31, 35, 40, 178 nn.12–13, 183 n.8
  "Marriage a la Mode" 183 n.49
Dubey, Madhu 13, 61

black nationalist discourses 193 n.25
Black Women Novelists and the Nationalist Aesthetic 179 n.21
"Gayl Jones and the Matrilineal Metaphor of Tradition" 193 n.24
Signs and Cities: Black Literary Postmodernism 192 n.20
Dudziak, Mary L. Cold War Civil Rights: Race and the Image of American Democracy 203 n.44
Dulles, John Foster 169–71
"Soviet Foreign Policy and What to Do about It" 169, 207 n.3

Ebert, Roger 12–13
"First Novels by Young Negroes" 179 nn.17–18, 191 n.8
Elam, Michele "Passing in the Post-Race Era: Danzy Senna, Philip Roth, and Colson Whitehead" 203 n.36
essentialism 19, 23–5, 43
ethnicity 27

Fabi, Giulia, *Passing and the Rise of the African American Novel* 163
Faulkner, William 6, 44
Felski, Rita 2–3
American studies: In *Beyond Critique* 2
Limits of Critique, The 177 n.4
Feminine Mystique (Friedan) 41, 186 n.34
femininity 35, 43, 54, 63, 134. *See also specific novels*
Fielder, Leslie 9, 31–2, 178 nn.13–14, 183–4 n.8, 184 n.9, 185 n.15
Love and Death in the American Novel 9, 184 n.8
"Up from Adolescence" 178 n.13, 183–4 n.8
Flagellants, The. See also BAM (Black Arts Movement); Polite, Carlene Hatcher
black American communities, depiction in 58, 61, 64, 72, 74, 81
Black Bottom 55–7, 65–8, 78, 80, 193.n.28
characterization 57–9, 63, 67, 69–72, 78–82

elder authority 66–7
feminist discourses 61–2, 68
gender relations 62, 71, 77, 88
Ideal in 55–7, 59, 63, 65–81, 193 n.28
Jimson in 57–9, 63, 68–81
narrative style 56–7, 63, 65–8, 70–9, 81
Papa Boo 72–3, 77
patriarchal ideology 77–82
prologue 55, 57, 62, 64–8, 70
racial discourse 78, 81
on racial treatments 57, 59–60, 62–3, 68, 71–2, 77, 80
Foucault, Michel 18
Franco, Dean 26–7
"Being Black, Being Jewish, and Knowing the Difference: *Human Stain*; or, It Depends on What the Meaning of 'Clinton' Is" 182 n.47
Frank, Andre Gunder, "No End to History! History to No End?" 91, 196–7 n.25
Franny and Zooey. See also Salinger, Jerome David
Beatrice 187–8 n.65
characterization 9, 16, 35, 37, 39, 42–4, 54, 187 n.65
cliché and modern womanhood 29–34, 36, 42, 49–54
cultural environment 30, 33, 36, 38–9, 54
dialogues 37–8, 42–3, 45–6
feminine identity discourses 2, 8–11, 14–15, 19–20, 27, 48–50, 53–4
gender relations 31–2, 37, 52
Glass, Buddy 32, 42–6, 48, 50–1
Glass, Franny 29–57, 80, 85–6, 88–9, 168–70, 178 n.12, 184 n.9, 185 n.16, 186 n.26, 187–8 n.65, 187 n.54, 188 n.74, 189 n.101, 190 n.105, 190 nn.108–9, 195 n.9
interpretive treatments 2, 8–11, 14–15, 19–20
Lane in 32–41, 46, 51
sociological concerns in 47, 52–3
Way of the Pilgrim, The 14, 47, 52–3
Zooey's statements/opinions 46–7, 49–51

Freedman, Jonathan 143, 155, 157
  The Human Stain 26
  Klezmer America: Jewishness, Ethnicity, Modernity 130
Freeman, Alan David, "Legitimizing Racial Discrimination through Antidiscrimination Law: A Critical Review of Supreme Court Doctrine" 203 n.38
Friedan, Betty 8, 11, 40–1, 43, 47–9, 53, 186 n.34
Fukuyama, Francis 5, 17, 20–1, 23, 28
  The End of History and the Last Man 4, 17–19, 84, 122, 181 n.34, 196 n.25
  Introduction to the Reading of Hegel 83
  "universal homogeneity" 19

Gans, Herbert J.
  Sociology and Social Policy: Essays on Community, Economy, and Society 180 n.29
gender relations. *See specific novels*
Gerring, John, "Ideology: A Definitional Analysis", *Political Research Quarterly* 196 n.19
Giovanni, Nikki, "Review of *The Flagellants*" *Negro Digest* 178–9 n.17
Goeman, Mishuana, *Mark My Words: Native Women Mapping Our Nations* 197 n.28
Grunwald, Henry Anatole, Salinger: The Classic, Critical and Personal Portrait 177–8 n.10, 178 n.13, 183–4 n.8, 185 n.15
Gutenberg 34

Halio, Jay 202 n.31
Harlem Renaissance 60, 163, 191–2 n.16
Harley, J. B. 98, 102
  New Nature of Maps, The: Essays in the History of Cartography 96, 197 n.26, 197 n.34
Harris-Perry, Melissa
  Sister Citizen: Shame, Stereotypes, and Black Women in America 194 n.38

Hegel, Georg Wilhem Friedrich 19–20, 83–5, 88–9, 92–5, 101, 106, 109–10, 113, 122
Henry, James, *Portrait of a Lady, A* 43
hooks, bell 75
  Ain't I a Woman? Black Women and Feminism 194 n.55
Human Stain, The. See also Roth, Philip; Zuckerman, Nathan
  Athena College 129–30, 132–3, 139, 151, 161, 200 n.3, 202 n.26, 202 n.31
  characterization 131–6, 138, 140, 146, 148, 150–1, 162–3, 165
  Farley, Faunia 133, 136, 151, 159–64
  gender relations 137
  on Jewish identity 129–30, 139–41, 143, 145–6, 153, 157, 161
  language, use of 132, 139–40
  Magee, Ellie 153–61
  narrator 132, 154
  Paulsson, Steena 136, 154, 156–8, 160–1
  racial discourse 129–33, 135, 137–46, 148–50, 152–5, 157–9, 162–4
  Roux, Delphine 133–4, 140, 159, 161–2, 201 n.16
  Silk, Coleman 129, 131–2, 152–65
  Silk, Ernestine 129, 131
  Victor, Zuckerman 147–8
  woman, depiction in 152–65
Hungerford, Amy 50
  Postmodern Belief 189 n.101
Hurston, Zora Neal 62, 64, 68
  New Essays on Their Eyes Were Watching God 193 n.26
Hutner, Gordon, *What America Read: Taste, Class, and the Novel* 178 n.14, 183–4 n.8

ideology 2–6, 8, 10–12, 14–20, 24, 28–30, 52–4, 56–8, 60–4, 68–70, 78–82, 90–2, 124–6
intellectuals 15, 47, 58, 61, 79
Irr, Carmen, Timelines of Almanac of the Dead, or a Postmodern Rewriting of Radical Fiction 182 n.40

James, Rawn Jr.
  The Double V 192
Jameson, Frederic 1, 3
  The Ideologies of Theory 177 n.1
Jones, Gayl 62, 64, 192–3 n.24
  Corregidora 193 n.25

Kant, Immanuel 83, 89
Kazin, Alfred 9, 15, 31, 42
  "Everybody's Favorite" 178 n.13, 183–4 n.8
Kebel, Herb 200 n.3
Kim, Claire Jean 135, 181 n.32
  "Clinton's Race Initiative: Recasting the American Dilemma." 181 n.32
Kinsey, Alfred C., *Sexual Behavior in the Human Female: By the Staff of the Institute for Sex Research* 184 n.11
Klein, Christina, *Cold War Orientalism: Asia in the Middlebrow Imagination, 1945–1961* 183–4 n.8
Klein, Viola 8, 40
Kojeve, Alexander 83–4, 89, 94
  Introduction to the Reading of Hegel Lectures on the Phenomenology of Spirit 83, 195 n.1

Lears, Jackson, "A Matter of Taste: Corporate Cultural Hegemony in a Mass-Consumption Society" 190 n.109
Leslie, Esther 4
Le Zotte, Jennifer, *From Goodwill to Grunge* 185 n.19
Lieberman, Robert C. "The Storm Didn't Discriminate: Katrina and the Politics of Color Blindness" 199 n.101
literary interpretation. *See also* American novels
  formalist approaches 3
  historical impulses 1–3
  New Critical principle 10
  plot of 1–2
  text's *meaning* 1–2
Lonely Crowd (sociological study) 44
Lundquist, Susan, *Native American Literatures: An Introduction* 181 n.39

Malcolm, Janet 9
  "Justice for J. D. Salinger" 8, 178 n.11
Malcolm X 58, 191 n.9
Marx, Karl 19–21, 109, 113, 115, 122–3, 181 n.36, 195 n.5, 195 n.7, 196 n.22
  Cubans' interpretation 87, 89–90, 93, 96
  Das Kapital 90
  Kojeve's interpretation of 83
  on labor's place 195 n.7, 196 n.22
Maslan, Mask 26
  "The Faking of the Americans: Passing, Trauma, and National Identity in Philip Roth's *Human Stain*" 182 n.46
mass cultures 1, 6, 8–9, 11, 15–16, 30, 43, 69, 80, 126
McCarthy, Mary 6–7, 9, 15, 31, 35–6, 40, 43–6, 184–5 n.14, 188 n.72, 189. n.104
  On the Contrary 43, 177 n.9, 184–5 n.14
  on *Madame Bovary* 43
  "Salinger's Closed Circuit" 189 n.104
McLuhan, Marshall 5, 8, 11, 30, 34–6, 48, 177–8 n.10, 183 n.5
  From Cliché to Archetype 177–8 n.10, 183 n.7
  The Mechanical Bride: Folklore of Industrial Man 30, 34, 177–8 n.10, 183 nn.6–7, 186 n.34
  Understanding Media 177–8 n.10, 183 n.7
Meggs, Philip B. 34
Morrison, Toni 62, 64, 67, 193 n.25, 200 n.6
  Bluest Eye, The 193 n.25
  Sula 193 n.25
Moynihan, Daniel Patrick 11
Moynihan Report 61, 74–5
  Negro Family: The Case for National Action 178 n.16
Myrdal, Alva 8, 40
  Women's Two Roles: Home and Work 40
Myrdal, Gunnar 145, 147–50, 155–6, 180 n.29
  An American Dilemma 142, 144–5, 182 n.43, 204 n.68
  on under-class 18, 180 n.29

Nash, Roderick, *Wilderness and the American Mind* 182 n.40
Neal, Larry, "The Black Arts Movement" 191 n.10
Newson, Adele, "The Poet's Distance Achieved through a Parisian Sojourn" 178–9 n.17
Nielsen, Aldon 13
  Black Chant: Languages of African American Post-Modernism 179–80 n.21

omissions 9, 25, 54, 87, 98, 111, 131
oppression 61, 75, 79, 88, 101
  racial 59, 62–3
Organization Man (sociological study) 44

Passos, John Dos 6, 44, 48
Peery, Patricia 69
  "Is the Black Man Castrated?" 190 n.7
Pinkney, Alphonso 59
  Red, Black, and Green: Black Nationalism in the United States 191 n.13
Polite, Carlene Hatcher 2, 10–11, 54–5, 62, 192–3 n.24. See also *Flagellants, The*

race. See also *specific novels*
  American conceptions 11, 14, 19–20, 22–7
  interstices 11, 61
racism 24, 27, 60–1, 64, 132–3, 135–6, 138, 140–2, 145, 149, 155, 163–5
Raise High the Roof Beam, Carpenters (Salinger) 42, 187 n.60, 188 n.66, 188 n.74
Raphael, Frederic 13, 178–9 n.17
Reid, Margaret, "Carlene Hatcher Polite and the French Connection" 179 n.17
Roth, Philip 11, 24, 26–7, 126. See also *Human Stain, The; Zuckerman, Nathan*
  American Pastoral 138, 183 n.50, 200 n.1
  Anatomy Lesson, The 202 n.29
  Counterlife 133

Exit Ghost 164, 206 n.117
Facts, The: A Novelist's Autobiography 202 n.30
Ghost Writer, The 133, 137–8, 146–8, 160, 203 n.36, 204 n.57, 207 n.5
I Married a Communist 138, 200 n.1
Prague Orgy, The 202 n.29
Zuckerman Unbound 133, 202 n.29
Royal, Derek Parker 27
  "Fictional Realms of Possibility: Reimagining the Ethnic Subject in Philip Roth's *American Pastoral*" 183 n.50
Ryan, Alan 22–3
  "An Inept *Almanac of the Dead*" 181 n.39

Safer, Elaine 201 n.16, 202 n.31
Salinger, Jerome David 7–9, 11, 14–17, 20–1, 26, 187 n.54. See also *Franny and Zooey*
  "A Perfect Day for Bananafish" 42, 53
  Cold War narratives 167–9
  contemporaries of 178 n.13
  "Down in the Dinghy" 42, 187 n.65
  Raise High the Roof Beam, Carpenters 42, 187 n.60, 188 n.66
  Seymour: An Introduction 42, 187 n.60, 188 n.66
  Teddy 42
Salzman, Sue 33–4
Sayre, Nora 12–13
  "Punishing", *The Nation* 179 n.19
Schraufnagel, Noel 58–9, 72, 191 n.12
  From Apology to Protest 178–9 n.17
Second World War 1, 4–5, 7, 10, 15, 29, 47, 53–4, 60, 63, 69, 81, 84, 139, 192 n.17, 203 n.36
Seed, David 42
  "Keeping It in the Family: The Novellas of J. D. Salinger" 187 n.58
Silko, Leslie Marmon 11, 18–23, 25. See also *Almanac of the Dead*
  A Collection of Critical Essays 182 n.40
Smethurst, James Edward 13, 60
  The Black Arts Movement: Literary Nationalism in the 1960s and 1970 179–80 n.21

Sontag, Susan 3
  "Against Interpretation" 177 nn.5–6
Spivak, Guyatri, *Death of a Discipline* 180 n.28

Tillet, Rebecca 23
  Howling for Justice 182 n.40, 182 nn.40–1
Trilling, Lionel 5–7, 15, 53, 172
  "Our Country and Culture" 177 n.8
Trudy, "On Misogynoir: Citation, Erasure and Plagiarism" 180 n.22
Truman, Harry.S. 61
  Executive Order No. 9981 60

Updike, John 9, 31, 177–8 n.10
  "Anxious Days for the Glass Family" 178 n.13
urban center 18, 112

visualization 86, 103, 111
vulnerability 38, 104, 173

Walker, Alice 62, 66–8
  "In Search of Our Mothers' Gardens" 68, 194 n.33
Washington, Cynthia 71
whiteness 139, 157–9, 164
Whyte, William, *The Organization Man* 6–7, 44
women 8–11, 14, 18, 29, 31, 36, 40–4, 47–9, 51, 54, 71, 74, 151–3
Wright, Richard, *Black Boy* 12

Young, Cynthia 13
  Soul Power: Culture, Radicalism, and 179–80 n.21
youth 25, 52, 80, 129–30, 134, 148

Zeigler, James, *Red Scare Racism and Cold War Black Radicalism* 192 n.17, 192 n.19
Zuckerman, Nathan 23–8, 200 n.2, 200 nn.5–6. *See also* Roth, Philip

www.ingramcontent.com/pod-product-compliance
Lightning Source LLC
Chambersburg PA
CBHW072232290426
44111CB00012B/2067